GATEWAY TO GLORIETA

GATEWAY TO GLORIETA

A History of Las Vegas, New Mexico

Lynn Irwin Perrigo, PhD

New Foreword
by
Maurilio E. Vigil

SANTA FE

This new edition is the end-result of an initiative by Sunstone Press, the City of Las Vegas, New Mexico Museum and Rough Rider Memorial Collection, and the Friends of the City Museum in their promotion of scholarly research and education.

New Material © 2010 by Sunstone Press. All Rights Reserved.

No part of this book may be reproduced in any form or by any electronic or mechanical means including information storage and retrieval systems without permission in writing from the publisher, except by a reviewer who may quote brief passages in a review.

Sunstone books may be purchased for educational, business, or sales promotional use. For information please write: Special Markets Department, Sunstone Press, P.O. Box 2321, Santa Fe, New Mexico 87504-2321.

Library of Congress Cataloging-in-Publication Data

Perrigo, Lynn Irwin.
  Gateway to Glorieta : a history of Las Vegas, New Mexico / by Lynn Irwin Perrigo ; new foreword by Maurilio E. Vigil.
    p. cm. -- (Southwest heritage series)
  Originally published: Boulder, Colo. : Pruett, c1982.
  Includes bibliographical references and index.
  ISBN 978-0-86534-785-4 (softcover : alk. paper)
  1. Las Vegas (N.M.)--History. I. Title.
  F804.L3P47 2010
  978.9'55--dc22
                          2010035391

WWW.SUNSTONEPRESS.COM
SUNSTONE PRESS / POST OFFICE BOX 2321 / SANTA FE, NM 87504-2321 /USA
(505) 988-4418 / ORDERS ONLY (800) 243-5644 / FAX (505) 988-1025

CONTENTS

THE SOUTHWEST HERITAGE SERIES / I

FOREWORD TO THIS EDITION / II

FACSIMILE OF 1982 EDITION / III

I

THE SOUTHWEST HERITAGE SERIES

"The past is not dead. In fact, it's not even past."
—William Faulkner, *Requiem for a Nun*

The history of the United States is written in hundreds of regional histories and literary works. Those letters, essays, memoirs, biographies and even collections of fiction are often first-hand accounts by people who wanted to memorialize an event, a person or simply record for posterity the concerns and issues of the times. Many of these accounts have been lost, destroyed or overlooked. Some are in private or public collections but deemed to be in too fragile condition to permit handling by contemporary readers and researchers.

However, now with the application of twenty-first century technology, nineteenth and twentieth century material can be reprinted and made accessible to the general public. These early writings are the DNA of our history and culture and are essential to understanding the present in terms of the past.

The Southwest Heritage Series is a form of literary preservation. Heritage by definition implies legacy and these early works are our legacy from those who have gone before us. To properly present and preserve that legacy, no changes in style or contents have been made. The material reprinted stands on its own as it first appeared. The point of view is that of the author and the era in which he or she lived. We would not expect photographs of people from the past to be re-imaged with modern clothes, hair styles and backgrounds. We should not, therefore, expect their ideas and personal philosophies to reflect our modern concepts.

Remember, reading their words and sharing their thoughts is a passport back into understanding how the past was shaped and how it influenced today's world.

Our hope is that new access to these older books will provide readers with a challenging and exciting experience.

II

FOREWORD TO THIS EDITION
by
Maurilio E. Vigil
Emeritus Professor of Political Science
New Mexico Highlands University

Las Vegas, New Mexico has been characterized as "two towns, one place," "The Town that wouldn't gamble," and "The Wildest of the Wild West." The descriptions are at least partially accurate, but they fail to capture the essence of this small city.

Much has been written about the history of Las Vegas. Narratives continue to appear in popular, scholarly and promotional articles and essays. In some cases, Las Vegas' history is presented as a back-drop to the telling of a story about a particular person, era, theme, event, or some other aspect of its story. But, there have only been six book-length works devoted entirely to the telling of the history of Las Vegas from its inception until a certain period in its development. Perhaps the first attempt at writing a formal history was a short treatise written by H. T. Wilson titled *Historical Sketch of Las Vegas, New Mexico*, in 1880 and printed in a promotional pamphlet designed to promote the town's resources for business and economic development.

Father Stanley [Crocchiola], the author of numerous short pamphlet histories and books on New Mexico towns, wrote the first book-length history, the *Las Vegas (New Mexico) Story*, in 1951. Father Stanley described his experience as "an adventure" since he experienced appearing for an interview and having a door slammed in his face and having his notes burned by a cleaning lady who thought they were "rubbish." He persevered and wrote about the uniqueness of Las Vegas being two towns in one: how Las Vegas had two of everything—two governing bodies, police departments, fire departments, post offices, even two high school teams that "would rather lose all games of the season and not feel bad if they licked the school across the river. . .two towns, one place."

Milton Callon, owner of a local gas service station and amateur historian, titled his 1962 work, *Las Vegas, New Mexico, The Town That Wouldn't Gamble*, in obvious reference to its more famous namesake, who did. Callon's theme is the "rise and decline of this unique and interesting city [whose] history of violence, commerce, politics, and all the fascinating phases of early western living that has made the West a storehouse of thrilling adventure stories."

Las Vegas Grandes on the Gallinas: 1835-1985 (1985), by Anselmo Arellano and Julian Josue Vigil, focused primarily on the impact of Hispanos in the founding, evolution and development of Las Vegas. The centerpiece of their discourse was the political activity of the Romero, Delgado, Martinez and Lopez families that figured so prominently in the history of Las Vegas and New Mexico. The work also focused attention on the long neglected literary contributions of Hispano writers and educators whose works helped to preserve Hispanic culture. They highlighted the continuously prominent role of Hispanos in the political, economic and social life of Las Vegas and New Mexico that was largely neglected by previous writers.

A book by Howard Bryon, *Wildest of the Wild West* (1988), focuses on the new town of Las Vegas that emerged following the arrival of the railroad in 1879. Max Evans' Introduction minces no words in describing how "the story of Las Vegas, New Mexico, causes one to ponder how most historians of the West could have missed a town as wild and full of bloody bullet holes and neck-stretched hemp as to make Tombstone and Dodge City look like the headquarters for a Billy Graham Crusade."

A monograph, *Pioneer Merchants of Las Vegas* (2004), by Marcus Gottschalk, provides a narrative of the origin, development and evolution of Las Vegas as a commercial center in the southwest. Gottschalk describes the pioneering merchants in the original Old Town plaza who thrived on the commerce of the Santa Fe Trail, then discusses the new merchants who arrived with the railroad to help build the new "rail town" on the east side of the Gallinas River. Together these merchants subsequently ushered in the era of large-scale commercial merchandising utilizing the railroad as the primary means of transportation.

Among these notable publications, appeared the book by Lynn I. Perrigo, PhD, *Gateway to Glorieta: A History of Las Vegas, New Mexico,* which is arguably the most comprehensive and authoritative book on the history of Las Vegas. Before this book was published, Perrigo wrote two previous monographs on Las Vegas that were never published. When he completed his first monograph, *The Original Las Vegas, 1835-1935,* a 700-page, two-volume work in 1975, he acknowledged that some ten theses and sixty-three seminar papers produced by students he supervised as Professor of History at New Mexico Highlands University were the inspiration in preparing his "synthesis" of Las Vegas history. That research not only facilitated his own research, according to Perrigo, but provided insights into some areas of Las Vegas history that were validated by his exhaustive investigation (including interviews and countless hours poring through old documents and decades of newspaper coverage). Perrigo launched his historical research shortly after he arrived at Highlands in 1947 and wrote prolifically. In addition to several general history textbooks on the American Southwest, New Mexico and Latin America, he also wrote dozens of essays and articles on Las Vegas for newspapers, magazines and promotional brochures. Indeed, many of the informational pamphlets, tour guide maps and similar brochures still used by the Las Vegas/San Miguel County Chamber of Commerce were authored by Perrigo. Moreover, the fact that Las Vegas has over 900 buildings listed on the National Register of Historic Places (more than any other city in New Mexico), is due to his exhaustive research. And, as much as his research on Las Vegas was of an historical nature, it was also a labor of love. He worked on it systematically over the course of the half century that he lived and worked in Las Vegas.

The voluminous nature of the *Original Las Vegas* manuscript, which included copious documentary footnotes, often as long as or longer than the text material, made it difficult for Perrigo to secure publication. While the treasure chest of information contained in the many footnotes was (and is) a valuable resource for local historians, it was deemed cumbersome, by publishers, for a general audience. This led Perrigo to produce a second monograph, completed in 1980, *The First Century of Las Vegas,* which he described as an "abridgement and revision" of his previous (*Original Las Vegas*) work. Still, this monograph was over 500 pages long and was bound in three (albeit shorter) volumes. Perhaps criticized for ending the first monograph's coverage in 1935, Perrigo decided to clarify that his intent was to limit the work to the first 100 years of Las Vegas history, thus the new title. This may have limited the public appeal of the work, since again the manuscript remained unpublished.

The barriers that Perrigo encountered in seeking publication of the first two Las Vegas manuscripts are typical of what authors, and particularly historians, face. That is, the need to write a comprehensive work that is yet concise and emphasizes popular themes in order to appeal to a wider audience. In some cases, the editing and necessary abridgement prove difficult for a serious scholar such as Perrigo, to accept. In addition to the difficulty of securing publication of a manuscript that contained an incomplete history (with the most recent developments left out), one other factor prompted Perrigo to prepare a third manuscript on Las Vegas. Unlike many historians who simply write a history of a topic but remain personally detached from the history itself, Perrigo was to be part of Las Vegas' most recent history. In 1967, a Joint Commission on Consolidation was formed to pursue merging of the two separate towns: the City of Las Vegas and the Town of Las Vegas. Chaired by District Judge Joe Angel, the nine-member Commission drafted a plan for consolidation and a charter for the proposed new municipality. Dr. Perrigo was enlisted as an "advisor" to the group. At Perrigo's prompting, the Commission adopted a new charter for the municipality that included an innovative hybrid form of mayor-council-manager form of municipal government. As a result of their effort, the city and town of Las Vegas were successfully consolidated as a single municipality in 1970, following a public referendum approved by voters in both communities. They continue to operate as a single municipality to this day. Needless to say, this first-hand experience in civic engineering prompted Perrigo to expand his previous manuscript to include the next half century and thus produce a more complete history of Las Vegas.

The original *Gateway to Glorieta: A History of Las Vegas, New Mexico* was first published in 1982 by the Pruett Publishing Company of Boulder, Colorado. It was the culmination of a long and determined struggle by Dr. Perrigo to get his overdue manuscript in print. While the 245 page book was much shorter than either of its predecessors, it had survived the trials and tribulations of the pre-publication process. This original edition has been out of print for years until Sunstone Press decided to publish this new edition in its award-winning Southwest Heritage Series.

Perhaps the most discussed feature of the Gateway book is, ironically, the title. What does Gateway to Glorieta mean? If Glorieta Pass was a universally known location in American or Western history, there would be no doubt about its meaning. However, even for native New Mexicans familiar with Glorieta, the significance of Las Vegas as being the gateway to it is lost. Perrigo's explanation of the title is simple enough: the natural geographic gap at Glorieta has served as a form of a gateway to the far Southwest for centuries of travelers from the ancient Indian tribes, to Spanish explorers and colonists, to travelers on the Santa Fe Trail, then the Santa Fe Railroad, and more recently, tourists on I-25. Las Vegas, as the principal city in northeast New Mexico, has thus served as the gateway to this natural pass. Perhaps, Perrigo strove for a grander title which certainly Las Vegas deserved, such as "Gateway to the West", or "Gateway to the Far Southwest." (Dr. Perrigo, who was most careful when titling a manuscript, was quite aware of this pitfall, agonizing over an appropriate choice.) Nevertheless, notwithstanding Perrigo's choice of a title, there is no doubt that he was writing an important book about an important city, and that he indeed saw Las Vegas as the gateway to New Mexico and the far Southwest.

On August 22, 1846, a soldier with General Stephen W. Kearny's Army of the West, passed through Las Vegas enroute to Santa Fe, and wrote of his perspective of the country he had just passed. He wrote: [This] "is a sandy, barren country covered with sickly vegetation and inhabited by a race of people but little superior to our Negroes living in low mud houses—in a word, the whole of Mexico that I have seen as yet is not worth the devil's fetching."

The natural geographic landscape that the soldier described in 1846 has not changed much since then, but Las Vegas has evolved and seen dramatic transformation in the 162-year period. As a gateway to New Mexico and much of the far Southwest, Las Vegas has a unique history shaped by the people, cultures and governments that impacted its development and evolution. The region that became Las Vegas was first traversed by Paleo-Indians and later settled by ancestors of the modern Pueblo Indians around the 12th century. Archeological excavations on a site ten miles southwest of Las Vegas uncovered a sizable pueblo abandoned about A.D.1300. In a way, modern-day Las Vegas began as Luis Maria Cabeza de Baca's dream of a great hacienda of vast agricultural fields of native crops and mammoth meadows where livestock grazed in open, unending range. The dream was dashed by the harsh realities of resentful Indian tribes who attacked incessantly and natural climatic disasters—fierce hail storms, floods, droughts and insect infestations that ruined more than one crop. Eventually, C de Baca abandoned his 1821 land grant.

A colonizing party from San Miguel del Bado arrived in 1835 and after facing the same vicissitudes that foiled C de Baca, established a struggling land grant community focused on subsistence agriculture. Time and location, however, intervened to transform the village into a thriving commercial center. The opening of trade with the United States and its location as the first community in New Mexico on the newly initiated Santa Fe Trail, assured the destiny of Las Vegas as a commercial center for the next four decades. In 1846, when General Stephen W. Kearny arrived from the United States with his Army of the West, the first declaration of American occupation took place atop a building on the Las Vegas Plaza. In 1848, Las Vegas, along with the New Mexico Territory became part of the United States following the signing of the Treaty of Guadalupe Hidalgo. The arrival of the railroad in 1879 catapulted Las Vegas into unprecedented growth and development as New Mexico's most important commercial center as it became headquarters for such prominent firms as Otero, Sellar and Company (later Gross Kelly), Browne and Manzanares, the Charles Ilfeld Company and the Romero Mercantile Company. It also spawned new tourist, industrial and agricultural development with the opening of the Montezuma Hotel and Hot Springs as a popular resort destination, opening of a brewery, a brick factory, an iron foundry, a slaughterhouse, a flour mill and the W. H. Shupp factory, a major builder of wagons and carriages for the Southwest market. Most importantly, the commercial growth associated with the railroad flooded the newly created "new town" with additional capital that financed dozens of new businesses such as hotels, restaurants, and bars. Progress was manifested in new business corridors along Douglas and Railroad Avenues and the fashionable

Victorian houses in residential neighborhoods on 6th, 7th and 8th streets.

A major effort at agricultural development was initiated in 1905 in what became known as the Storrie Project. It extracted 40,000 acres of the Las Vegas grant land, for irrigated farming. The railroad also wrought developments that would affect the "political" future of Las Vegas. The "new town" created in East Las Vegas ushered in a 90-year period when "Old" and "New" Town would co-exist as two separate and distinct communities. For the first two decades, East Las Vegas cultivated a reputation compared to Dodge City, Kansas, and Tombstone, Arizona, as one of the "wildest of the wild West" and many Wild West characters such as Bat Masterson, Dave Mather, Dave Rudabaugh, Jesse James and Billy the Kid once walked these streets.

In 1900, Las Vegas was New Mexico's largest and most prominent community, so prominent, in fact, that territorial leaders briefly considered locating the state capitol in there when statehood was finally granted in 1912. Las Vegas was also an early center of the silent film industry with such film pioneers as Romaine Fielding and Tom Mix. It also hosted a world boxing championship match between Jack Johnson and Jim Flynn. In the 1920s, Las Vegas began to decline as a railroad and commercial center after its discontinuance as a division headquarters and moving of key rail offices to Albuquerque. Nevertheless, it retained two gems that it had acquired during its heyday, New Mexico Normal School (later New Mexico Highlands University) and the New Mexico State Hospital (later the New Mexico Behavioral Health Institute) which continue to serve as two main bulwarks of its economic livelihood.

Today there are many remnants of the elements, style and physical character that Las Vegas experienced in its history. Among the 900 or so buildings in its historic registry are many elegant business establishments, churches and private homes that are a constant reminder of a storied past. These buildings are, in effect, as reflective of the diversity in population, cultures, architecture and style that comprised this once cosmopolitan city. And these elements of its character have remained basically the same even after 150 years of general change.

Diversity is a word that correctly reflects the character of Las Vegas: diversity among the many people (Hispanic, Anglo, Native American, Jewish, Italian, Irish, and Lebanese) who have lived and worked there; diversity in the cultures and customs that have existed and interacted; diversity in the architecture; diversity in the many religions; diversity reflected in the occupations of its people; and diversity manifested in the individuality, tolerance and acceptance of differences that have become part of its character.

While Las Vegas in the 19th century preceded the development and evolution of other important New Mexico cities such as Santa Fe and Albuquerque, exogenous technological developments, among other factors, determined a different destiny for Las Vegas. Being the first city at the western end of the Santa Fe Trail, and later the arrival of the railroad, Las Vegas, as stated, went through various stages in the 19th century. However, as the fortunes of its sister cities blossomed in the 20th century, Las Vegas' declined and entered a downward spiral.

It began as a small community peopled by Hispanic colonists struggling to make a living as subsistence farmers and ranchers in a hostile environment. In one century, Las Vegas evolved into a dynamic, commercial, industrial and agricultural center with a cosmopolitan population, only to fade after the changes in the railroad infrastructure led to closing of the railroad machine shops in the early 20th century.

In the last 75 years, it has survived as a small but vibrant community, populated by a Hispanic majority population, an enviable geographic landscape, and a rich historical legacy. *Gateway to Glorieta* addressed issues in the development of Las Vegas, New Mexico, and the Southwest that remain quite relevant in the 21st Century. Among these are an increased socio-cultural diversity that impacts the hegemony of this population and its effects on inter-cultural relations; Spanish/Mexican sovereignty versus American expansionism; conflicting conceptions of land and water rights; and resolving local community problems and public policymaking in the wake of divergent political cultures. The book remains an important treatise since it is a well researched biography of an important and vital town that figured prominently in the growth, evolution and development of New Mexico and the far Southwest.

III

FACSIMILE OF 1982 EDITION

GATEWAY TO GLORIETA
LYNN PERRIGO

A History of Las Vegas, New Mexico.

© 1982 By Lynn I. Perrigo
All rights reserved, including those to reproduce
this book, or parts thereof, in any form, without
permission in writing from the Publisher.

Printed in the United States of America

Contents

Preface

I   **Three Towns Grow In The Gateway**   1

Antecedents • Neighbors • C. de Baca • Subsistence • Santa Fe Trail • Ilfeld • Plaza • New Allegiance • Resistance • Defense • Stagecoaches • Civil War • Railroad • Improvements • Montezuma Hotels • Mercantile Companies • Banks • Hotels • Water Works • Fire Companies • Utilities • Trolley Line • Ranches

II   **Reverses Force Readjustment**   37

Setbacks • Insane Asylum • Rail Traffic • Sanitaria • Fairgrounds • Scenic Road • Championship Bout • Movie Production • Storrie Resort • Chautauqua • National Guard • Camp Luna • Rodeos • Automobiles • Aviation • Early Depression • Poverty • New Pattern

III   **Citizens Seek Order Amid Troubles**   67

Initial Government • The County • Disorder • Gambling • Girls • Gunmen • Fires • Smallpox • Politics • One City • New Town • Silva's Gang • War with Spain • Rough Riders • Floods • Conflicts • Local Government • Statehood • Politics • World War • Magee Episode • Turmoil • Consolidation

IV Much Land And Little Water Require Action   101

Land Grant • Colonists • Confirmation • Confusion • Transgressors • Milheiser Case • White Caps • Legal Proceedings • Land Grant Board • The Town • Getting Control • Small Tracts • Land Sales • Dry Farming • Audit • Reservoir Site • Water Rights • Camfield's Failure • Storrie Dam • Frustration • Outcome

V Education Promises Enlightenment   133

Informal Beginnings • Sisters' Academy • Presbyterian School • Jesuit College • Christian Brothers • Congregational Academy • Methodist Seminary • County Schools • Town Schools • City Schools • Normal University • Upheaval • Revival • Troubles • Stabilization • Baptist College • Library • Radios • Newspapers • New Journalism

VI Diverse Peoples Form Many Societies   157

Early Dons • New Dons • O.L.S. Church • The Hermit • I. C. Church • Penitentes • Social Customs • Newcomers • Presbyterians • Episcopalians • Methodists • Baptists • Hebrews • Other Churches • Fraternal Orders • Women's Organizations • Hospitals • Y.M.C.A. • Service Clubs • Social Activities • Brass Bands • Theatricals • Motion Pictures • Sports • Later Recreation • The Centennial

VII The Community Becomes Contemporary 187
Population • Frustrations • Achievements •
Institutionalization • Crises • Public Schools • State
Hospital • Community Hospital • University •
Standardization • Observations

Bibliography **209**
Index **237**

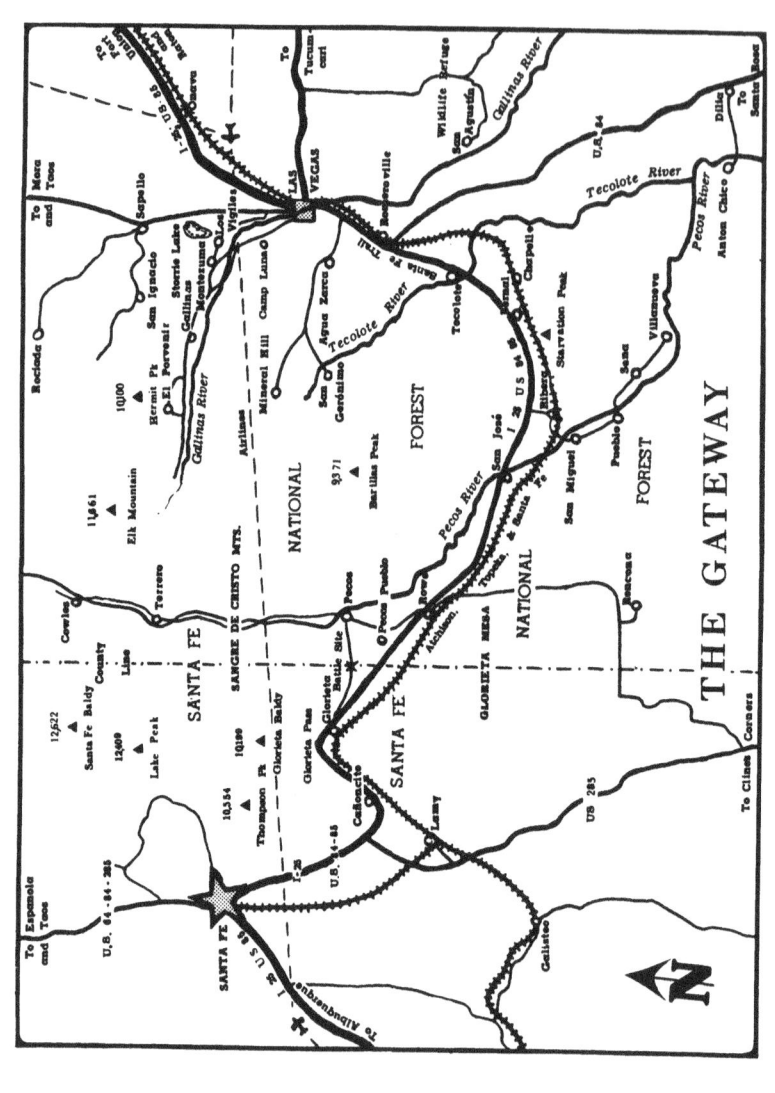

Preface

After a town was founded in 1835 at the eastern gateway to Glorieta Pass and all of the Far Southwest, within one century the present pattern of that community had become established, with a few subsequent exceptions; therefore, the year 1935 has been settled upon as the approximate terminal date of the detailed narrative.

Much of the inspiration for its preparation has been derived from twelve theses and seventy-three research papers on local history which I had the good fortune to supervise while employed as professor of history at New Mexico Highlands University from 1947 to 1971 and which have been duplicated and placed in both local libraries. Afterward I extended my research into 470 additional sources, all of which are listed in the appended bibliography.

I am obligated, therefore, not only to all of the persons who prepared those materials but also to the staff of the several repositories who lent courteous assistance, specifically those of Donnelly Library of New Mexico Highlands University, Las Vegas Carnegie Library, Las Vegas City Museum, the State Records Center and Archives, the Library and Photo Archives of the State Museum, the Special Collections of the University of New Mexico, and the offices of the San Miguel County Clerk, the Clerk of the District Court, and the City Manager of Las Vegas.

In addition, I remain indebted to Charles Morrison for granting access to a large collection of glass photographic plates and to Elmo Baca for providing copies of several of the pictures collected in the local photographic survey.

To my partner, Vera, I remain grateful for her typing not only of this manuscript but also of two others upon which it is based. "The Original Las Vegas," a 700-page manuscript prepared in 1975, is replete with footnotes in which sources are cited and supplementary details are presented. "The First Century of Las Vegas," a 540-page volume, omits the footnotes but contains an index and minor revisions and corrections found necessary by continuation of research to 1980. Copies of both have been placed in the two local libraries for use by researchers and antiquarians.

Finally, I want to express my appreciation to six natives of this locality who have a close acquaintance with its history. They critically read the original, more detailed manuscript at my request and appraised its contents and accuracy. These persons are S. Omar and Elsa Barker, authors; Carol Tinker, former state representative; Joe Angel, district judge; Ray John de Aragón, teacher and author; and William L. Erb, retired realtor.

Lynn I. Perrigo

1 | Three Towns Grow in the Gateway

A long procession of hopeful colonists made its way over the ridges from the Mexican town of San Miguel del Bado in 1835 to the promising site for a new settlement on the grasslands in the valley of the Gallinas River. On April 6, thirty-seven of them, men only at first, obtained small tracts of land along the river with the approval of their *alcalde* and immediately planted crops, mostly beans. Some of the men, when interviewed by a visitor in 1880, said that a hailstorm which destroyed their crops caused them to return to their previous homes for the winter.

They returned in the spring of 1836 with their families. Then they hastily built temporary log huts, planted crops, dug irrigation ditches, began work on an adobe church building dedicated to Our Lady of Sorrows, and constructed an adobe wall around the Plaza so that it could be used as a corral for the safekeeping of their cattle. When others arrived, a few founded an adjoining settlement in 1841 north of the first one. As it grew in the neighborhood of its Church of San Antonio, it came to be known as Upper Las Vegas and Upper Town.

This founding of the first two towns of Las Vegas came as the culmination of a long series of activities by others in that propitious location. First, Folsom Man had hunted in the vicinity as far back as 10,000 years ago. Next, after the emergence of the Basketmaker culture shortly before the time of Christ in what would later become the Four Corners area, those Pueblo Indians discovered the mountain pass and crossed eastward to establish several villages of stone houses in the foothills.

In 1961 in the Tecolote ruins, a Pueblo II site about ten

miles southwest of present-day Las Vegas, excavations by university students under the supervision of professors Floyd W. Snyder and Clark S. Knowlton yielded fragments of pottery which had been brought there from other pueblos, some as far away as Arizona. Currugated pottery, serrated arrowheads, mica ornaments, bone tools, an unusually deep *kiva*, and a grinding room containing *manos* and *metates* were also found. Scraps of timber were dated at A.D. 1171 and 1200 by the pattern of their tree rings. Evidence suggested that the pueblo had been abandoned in about A.D. 1300.

In 1981, a survey of a large ranch five miles southwest of Las Vegas by Professor Robert E. Mishler revealed the location of twenty-four archeological sites, and one of them excavated by his university students turned out to be an unusually large pitroom containing *manos, metates,* arrowheads, awls, beads, corn, beans, bones of animals, and much broken pottery, some of which had been brought there as trade wares from the Río Grande Valley. The last intensive heating of the fireplace rim was dated archeomagnetically at approximately A.D. 1295.

All of the Pueblo People departed from their eastern villages, due either to the great drought of A.D. 1276 to 1298 or to the pressure applied by the newly arrived nomadic Jicarilla Apaches. When they were followed in about A.D. 1500 by Comanches—sturdy, nomadic buffalo hunters—next it became the turn of the Apaches to withdraw farther into the mountains.

The harassed Pueblo Indians founded Pecos Pueblo in about A.D. 1200 and continued to arrive there until it became an impressive stronghold having a population of over 2,000. Campaigns of nomadic Indians against that pueblo occurred in almost every year for which records are extant. Thus, the site of Las Vegas then witnessed much traffic, as Plains Indians camped there while traveling back and forth on raiding and trading expeditions.

Next came the Spanish explorers. Francisco Vásquez de Coronado was the first to visit the site when he and thirty of his horsemen returned by way of the crossing of the Gallinas and the mountain pass in 1541 after having made a futile search for riches in an Indian village called Quivira in present-day Kansas. Between 1581 and 1808, at least fifteen other Spanish expeditions traveled over Glorieta Pass and crossed the Gallinas somewhere near the site of what is now Las Vegas. Notable among them were the army led in 1600 by Juan de Oñate, founder of the first Spanish settlement in San Juan, New Mexico, and the party led by Pedro Vial, who was exploring for the opening of trails between San Antonio, Texas, and Santa Fe and St. Louis from 1787 to 1792. Other trailbreakers were parties of Frenchmen, including the one led by Peter and Paul Mallet in 1751 in their endeavors to establish a trade route between St. Louis and Santa Fe.

Much traffic over the pass enhanced the prospect that offshoots would be planted at favorable sites on the eastern slope as soon as the colony founded in Santa Fe in 1610 should acquire sufficient strength, but vicissitudes there caused a delay for almost two centuries. In that time, the only penetration to the southeast was the founding of a mission at Pecos Pueblo by Franciscan friars.

Finally, in 1794, Spanish soldiers settled fifty-two families, mostly *genízaros,* or Indians cast out of their tribes because of their conversion to Christianity, in San Miguel del Vado, a village in the valley of the Pecos River. They were joined by Spanish colonists mostly from Peña Blanca and Santa Fe, causing San Miguel to become the Mexican equivalent of a county seat for the settlements east of the mountains. Other early villages were San José, founded in the Pecos valley by colonists from Santa Fe in 1803, and Tecolote, over the ridges in the valley of a stream by that name, in 1824.

The opening of the Santa Fe Trail by William Becknell in 1821 made San Miguel a thriving New Mexican port of entry which grew to a population of over 2,000 in the 1830s. Then the overcrowding caused a group of colonists to move farther down the river to Antón Chico in 1834. They and those in Tecolote, and those in San Miguel and San José jointly, were awarded community land grants by Mexican officials. In addition, in 1835 a community land grant was forthcoming for Mora, first settled in 1819.

Glorieta Pass in 1925 *(Museum of New Mexico; T. Harmon Parkhurst)*

There was another popular type of land grant—a large tract for a private ranch—which was available to citizens who had the influence that could obtain favorable dispensations for themselves. As early as 1819, Antonio Ortiz had been awarded such a *sitio* of 163,921 acres along a branch of the Canadian River southeast of the future site of Las Vegas, and in 1823, Juan Esteban Pino received a similar grant in the lower valley of the Pecos River, north of present Santa Rosa. A year later, Pablo Montoya obtained a mammoth ranch of 655,408 acres far to the east, in the valley of the Canadian River, where ultimately it would become the nucleus of the Bell Ranch.

As settlements were surrounding the Meadows, naturally that site was not overlooked. Prior to 1820, a few of the ranchers in San Miguel del Bado had taken their flocks of sheep there for grazing in the summers, and eight of them had petitioned Spanish officials for land there. It was one of them who spoke favorably about the site to Luis María C. de Baca when he visited San Miguel in search of a favorable location. Don Luis, who claimed to be a descendant of one of the first explorers of New Mexico, the famous Álvar Núñez Cabeza de Vaca, had resided in Peña Blanca since 1803. However, because of Indian harassment, he had abandoned a large ranch which had been granted to him in the Jémez Mountains. Next he joined with the other eight in filing an application which obtained a land grant for them in 1820. Immediately he moved his cattle to the Meadows, and in January 1821, he filed a petition again, this time for himself and his seventeen children. Two years later, because the eight other prior applicants had not occupied the site, the political chief in Santa Fe ordered the *alcalde* there to place Don Luis in sole possession.

The grant to Don Luis had grandiose dimensions, from the Chapellote (Sapelló) River on the north, the boundary of the San Miguel Grant on the south, the Pecos Mountains on the west, and the boundary of the Ortiz Grant and the *Aguaje de la Ilegua* (Watering Place of the Mare) on the east, containing close to one-half million acres. Although the location was favorable for ranching and for the development of a trading post on the Santa Fe Trail, it was too exposed for one family to hold. Indians kept making away with the C. de Baca livestock until Don Luis gave up and returned to Peña Blanca.

Others from San Miguel continued to graze sheep seasonally on the Meadows. One of them, Miguel Romero (but not the man of eminence by that same name), said in 1880 that he had begun doing that in 1833. Two years later, the push of overpopulation in San Miguel induced twenty-nine citizens to apply for a land grant on the Meadows. It was approved, and the aforementioned settlements were founded. For mutual protection, most of those pioneers built their houses in the town located on the west side of the stream. From there, they went forth to tend the crops raised on their small, arable strips of land and to graze sheep on the common pastures.

Theirs was a subsistence economy. From local materials, they constructed adobe dwellings with dirt roofs supported

An outfit like on the Santa Fe Trail *(Rex Studio)*

by *vigas*. They shared in work on the roads and ditches and periodically formed a caravan of carts for trips to distant *salinas*, where they shoveled up loads of salt. Those who possessed muskets and good tools had to purchase them in distant markets or trade for them, and scraps of iron were brought from outside for reshaping for local use. Otherwise, most necessities were provided by ingenious and laborious utilization of local resources. Men and boys worked long hours outside, while the women prepared foods, spun thread, wove cloth, made clothing and bedding, and produced beautiful lace and embroidery.

A visitor in 1862, Ovando J. Hollister, observed that the houses were

> very neat and cozy, the walls nicely whitewashed; the fireplaces small and handy, shaped like the half of an old fashioned bee-hive, with a small flue leading out for the chimney.

Mattresses rolled up in day into a settee around the walls. A table, stools, skillet, coffee pot comprise the furniture. The ornaments, even among the best class, consist wholly of ordinary prints of sacred subjects mounted in tin frames, and images of saints roughly carved in wood.

One of the cooperative endeavors was the annual buffalo hunt for the acquisition of robes and meat. Sometimes as many as 100 men, selected for their skill as horsemen, rode forth on those forays. The nimble, experienced hunters served as lancers, while the others aided as skinners and wagon drivers. After a kill, the hunters made camp in order to dry the hides and to cut the meat into strips for drying. Ultimately, the extinction of the buffalo made those expeditions unprofitable.

Other colorful characters known as *Comancheros* traveled out onto the plains to meet with Comanche Indians at an agreed place, where they engaged in trade profitable to both parties. They exchanged cloth and attractive trinkets such as mirrors and beads for horses, mules, and buffalo hides. The majority of the townsmen condemned those who for profit established friendly relations with Indians who were a feared menace; consequently, most of this trade was conducted surreptitiously. When cattle obtained from Comanches were identified as having been stolen, the army tried to suppress this trade.

Vistas to the east were opened seasonally also by trade conducted over the Santa Fe Trail. In the year of the founding of Las Vegas, the merchandise transported in seventy-five wagons had a value estimated at $140,000 and contributed to the employment of 140 men. The trade continued at about that pace until 1843, when it boomed to a value near $250,000.

The wagons on the trail transported to New Mexico cloth, ribbons, shawls, hose, shirts, thread, combs, buttons, nails, spoons, scissors, knives, files, padlocks, and hoes. Some wagons returned empty, with many mules towed along for sale in Missouri, while others carried wool and handcrafted products. Because the route was considered a westward extension of the Old National Road in the East, it was commonly called the National Highway in its course through Las Vegas.

The caravans stopping in the Plaza not only provided merchandise for the stores but also created employment. Young men hired out as drivers, others tended the livestock gathered in the corral west of the Plaza, and townsmen sold the wagoners vegetables, fruit, milk, and cheese. Young men also rode forth to meet the returning caravans and replace their fathers as drivers so that the latter could ride ahead into town and clean up in preparation for the *fandango* that would celebrate the arrival of the wagons.

Local entrepreneurs who could purchase wagons and oxen for the freighting business usually emerged as men of affluence and influence in the community. Although books about the Santa Fe trade portray it as a project of Midwesterners (and it did begin that way), it soon became to a remarkable extent the enterprise of Las Vegans, notably F. O. Kihlberg, Andrés Dold, Charles Blanchard, Francisco López, and Miguel Romero and sons.

An early Anglo enterprise was the Exchange Hotel and its barroom called Buffalo Hall, built in 1852 facing a corner of the Plaza. The early proprietors, Dr. Henry Connelly and E. F. Mitchell, also acquired a large lot back of the hotel for accommodation of vehicles and draft animals. Inside, the rooms for guests were separated by partitions which did not reach the ceiling, so that a guest could hear all of the noises of other rooms. Nevertheless, businessmen, lawyers, and cattlemen congregated there. Later that hotel also became the local stagecoach station and housed the telegraph office.

Quite early, a few other Anglos as well as Germans and French Canadians settled in Las Vegas and became eminent in the business community. In 1867, a German Jew, Charles Ilfeld, joined them and ultimately developed the leading mercantile business in the territory. First, he was employed in 1865 by Adolph Letcher in Taos, but the latter decided that Las Vegas offered greater opportunity. He and Ilfeld loaded their wares on 100 burros and traveled over the mountains to take over a store that faced the Plaza and was formerly man-

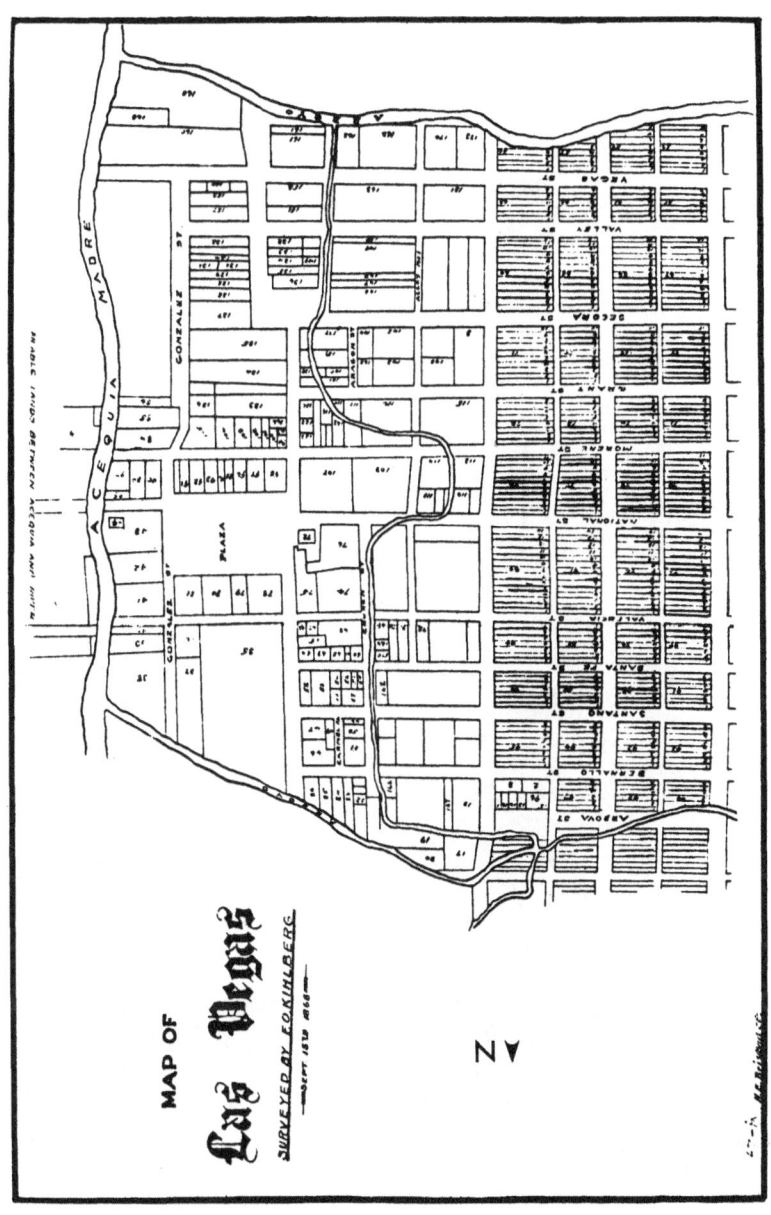

Kihlberg's Plat, 1868 *(H. E. Beisman)*

Charles Ilfeld *(Highlands University Collection)*

aged by Frank O. Kihlberg. Soon Ilfeld bought a partnership in the business, which, by marking up prices as much as 100 percent, made a profit of $18,000 for each partner in their first year at this location.

By 1875, when Ilfeld bought out his partner, this mercantile business had outlets in the neighboring villages of Los Alamos, Tecolote, and Watrous. Subsequently, eight more branches were added, as well as three local warehouses. The original store on the Plaza was replaced by a three-story stone building in 1882. An addition doubled its size in 1890. Ilfeld's great success and civic interests enabled him to emerge as the community's major financial benefactor.

The emergence of Las Vegas as the leading early center for commerce in New Mexico effected a remarkable transformation of the Plaza. It became an alternately dusty and muddy arena for the parking of wagons while loading and unloading. Stores had been built where houses once had stood. Because the lots had been laid out haphazardly, and selected spontaneously, much confusion ensued when those lots became valuable. In 1867, therefore, the county commissioners designated Frank O. Kihlberg as commissioner of the Plaza. He was to settle disputes and draw a plat of the town. Nine years later, the merchants employed Orlando Smith to dig a well in the center of the Plaza and to build a windmill; but the well soon went dry, and the derrick became a conspicuous place to hang culprits caught by the vigilantes.

Incidentally, on the west side a conjecture persists that the Plaza originally had been square and larger than at present, and that in the 1870s Anglo merchants had appropriated two rows of lots from the north and south sides of it, thereby creating Moreno and Valencia streets behind those lots. However, the Plaza had its present shape and size on all pictures from the 1870s and on the plat drawn by F. O. Kihlberg in 1868. In addition, in a few titles to lots dating back into the late 1840s, there is mention of Moreno and "Courthouse" (Valencia) streets. Therefore, if ever the Plaza had been reduced in size, it had to have been done by the Hispanic pioneers very early in its history, by consent of the *alcalde*.

While the Hispanos of Las Vegas were witnessing the rise to eminence of a few *extranjeros* in their business community, they also experienced an abrupt change in their national affiliation. It was an outgrowth of the declaration of a "defensive war" by Mexico against the United States on April 23, 1846, followed by the adoption of a resolution on May 10 by the Congress of the United States recognizing that a state of war existed. Las Vegas was destined to become the first Mexican community in the present Southwest to feel the effects due to its location at the eastern entrance to the Glorieta Gateway.

By late June, the Army of the West had started westward on the Santa Fe Trail. On the evening of August 14, the soldiers encamped about a mile from Las Vegas, where several townsmen visited them, some out of curiosity and others to sell them milk, bread, mutton, cream, and cheese, for which one soldier remarked that "they took care to demand a very high price."

A pioneer, Mrs. Gallegos C. de Baca, recalled later that when she was nine years old, she saw tents and cannons on the hill where the university would later be located. Then the women and children were sent up to hide among the rocks and trees on the *Crestón*, while the men assembled in the Plaza. There General Stephen Watts Kearny spoke to them

The Plaza in the 1870s *(Las Vegas City Museum; J. Furlong)*

from the roof of a building which she called the Plaza Apartments, later known as the Dice Apartments.

Early that morning, a messenger had delivered to Kearny a notice of his promotion to the rank of brigadier general; therefore, it was General Kearny who requested the *alcalde* and two of his aides to climb with him up a "rickety ladder" to the roof of that house. There he proclaimed to the assemblage of 150 men that the United States claimed possession of New Mexico and that Manuel Armijo therefore was no longer their governor. He sought to offer assurance that "We come amongst you as friends, not as enemies; as protectors, not as conquerors." Then he administered the oath of new allegiance to the *alcalde,* Juan de Dios Maese.

Immediately the soldiers, who had been waiting nearby, marched southwestward on the Santa Fe Trail, where they proceeded with caution as they entered *El Puertocito,* later known as Kearny's Gap, because they had heard a rumor that 600 Mexican soldiers were waiting there to do battle. Nobody stood in their way, however, whereupon one soldier wrote in his diary that "We are disappointed in not meeting the enemy today, as all appeared eager for the fray."

The Army of the West marched unimpeded on to Santa Fe, and then General Kearny reported to his superiors that the people of the entire territory were friendly and "contented with the change of government." Nevertheless, he exercised the precaution of leaving a small detachment in Las Vegas and a company in Santa Fe while he hastened on toward California, and those soldiers soon saw action.

First, the Pueblo Indians of Taos arose in rebellion in January 1847 and murdered all of the Anglos they could find, including Charles Bent, whom Kearny had appointed as civil governor. While Colonel Sterling Price was marching his command north from Santa Fe to crush that rebellion, the uprising spread next to Mora, where insurgents killed five transient Anglo merchants. Captain J. R. Hendley in Las Vegas increased the size of his small detachment to eighty by enlisting volunteers and marched his mixed company to Mora, where 200 insurgents fought back the invaders in a battle in which Captain Hendley was killed. On January 30,

Connecting East and West *(National Park Service)*

the soldiers returned, and, as they renewed the assault with the aid of a cannon, they almost destroyed the village of Mora.

A leader of the opposition, Manuel Córtez, escaped, along with approximately 200 Mexicans and Indians. They camped at the junction of the Mora and Canadian rivers and retaliated by attacking wagon trains and pillaging ranches. No doubt they considered themselves to be a patriot army, fighting for freedom, whereas the Anglos in Las Vegas regarded them as bandits. Finally, Major D. B. Edmonson, next commander of the detachment in Las Vegas, had a skirmish with those opponents and chased them far into Texas in May 1847.

Near Las Vegas, soldiers and settlers continued to be harassed by Mexicans and Indians. Convinced that the assaults were being committed by conspirators in the town, Major Edmonson raided the houses of suspects, burned down the mill owned by the *alcalde,* arrested him and about fifty others, killed ten who resisted, and sent the others as prisoners to Santa Fe. There, in a trial conducted on August 3, 1847, six of the suspects were found guilty and were hanged, while the others, including the *alcalde,* were exonerated and released. Although the occupation of New Mexico often has been lauded erroneously as a "peaceable" achievement, actually it ultimately had precipitated considerable bloodletting in Taos, Mora, and Las Vegas.

More troubles ensued, as Indian depredations soon resulted in the loss of thousands of livestock in the vicinity of Las Vegas. For protection of the ranchers and of the travelers on the Santa Fe Trail, the army posted two companies of Illinois Volunteers at Las Vegas as a "grazing detachment" of cavalry in February 1848. They did more than grazing, however, because the post records report the rushing forth of detachments frequently to try to frighten Indians away from neighboring villages.

In 1851, the departmental commander, Colonel Edward Vose Sumner, concentrated the previously scattered detachments at one post, Fort Union, built in that year north of Las Vegas near the junction of the Mountain and Cimarrón branches of the Santa Fe Trail. Through the ensuing decade, the expeditions operating from that fort were fairly effective in curtailing Indian depredations.

The presence of military establishments had a by-product in the stimulation of the local economy. As the army bought flour, corn, and beef, the ranchers expanded their production and built several grist mills, from which the profits were great. Also, the freighting of supplies from St. Louis to the forts became a big business. The economic development of northern New Mexico, therefore, was being stimulated by federal aid in the form of expeditures for maintenance of the military establishments.

The boom in freighting on the trail was accompanied by an improvement in facilities for transporting passengers. In 1850, the Post Office Department let a contract for operation of a mail and stage line from Independence, Missouri, to Santa Fe; but the first luxurious coach sent westward was attacked by Kiowa Indians near Wagon Mound. The Indians burned the coach and killed the driver and guards.

After that massacre, the service was continued irregularly, and wagons were accompanied by armed guards. At night the drivers pulled the wagons into a triangle, within which they and the few passengers slept on blankets on the ground. When the Civil War ended, Congress granted a subsidy of $39,999 a year to the Hall and Hockaday Company for trips twice a month, and that contract was taken over immediately by the Barlow and Sanderson partnership. Then new coaches were acquired and stage stations were built along the way. Thenceforth, Las Vegas had regular and comfortable stagecoach connections with the East, until they were superseded by the railroad in 1879. Even then, for several years feeder lines operated over primitive roads from Las Vegas to other towns.

The Civil War, although fought mainly in the East and Midwest, also extended into New Mexico, which became a western border state fought over by Texans against Coloradans, Californians, and New Mexicans. At first the large Hispanic population remained indifferent about a war over issues not well understood by them, but as soon as they heard that Texans were marching up the valley of the Río Grande in an effort to conquer New Mexico, over 4,000 enlisted in the Union Army, including a company from Las Vegas commanded by Captain Arthur H. Morrison.

When the Confederates were approaching Santa Fe early in March 1862, the commander at Fort Marcy had all of the supplies there loaded into wagons and transported to Fort Union. On March 4, the territorial governor, Dr. Henry Connelly, moved the executive offices to Las Vegas in a building which he owned—the Exchange Hotel.

Since most of the New Mexico Volunteers had been concentrated in Fort Craig, far to the south where the Confederates had bypassed them, Governor Connelly sent a plea for help to the governor of Colorado Territory. Immediately a regiment of Colorado Volunteers commanded by a lawyer, John P. Slough, who had been given a commission as colonel, made a hasty march south.

As the Colorado Volunteers advanced toward Santa Fe,

a detachment had a skirmish with a reconnaissance party of Confederates in Apache Canyon on March 26. Two days later, when the opposing regiments met in Glorieta Pass, the Confederates appeared to be winning the battle. The Colorado regiment had been weakened when a detachment had been sent over the mesa to swoop down upon and destroy the Confederate camp at Cañoncito—a loss that forced the Texans to withdraw. Governor Connelly was back in Santa Fe again by April 20. The reversal in northern New Mexico prevented the Texans from overwhelming the weak defense in Fort Union and marching on to a probable easy conquest of Colorado—a victory that would have placed the gold mines in the hands of the financially distressed Confederacy.

The Texans caused no more trouble in New Mexico, but the Indians did, as they sensed that they could take advantage of the crisis. They raided ranches, waylaid stagecoaches, and destroyed wagon trains. Then Colonel Kit Carson and the New Mexico Volunteers crushed the Navajos in their stronghold and marched them as prisoners to a compound called Bosque Redondo at Fort Sumner. Las Vegas citizens protested about the concentration of so many Indians near their homes and became convinced that renegades departing from Fort Sumner were responsible for continuing depredations. Soon, in 1868, the United States Peace Commission made a treaty with the Navajos and released them for the "long walk" back to their devastated homeland.

The termination of warfare permitted improvements in Las Vegas, especially in the churches and schools and in the publication of newspapers (as will be described in appropriate chapters). Next, in 1879, came another improvement—the arrival of a railroad—which truly brought the dawn of a new era.

The attention of promoters had become focused upon all feasible routes for a railroad to the west coast, one of which naturally would lie along the old Santa Fe Trail into New Mexico. There stood Las Vegas, directly in the pathway at the eastern entrance to the gateway to all of the Far Southwest. In 1878, the Atchison, Topeka and Santa Fe was approaching New Mexico, and on December 1, the first

"Baca's Folly" in later years *(Museum of New Mexico; M. Otero)*

Building a railway *(National Archives; A. R. Waud)*

locomotive climbed over Ratón Pass.

One pioneer recalled later that among the Hispanos, many expressed misgivings, because a railroad would bring in a flood of strangers, as indeed it did. Others welcomed the prospect. Among them was Rumauldo Baca, who owned a lot west of the Exchange Hotel somewhere near the place where surely the Santa Fe Railroad would locate the depot. On it he built a mammoth, four-story building with rooms for stores on the first floor and for meetings and offices upstairs. After his expectations failed to materialize, his big house became jestingly referred to as "Baca's Folly."

Hopes of the townsmen had a foundation, because an agent of the railroad had obtained pledges of sums of money from businessmen around the Plaza to be used for building the depot. One can imagine their consternation when they learned that the track would miss Las Vegas and that the depot would be built in previously open country a mile to the east.

When the first train arrived on July 4, the locomotive was bedecked with evergreens and colored bunting, and the hills all around were covered with the wagons of spectators who had come from up to 200 miles to see *El Diablo*, their name for the puffing locomotive. A party of excited townsmen had even made the arduous trip to Trinidad in order to ride into New Town on that train, to the cheers of the welcoming crowd. A reporter for the Boston *Herald* observed that near the mechanical giant, "a Mexican was driving oxen and plowing with a crooked piece of wood."

Already a new town was rising rapidly in frame structures built hastily along Railroad Avenue. In one of them, Close and Patterson's Hall, a grand ball would celebrate the event that evening, and another would be held in the Exchange Hotel on the west side. That was the beginning of the conducting of two of almost everything for several decades afterward.

On February 9, 1880, when the first train pulled up at the new depot in Santa Fe, the people there celebrated by staging a great parade. New Mexico then was wrought up with a mania for railroad building. In the decade of the 1880s, promoters filed incorporation papers in Santa Fe for sixty-two railroads. If all had been built, Las Vegas would have had ten more of them.

Travel by rail, however, did not turn out to be all glorious, as a train wreck near Las Vegas late in 1879 injured several persons. Other accidents occurred periodically in subsequent years. The worst of the era happened in 1895, when a head-on collision near Shoemaker killed three trainmen and injured numerous passengers. One engineer expressed pride that he had never had a wreck, but it is a wonder. As he related it, "In those days we never got any train running orders. We ran exclusively by smoke and headlight."

The arrival of the steel trailway stimulated several improvements in Las Vegas and inaugurated an era of two decades of prosperity arising from the temporary eminence of this terminal. In that era it had a near monopoly as the commercial center for all of eastern New Mexico, and the population which had been 1,730 in Old Town in 1870 increased in one decade to 4,697, largely by the addition of New Town.

As an immediate improvement, hacks began hauling passengers from the trains across the river, where a wooden

Wagonloads of wool on Railroad Avenue *(Rex Studio)*

Ice houses and ponds, about 1890 *(Rex Studio)*

bridge was built in December, to restaurants on the Plaza. As soon as work was finished on the new depot, a telegraph office was housed in it. Then orders of train passengers were wired ahead so that meals could be ready in the newly built frame Depot Hotel, across the tracks, allowing a stopover of only thirty minutes.

In 1882, an associated company built nine dams to create ice ponds in the canyon of the Gallinas River, just above the Hot Springs, and the Santa Fe built a spur track up along the river to the ninth pond. In that era, ice was so much in demand for use in dining cars and refrigerated freight cars that this became one of the major ice-producing centers in the West. It employed up to 300 men seasonally for the cutting, storing, and shipping of 50,000 tons annually, until it lost out to mechanical refrigeration in the 1930s.

Moreover, in 1884, the Santa Fe built a company hospital on the west bluff of the Gallinas valley about two miles north of town. In its eleven rooms during the first six months of operation, the physician employed by the company cared for 108 ill and injured railroaders, whose hospital expenses were paid for from a fund built up by employee contributions.

By far the greatest project was the hotel at the Hot Springs, which had been named Montezuma due to a legend of the Pecos Indians that the famed emperor of the Aztecs had journeyed to those springs for beneficial bathing. Back in 1841, Julian and Antonio Donaldson, aware of the prospective value of those springs, had obtained a grant of the site by the *alcalde,* and by 1846 they had a small bathhouse there, which could be utilized for a fee. By 1856, they had apparently overextended themselves by building a log bathhouse containing six rooms, because the very next year the United States Marshal seized the property for debts and sold it to others. Then the army assumed management of it in conjunction with Fort Union, but that affiliation ceased during the Civil War.

As the property changed hands several times, O. H. Woodworth emerged as the new owner in 1864 and advertised "The wonderful effect of these springs in curing Syphilitic and kindred diseases, Scrofula, Cutaneous diseases, Rheumatism, etc." For a decade after 1868, the bathhouse was managed by Dr. and Mrs. S. B. Davis, and then W. S. Moore bought the property and built the Adobe Hotel. Jesse James and his friend Billy the Kid spent three days there quietly as guests in July 1879.

When the railroad arrived, a Boston capitalist organized the Las Vegas Hot Springs Company, in which the railroad was the controlling shareholder. This company purchased the property on August 1, 1879, and built a stone, two-story bathhouse costing $17,000. Twenty of the forty springs were walled up, and the hot water was pumped into the fourteen bathrooms. Next, in 1880, the company built a three-story stone hotel containing seventy-five rooms available to guests for four dollars a day. Its opening was celebrated on February 6 by a grand ball lasting all night.

The first of a series of disastrous fires destroyed the

The lobby in the second Montezuma Hotel *(William L. Erb)*

bathhouse in 1881. Undaunted, the promoters immediately built a new $20,000 stone bathhouse which could accommodate 500 customers daily. In addition, they engaged John Wellborn Root of Chicago as the architect for a new, large, frame hotel, which was built in 1882 at a cost of $150,000. It housed a dining hall, bowling alleys, a billiards room, and 240 guest rooms, and it had gaslights. Across the river south from it was the power plant and the depot of the spur railway, which was completed on April 5, 1882, in time to facilitate the attendance of 400 guests for the grand opening two days later. In his oration at the banquet, Miguel A. Otero, Jr. described how the emperor, Montezuma, had "disappeared from view amid clouds" but with a promise that he would return "in glory from the East." He concluded that "Tonight we hail his coming in the new and splendid halls of Montezuma."

The proprietors contracted with Fred Harvey to manage the hotel and dining service. For the wealthy clientele, fresh vegetables and fruit were obtained in Mexico and foreign delicacies were imported, included green turtles and sea celery. For the guests, several carriages, thirty carriage horses, and twenty-five saddle horses were kept in the stable, and the park contained rustic bridges, an archery range, and courts for tennis and croquet.

Fire struck again in January 1884. It started in the naphtha of the gas generating plant and spread so rapidly that it destroyed that building in less than an hour. Immediately the company began construction of a new, larger, brick and stone hotel, designed in the Queen Anne style. Upon its completion in 1885, its guests reveled in luxurious furnishings said to have cost a million dollars. It had 300 rooms in addition to auxiliary facilities, and the Fred Harvey System continued to serve exotic foods in the spacious dining hall. Moreover, its owners could boast that it was the first building in New Mexico to be lighted by electricity.

Within four months of the opening of that palace, fire ruined much of it. The blaze started in the attic, and the water sprayed from the hoses of the volunteer fire companies could not reach it; but the firemen were able to save the first two floors. After the hotel was rebuilt, with three floors instead of four, the management named it the Phoenix for having risen from ashes; but that name failed to win popular acceptance. It continued to be called the Montezuma.

In its heyday, the resort at the Hot Springs was advertised by a series of widely distributed brochures which described the salubrious mineral composition of the hot water, along with the variety of available bathing—such as shampoo $1.00, tub and pack 75¢, massage $1.00, electric $1.00, vapor 75¢, and mud pack $3.00. Those baths allegedly would cure, or alleviate, almost every disease and ailment then known.

In response to the promotion, visitors came from far and near. In addition to former President U. S. Grant and other prominent officials, businessmen, and honeymooners, eminent guests came from England, Germany, and Mexico. Probably the largest aggregation was the national convention of the Oddfellows Lodge in 1888, when 1,000 came on two special trains.

Before long, this spa no longer attracted numerous

guests. One temporary cause, of course, was the Panic of 1893. Additional reasons were the opening of other resort hotels farther west, also accessible by railroad, and the launching of luxurious steamships for travel abroad. The first intimation of final failure came in 1903 when the management revealed that it had sought, without success, to sell the idle plant to the government for use as an army sanitarium. Lack of patronage had made this aging facility a "white elephant," and, to make matters worse, in 1904 a flash flood washed away the large bathhouse. An era of brilliance had gone into eclipse.

That succession of luxury hotels was not the only evidence of the boom that Las Vegas enjoyed in the 1880s. Because this was the era when Charles Ilfeld emerged as the leading merchant in the territory, others emulated his success. The Otero, Sellar Company, which later became the Gross, Kelly Company and simultaneously the Browne and Manzanares Company, established wholesale businesses in frame buildings located alongside the railroad tracks in New Town, and both flourished so well that they built large brick buildings, the former in 1899 and the latter in 1889. Both also added branch outlets in other towns and did a big business in wool, mining tools, groceries, ranching implements, wagons, and household wares. Ranchers came from as far away as Carlsbad to trade at those stores.

Over on Bridge Street, the partnership of Stern and Nahm also handled much wool, retailed a variety of wares, and acquired a wool-scouring plant, a sawmill, a brick plant, and a lime kiln.

Likewise, on the west side, the sons of Miguel Romero, who had been associated with him as wagonmasters on the Santa Fe Trail, founded the Romero Mercantile Company in 1878. In three successive buildings facing the Plaza, it became the leading store in the Southwest in the wholesale distribution of dry goods. Trinidad Romero, erstwhile delegate in Congress, was active in the promotion of that profitable business. In 1880, he built a thirty-two-room mansion five miles southwest of town at a cost said to have been near $100,000. In it he and his family, aided by several Indian servants, enter-

An early mercantile center *(Museum of New Mexico)*

tained distinguished guests from the East.

In those times, when numerous patent medicines were being advertised as cures for almost everything, Benigno Romero acquired wealth by heading a drug company which advertised and sold widely a concoction called *La Sanadora*. Allegedly it was good for all ailments, and he obtained many testimonials as to its benefits, until finally its advertisements were condemned by the Food and Drug Administration.

Another beneficiary of the boom in business was the Central Bank founded in 1876 by Jefferson and Joshua Raynolds. In 1880, the partners had it incorporated as the First National Bank and built for it an imposing stone building at the corner of the Plaza and Bridge Street. Jefferson gave his attention to the profitable management of that bank as well as to his numerous community services, for which he was regularly a leading donor of funds. His brother, while continuing to reside in a fine home in Las Vegas, founded two more First Nationals in Albuquerque and El Paso.

In 1879, Miguel A. Otero, Sr. withdrew from the Otero, Sellar Company in order to open the San Miguel Bank in a room on the Plaza, but soon he moved it to a large building located on Grand Avenue in East Las Vegas. In 1890, the board of that bank founded a branch, the Las Vegas Savings Bank, which continues today as the Bank of Las Vegas. In 1920, the parent and the First National merged and two years later built a magnificent stone building that now is the home of the Bank of Las Vegas. By that time, the addition of other banks had increased the total number to six.

The boom also created a need for hotels better than the old Exchange and the other large rooming houses. Outstanding among the new ones were the large, brick Plaza Hotel built in 1880 by a company headed by Benigno Romero and the luxurious brick Castañeda built by the Santa Fe Railroad alongside the track in 1898 for lease to the Fred Harvey System. Much later, in 1923, local businessmen formed a company and bought shares in it for the construction of the large Meadows Hotel on Grand Avenue. This was to be a community project, but it later passed into individual ownership under a new name, the El Fidel.

The opening of a vast new frontier also created an opportunity for several producing enterprises which did well for about three decades, on the average. They included a brewery, a brick kiln, an iron foundry, a slaughterhouse, a flour mill, and, especially noteworthy, the W. H. Shupp factory on Bridge Street which supplied the market for carriages and wagons throughout much of New Mexico and Arizona.

Meanwhile, because the Plaza no longer needed to be reserved for parking wagons, the editors of both local newspapers proposed in 1879 that it be made into a nice park. Impatient about the lack of response, the editor of the *Optic* in 1880 condemned the "lack of public spirit" and added that "The merchants who trade and live around this dusty exposure seem to have been perfectly content to live and trade in dust and dirt as well as in wool and merchandise." Then donations were received for the building of a small bandstand in 1880 and for the planting of trees and the building of a picket fence around the Plaza in the ensuing year. In addition, two of the town companies which began selling lots on the east side in 1880 fortunately reserved two entire blocks for parks—Lincoln and Hillsite.

Don Margarito in the office of the Romero store, 1904 *(Our Lady of Sorrows Collection)*

The growth in population and in buildings required improved community services. Prior to 1880, residents had carted water from the river in barrels for domestic use. In that year, the Agua Pura Company was incorporated. It built a dam to create a small reservoir in the bed of the Gallinas River and piped the water to homes and fire hydrants. That reservoir accumulated much filth, which made the murky water, one consumer said, have the effect of "creating an eruption in the gastric neighborhood similar to that brought on by the eating of green apples."

Controversies over rates and service ensued until finally in 1910 the water company built Peterson Dam for the creation of a larger, secluded reservoir capable of containing eighty million gallons. Water was conveyed to it from a diversion dam upstream by means of a wooden flume supported by spikes in the granite cliff high above one of the ice ponds. Thenceforth, the two communities had a better water supply except in times of prolonged drought.

Another service, fire extinguishing, required both a supply of water under pressure and the mustering of manpower for utilizing it. Townsmen organized a volunteer hook and ladder company in 1881, and when a serious fire swept through much of a block on Railroad Avenue in November, the members of that company, who were attending a dance, rushed out and fought the conflagration while wearing their long-tailed dress suits.

As fire hydrants were being installed in 1881 and 1882, the hook and ladder company divided and enlisted others to found two hose companies almost simultaneously in order to have one in each business district. Number One on the east side moved into the new brick town hall in 1894. The company on the west side, named E. Romero after the man who was mayor in 1882 as well as the largest donor of funds for equipment, acquired a brick fire station on Bridge Street in 1909. Those two companies can claim to have been the second in the territory, after Socorro (1872), because as successors of the hook and ladder company of 1881, both antedate the two companies organized in Santa Fe in May 1882.

In 1899, the E. Romero Company acquired a Seagram hose and chemical wagon, as did Number One a year later. Lacking horses then, the first team to arrive at the station was hitched hastily to the fire wagon. In 1902, the city bought a team, and the town did likewise the next year. In 1916, both companies acquired fire trucks. When the next alarm was sounded after the town team had been sold to some gypsies,

West side of the Plaza in the late 1870s *(Museum of New Mexico; J. Furlong)*

Three Towns Grow in the Gateway

those horses came on the run, dragging two gypsy tents to which they had been tied.

In the era of the two-wheel, man-drawn hose carts, the two teams engaged in annual races and participated in state contests. Much excitement and rivalry were engendered by those contests, but otherwise the two companies engaged in friendly competition to be first, and best, in effective firefighting. They also cooperated in conducting Fourth of July celebrations and invited one another to annual fund-raising balls.

Protection of another type appeared to be urgent in 1880 when Victorio's band of Mimbres Apaches was committing depredations in the southern part of the territory. The townsmen organized a Home Reserve of forty volunteers and began drilling twice a week, until by 1882 the company took pride in being the most precise and flashy in the territory. Then interest declined but was revived periodically in the reorganization of new companies of home guardsmen. The one enlisted in 1897 was known as the Otero Guard, named after the territorial governor of that date. Its fifty-five members gave exhibition drills which caused that company to be dubbed "the best in the West." Hopes that it would be enrolled as a unit in the regiment of volunteers enlisted for the war with Spain failed to materialize.

For better street lighting, a company obtained a franchise from the county and built a brick gas works in 1881. The county commissioners specified that the gas street lanterns be lighted every night "except when the moon produces sufficient light which would be fully equivalent to the light produced by all the said street lamps in the City."

As soon as the technology became available for the transmission of electricity to arc lights, a franchise was granted in 1891 to the Las Vegas Light and Fuel Company. Immediately the governing bodies had trouble finding the means for installing those new marvelous lights at all locations where townsmen petitioned for them.

Another electrically operated convenience—the telephone—came quite early to Las Vegas, where the first line in the territory connected a telephone in the store of Charles Blanchard to one in his home in July 1879. Immediately banker Miguel A. Otero, Sr. organized a company, also the first in the territory. In 1881 it had lines in operation in town and one out to the hotel at the hot springs. A year later, the number of local telephones had increased to 173. As lines were extended northward to the villages of Los Alamos and Rociada, the agent reported that he was having difficulty in selling the service because some of his prospects doubted that that American mechanism could speak Spanish.

By 1889, the Colorado Telephone Company had strung a line from Trinidad to Las Vegas and had obtained a franchise for installing telephones; consequently, for a while the community had two competing companies. In 1903, the local manager for the Colorado company invited prospective patrons to come to the office and try out the long distance service whereby calls could be made to cities in Colorado, Wyoming, and Utah. Then that company bought the independent Las Vegas company and immediately extended the

Hose and Fire Company No. 1, about 1910 *(Museum of New Mexico)*

From the depot to the Plaza *(Our Lady of Sorrows Collection)*

The trolley car junction on Bridge Street, 1904 *(Museum of New Mexico)*

lines through Santa Fe to Socorro. Thus, modernization into the later Bell System had been inaugurated.

Facilities for improving local transportation became an urgent need as soon as the populous New Town arose east of the Gallinas River. To replace the hack service, the Las Vegas Street Railway Company obtained a franchise from the county in 1880 to lay tracks from the depot to the Plaza for operation of small streetcars to be drawn by "horse or mule power." Early in 1881, those streetcars began operating on a regular schedule between the two business districts.

Proposals soon arose for converting the streetcar line to electric power. In 1901, an applicant, Dr. E. L. Epperson of St. Louis, obtained a franchise, whereupon he and associated capitalists invested $100,000 in the project. That company improved the old streetcar tracks, hung a trolley line above them, built a depot by the bridge, and from it adapted the track of the spur railway to the hot springs for use by trolley cars. Because that line left Old Town without service, Jefferson Raynolds raised subscriptions of stock amounting to $20,000 for extension of the track west on Bridge Street and around the Plaza. The trolley cars began operating on a regular schedule in 1903, at a time when the patronage of the Montezuma Hotel had almost ceased; therefore, the principal revenue obtained from that branch was gained by transporting ice on freight cars drawn by a powerful electric locomotive.

In 1905, William A. Buddecke, representing capitalists in St. Louis, and Margarito Romero, proprietor of a resort at El Porvenir, purchased the trolley line and the electric power company and combined them as the Las Vegas Railway and Power Company. Those investors expended $100,000 to improve the track, purchase new cars, and build a large stone car barn and power plant, as well as to lay track out the boulevard to the Insane Asylum. They overextended themselves. In 1906, Buddecke ceased the operation of passenger cars from the bridge to Montezuma, and two years later he returned to St. Louis. By that time the company was in default in payments amounting to $300,000 due the purchasers of bonds. By court order, the company was placed in the hands of a receiver who sold the system to Denver capitalists. They continued the operation on a more modest scale so that it survived as an expanding electric utility after the use of automobiles put the trolley line entirely out of business in 1927.

In the vicinity of Las Vegas, mining excitement in the 1880s and a revival of it after 1900 brought rushes of prospectors and investors to each camp, notably at Mineral Hill and Rociada. However, the boom turned out to be more speculative than productive. In both 1910 and 1920, the United States Bureau of Mines had no reports of production or processing of minerals in San Miguel County in the two decades preceding those dates.

Farming and ranching fared better. Already mention has been made of the stimulating effect of the market for meat, grain, hay, and flour at Fort Union. The building of a four-story roller mill in town in 1886 was hailed as a sign of progress, because it would "bring the wheat raisers to Las Vegas to trade." A man who made a trip up through the Mora valley then remarked, "never in my life have I seen such an abundant harvest of cereals."

On ranches the sheep industry had been paramount back in the Mexican period, and it continued to prevail. By 1872, the estimate was that over one-half million sheep were being grazed in San Miguel County. Old-timers recalled later that at shearing time wagons lined up all the way out to Romeroville while awaiting their turn to unload at one of the several dealers' barns. At this leading wool shipping center in the Southwest, the amount sent out brought in over one million dollars annually in the 1890s and reached a peak of twenty million pounds in 1902.

Much of the wool was produced under the *partido* system, which is illustrated by the liberal terms of Charles Ilfeld's contracts. He once had 38,000 sheep let out to ranchers, who were to return two pounds of wool annually for each ewe. The remainder of the wool they could keep, as well as the lambs, but they could not sell any of the latter without Ilfeld's consent.

The third Las Vegas, Upper Town, fared well in the

early years as a center of farming and sheep raising. When in 1912 Margarito Romero prepared to publish a list of eminent *dons* whom he had known there and who had property valued at from $5,000 to $100,000 each, he named twelve, including six Bacas. That community reached a peak population of 796 in 1870 but declined gradually thereafter. As a result, it remained a suburban village which did not merge with either of the two larger neighboring communities.

The Hispanic pioneers had raised some cattle, but a greater expansion in that industry followed its Anglo promoters westward onto the usually lush grasslands of eastern New Mexico. Again the market at Fort Union was a factor, but cattle were shipped to the Midwest, too. As early as 1885, the car loadings were reported to have been over 5,000 head in that year.

Often ranchers bought some of the old Spanish land grants, but more often they merely acquired a watering place around which the branded cattle could be grazed upon the open range. One promoter, J. W. Lynch, was credited with persuading buyers in Wyoming and Montana to come to Las Vegas for the purchase of cattle, and he was said to have been the first to introduce Hereford cattle in San Miguel County.

Another big name in the cattle business was that of Wilson Waddingham, a millionaire from Kansas City who had a mansion in Connecticut and nationwide investments. In 1870, he bought the Pablo Montoya Land Grant and subsequently added neighboring tracts, all located in the eastern part of the county. He combined those vast holdings into the Bell Ranch. After he came to Las Vegas for his honeymoon, he also bought the Antonio Ortiz Land Grant from Thomas B. Catron. On his ranches, containing approximately one million acres, his foreman grazed cattle estimated at from 30,000 to 50,000 head. He became, therefore, a frequent, well-known visitor in Las Vegas.

"Dude" ranches were introduced quite early. In 1882, H. A. Harvey, who had come west from Boston for his health, found a secluded spot on El Cielo Mountain above Gallinas Canyon, and there he and his wife founded a guest ranch which was accessible only by riding burros up a primitive trail. Eight years later, Margarito Romero, previously engaged with his brothers in the mercantile business, marveled at the beauty of a site up the right fork of the Gallinas, which he called El Porvenir. There he built a resort hotel where guests came up in carriages and received room and board for $7.00 a week. After the original building burned down, he built another in 1906. Those two resorts and others that followed became quite popular and therefore usually were profitable.

Altogether, the large trade area produced much revenue for the Santa Fe Railroad. From 1886 to 1891, the cash receipts from shippers at this one point amounted to two and one-half million dollars and from passengers one-half million. Moreover, in 1886, the two banks in Las Vegas reported total resources of $1,300,000 and deposits of $600,000, whereas the two in Albuquerque then had only $700,000 and $300,000, respectively. The effect was reflected also in the census reports, which show that in 1890 the three contiguous Las Vegases had a population of 5,238 as against only 3,785 in Albuquerque. A decade later, Albuquerque was gaining on the Las Vegases, which then were only slightly ahead—6,818 to 6,238.

For several decades afterward, residents who had been present in that era shared pleasant memories of the thriving enterprise and unbounded optimism which had prevailed when these original towns of Las Vegas had been the "capital" of New Mexico in many capacities, with the exception of territorial government.

II | Reverses Force Readjustment

In the 1890s, Las Vegas began losing its territorial hegemony. The first serious blow fell when the army abandoned Fort Union in 1891. As the two companies rode on the train from Watrous to their new assignment at Fort Wingate, they sang, among other old favorites, *There's a Land That Is Fairer Than This,* and the editor wrote in the *Optic* a toast that almost came true: "Fort Union, may the pale moon and shining stars look down upon thee until thou shalt, by unseen power, sink into everlasting oblivion."

Immediately afterward, the nationwide Panic of 1893 bore down hard upon Las Vegas. The published list of tax delinquencies filled eight pages of the newspaper. Citizens established a Committee of Charity to solicit gifts of cash and clothing for the needy, and the city opened a soup house to feed tramps and others. As railroad revenue declined, the Santa Fe laid off employees, and the machinists at the roundhouse went on a strike in 1894. In response to false reports about destruction and looting, the governor sent a company of the Territorial Guard to patrol the streets and protect the railroad properties.

Recovery from that crisis was impaired by a serious decline in the wool market. By that time, too, other railroads penetrating New Mexico were reducing the trade area from a former "empire" to only the central part of this one county. The once great mercantile establishments held on tenaciously for half of a century, but in that time they were declining more and more into merely local outlets.

Meanwhile, the Santa Fe Railroad had built a branch across the Texas Panhandle to Belén, New Mexico, mainly for the handling of freight. Las Vegas was left principally

Bridge Street in 1892 (*Museum of New Mexico*)

with the passenger service, which had become transcontinental in 1885. One day in 1909, a newspaper reporter counted on one train 164 passengers headed for California. Arrival and departure of local passengers at Las Vegas had not yet been curtailed much by the use of automobiles, but they had been greatly reduced by the decline of patronage at the Montezuma Hotel and its final closing in 1903. That loss had been disastrous to the local economy in many other ways, too.

Obviously, if Las Vegas were to continue to thrive, the community was going to have to put down new roots. To that end, enterprising citizens sponsored promising projects, the energetic Commercial Club, organized in 1901 and converted into the Chamber of Commerce in 1923, engaged in strenuous promotion, and local representatives in the legislature sought plums for Las Vegas.

Pressures applied in Santa Fe were the first to get results. Because insane persons in those times were simply locked up in the jail, sometimes for many years, the territorial legislature enacted a statute in 1889 to found an asylum in Las Vegas. However, Benigno Romero, who, out of sympathy for the deranged persons took some into his home, also had to present strong appeals in Santa Fe until the legislature finally made an appropriation for a building in 1891. When it was ready in 1892, another year passed before funds were forthcoming for its opening.

By 1895, the forty-one patients in the Insane Asylum crowded the limited facilities, and those who were able were raising much of the food in the garden on the grounds. Two years later, a new brick wing added 110 rooms, and by 1902, the patients, numbering over 100, were reported to be having a recovery rate of about 15 percent.

In 1903, a sensational scandal disturbed the serenity of the institution. A local newspaper, the *Advertizer,* reported that the bones of a patient had been found scattered about the grounds and alleged gross mistreatment. The governor immediately appointed an investigating committee, which first heard testimony by two former employees about mistreatment. However, others testified next that those two had been dismissed by the superintendent, Dr. W. R. Tipton,

The first building of the Insane Asylum *(Las Vegas City Museum; Chamber of Commerce)*

because they had been guilty of misconduct themselves.

Dr. Tipton admitted that when a patient without relatives had died, he had first performed an autopsy and next had scraped the flesh from the bones in order to have a skeleton for study. Hints were forthcoming that a young, insubordinate physician on the staff had purposely scattered those bones on the grounds in an effort to get Dr. Tipton removed. In a majority report, therefore, the committee exonerated Dr. Tipton and staff members with only a mild scolding about the careless handling of those bones.

After that interruption, another building was added to the asylum in 1903, followed by a two-story annex two years later. The patients then numbered 115, and the recovery rate had increased to 31.5 percent. Patients working on the farm were producing crops valued annually at $14,000 under the supervision of the steward, George W. Ward.

Construction continued apace but always was a little behind the increase in admissions. In 1935, there were twenty-one buildings housing 716 patients and some of the employees, and the farm operation. Most of the employees, however, resided in Las Vegas, whence went a considerable

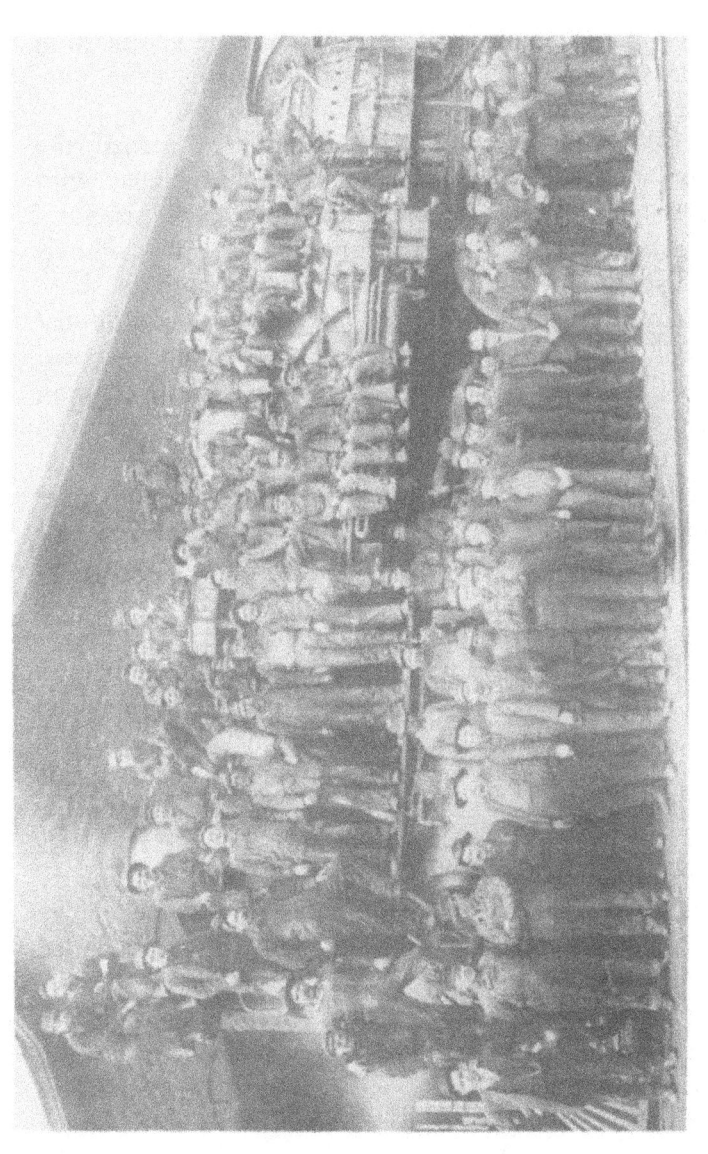

One shift of mechanics at the Roundhouse in the 1920s (*Our Lady of Sorrows Collection; Margaret Sanchez*)

portion of the expenditures amounting to near $200,000 in that year. Certainly this institution, later renamed the State Hospital, had become a major asset of Las Vegas.

In 1893, the year when the asylum was opened, the legislators had been persuaded to favor Las Vegas with another dispensation—selection of the town as the site for a territorial normal school. At that time, too, the public schools were beginning their phenomenal growth. Both of those institutions, despite periodic ups and downs, contributed much to the local economy while serving also a more exalted purpose. On the other hand, a big flurry of experimentation with dry farming from 1906 to 1908 followed by efforts to make a great success of commercial farming by irrigation in the 1920s both fizzled out. The first two of the above are more fully, and more appropriately, described in the chapter on education and the latter two in that dealing with land and water.

The water, electric, and telephone utilities became leading employers as their expansion accompanied the population growth. The railroad, too, although its freight loadings had been curtailed, still contributed much seasonal employment in the ice industry. In addition, 500 railroaders resided at this division headquarters. The Santa Fe enlarged the roundhouse in 1909 and built a new one of the thirty stalls eight years later. Here the steam locomotives were overhauled regularly by three shifts of mechanics totalling close to 400 men.

Other employees associated with the railroad included numerous "Harvey Girls" recruited in the Midwest to serve as waitresses in the Hotel Castañeda for $40.00 a month plus room and board. In the late 1920s, however, the increasing dependence upon automobiles and trucks was beginning to hurt the railroad, and later Las Vegas suffered a severe shock when conversion to diesel locomotives, which needed less frequent servicing, caused the elimination of this point as a division headquarters.

All of these activities were mere humdrum in contrast to what once had been the exciting role of this community. Townsmen therefore sought new means for restoring local eminence. On the basis of his necrology records, a

Dr. Francis A. Atkins suggested exploitation of the climate. For the year 1889, he found that nobody had died of disease excepting nine consumptives who had arrived too late for their ailment to be arrested. Las Vegas was not a good place for doctors, he concluded, because "Spells of weeks and months occur when one's practice hardly justifies his plant."

Advertising of this location as favorable for the curing of pulmonary ailments brought out Sisters of Charity from St. Louis, Missouri, and Leavenworth, Kansas. By 1897, this organization had raised funds to build St. Anthony's Sanitarium on a full city block purchased for them by local philanthropists. Immediately it became the "mecca of invalids" to such an extent that an annex had to be added in 1911. Meanwhile, in 1900, Dr. F. W. Seward of New York had rented the mansion built at Romeroville in 1880 by Don Trinidad Romero and had converted it into a sanitarium. Four years later, Dr. William T. Brown, also of New York, became his partner, but in 1905 he withdrew in order to open another sanitarium at Valmora.

In that era, when life out-of-doors in a dry climate was the only known cure for tuberculosis, victims of that disease, coming from afar, filled all of these facilities, as well as the Plaza Hotel and the small community hospital. They also resided in tent camps which sprang up on several vacant lots. Then Dr. W. R. Edison of St. Louis promoted a plan to have all of the national lodges unite to maintain a sanitarium for

A haven for "consumptives," 1897 *(Rex Studio)*

Reverses Force Readjustment

members in the idle Montezuma Hotel. He claimed that forty-nine lodges had agreed to support this by collecting one cent a month from their members, and sent a committee to Las Vegas in 1905 to negotiate terms for use of the Montezuma facilities. There was great rejoicing in the community when a conditional deed was executed. Las Vegas would get that sanitarium! However, the assessments failed to come in, and this endeavor came to naught.

In 1908, the Knights of Pythias proposed the founding of a sanitarium in Las Vegas, and businessmen almost overnight raised $8,000 to purchase a full city block of vacant lots. Citizens then were confident that this deal was wrapped up, but in October came the disappointing news that the Pythians would not be able to locate their sanitarium in Las Vegas.

The Commercial Club tried hard to land something that would make profitable use of the idle Montezuma Hotel, without immediate success. In 1914, therefore, the Santa Fe Railroad deeded the million-dollar facilities to the local Young Men's Christian Association, which held a few dinner dances there but lacked the means to maintain the property. A year later, the Y.M.C.A. sold it to the National Bible Play Society, which produced a few short motion pictures there on biblical topics before also giving up possession. Finally, in 1920, the Commercial Club negotiated transfer of the property to the Baptists for a college, but the school continued only for seven years. Hence, the quest for a profitable successor would continue.

At the time when the luxury hotel had been closed, the electric trolley line had begun operating passenger cars past it to the ice ponds. The Elks Lodge then promoted a proposal to create a fairgrounds on the flats west of the river near where the car track bridged that river, about three miles north of town. Soon an organization formed for that purpose—the Las Vegas Driving Park and Fair Association, under the presidency of a local attorney, Ralph Emerson Twitchell. This organization raised subscriptions to prepare a racetrack, a grandstand, and an athletic field better than Las Vegas had ever had.

A great crowd turned out for the horse races, baseball game, and fireworks on the opening day of the new fairgrounds on July 4, 1903. Plans were made for a northern New Mexico fair there the next year, which the promoters believed would surpass the territorial fair in Albuquerque; but that time a big flood washed away the grandstand and ruined the racetrack, so that the event had to be canceled. Undaunted, the promoters restored the property and promoted a fair there with great success in 1905. It included horse races, Indian dances, a baseball tournament, rodeo events, and races by volunteer firemen coming from other towns. A year later, similar events were repeated, but this was the last time. No reason for the cessation was published, but no doubt it was caused in part by the shutting down of the electric trolley line.

Another disappointment ensued. Persons who marveled at the scenic beauty of Gallinas Canyon imagined what stunning vistas would be unfolded for many more people if the road could be improved and extended over the range through Pecos to Santa Fe. In 1903, a large delegation from Las Vegas went to Santa Fe and obtained an appropriation to have the scenic road constructed by convict labor. Work was begun immediately under the general supervision of F. H. Pierce, superintendent of the local Agua Pura Company and also then president of the board of the penitentiary. Instead of improving the old road down in the canyon, where high waters sometimes washed out the bridges, a highline was built up along the cliffs.

A promotional brochure proclaimed that "Words are feeble, weak, impotent, when one undertakes to depict the beauties that this road will bring within easy reach of all." However, the laborious chiseling out of that highline proceeded so slowly that by 1907, when the funds were exhausted, the road had been built only to within three-fourths mile of the boundary of the national forest. In subsequent years, local citizens clamored in vain for the Highway Department or the National Park Service or somebody to construct an extension of the scenic road on over the range as originally authorized.

The new Scenic Road *(Rex Studio)*

In those years, the ambition of local sportsmen knew no bounds; they would even make Las Vegas the national capital of boxing. When Jack Curley, a promoter, planned to arrange a bout between Jack Johnson, heavyweight champion, and Jim Flynn, a contender who was emerging as "the great white hope," Charles O'Malley, a local former athlete, enlisted financial support and persuaded Curley to stage the event in Las Vegas on July 4, 1912. Early in May, Flynn arrived at training quarters prepared for him at the Montezuma Hotel. Later that month, Johnson moved into a house that was leased from Francisco Baca y Sandoval and located a block north from the Plaza. Years later, Eduardo F. Baca said that he arranged plank seats in the front yard, where spectators could watch the champion work out against sparring partners by paying ten cents for a seat.

The champion came to Las Vegas *(Our Lady of Sorrows Collection; Delfino Garduno)*

At first, tickets for the fight sold well at ten and twenty-five dollars each, but then everything went wrong. O'Malley and the contractor had a serious dispute about the arrangement of the seats in the stadium being built east of St. Anthony's Sanitarium, and late snows hampered the outdoor training of the contenders. Worse yet, the territorial ministers presented a petition to Governor W. C. McDonald to prevent the "brutal exhibition," and the Laguna Indians did likewise because the government would not let them fight anymore. After the legislature failed to respond, the governor announced that he would stop the fight anyway, but he later retracted that vow.

Reverses Force Readjustment   47

The confusion slowed down ticket sales so that only $36,000 were collected. The Santa Fe canceled the special trains, and only 5,000 fans showed up. As the bout progressed, Jack Johnson coolly taunted the challenger and mauled him so badly that in the ninth round, Captain Fred Fornoff of the Mounted Patrol jumped into the ring and ordered the fight stopped. The promoters did manage to scrape up the money guaranteed to the two combatants, but nobody else profited from this bout, which Milton W. Callon later dubbed "Boxing's Greatest Fiasco."

Las Vegas would have to try something else, and an opportunity appeared in 1913 when Romaine Fielding, early motion picture star, was acting in a movie being produced in Silver City. The Commercial Club invited him to come to Las Vegas, which he did in August of that year. At first, his crew prepared for him a studio in a house leased at 920 Gallinas Street, but a month later, Fielding's party took over the Plaza Hotel and renamed it temporarily the Hotel Romaine.

The first picture produced by Fielding in Las Vegas was *The Rattlesnake*, a story of a young Mexican's rivalry with another in a love affair. Four more followed within a month. Those early films, then hailed as masterpieces, won for him first place by a wide margin in contests conducted in 1913 and 1914 to select the nation's most popular motion picture actor.

Next, Fielding wrote the scenario for a five-reel thriller, *The Golden God*, about a labor revolution that he prophesied would occur in 1950 against the "consolidated industries. He spent close to $50,000 for the cavalry and artillery charge through the streets of Old Town in the assault upon an infuriated mob. The number of local "extras" employed in the battles was estimated at about 5,000, and an officer of the National Guard, Major Ludwig Ilfeld, won praise for his part in "the wonderful control of the fighting men."

The first "aeroplane" to be flown over Las Vegas, by R. C. McMillen, a stunt aviator, injected the climactic action in spectacular battle scenes witnessed by close to 10,000 spectators who jammed the town and covered the slopes of the Crestón. A local newspaper published a vivid description of the action:

> Overhead . . . the new terror of war, the dreadnaught of the skies, with death at the helm spread his grim toll of war . . . Bombs were dropped from the plane, which exploded in mid air. The mob, with flaming torches and rifles, tried to stop the terror of the clouds which spread in its path the vivid death of the cruiser of the air.

Immediately afterward, Fielding departed for Galveston, Texas, where he said he would have "a warmer climate for the winter months." So ended the productive but brief sojourn in Las Vegas of the most popular movie star of 1913.

Another actor soon came. For the first local rodeo in July 1915, Ludwig Ilfeld invited Tom Mix to participate in stagecoach races. He came, but the vehicles failed to arrive in time. Greatly impressed by the local setting, he then moved into the studio formerly prepared for Fielding on Gallinas Street and acted in motion pictures produced there, on the lot next door, in the streets of Old Town, and out on a ranch. The first picture, *Never Again,* was followed by five more within a year, of which two, *The Rancher's Daughter* and *The*

Watching the making of a Fielding movie *(Father James T. Burke)*

The first "aeroplane" in Las Vegas, 1913 (*Father James T. Burke*)

Country Drugstore, were pioneers of the type that came to be known as westerns. After Tom Mix departed, he became one of the nation's famous actors in pictures produced elsewhere. A by-product was the launching of the career of Leo Carrillo as a popular actor in motion pictures and on television, after he had started as a youthful "extra" in pictures made by Tom Mix. In 1928, Mix returned for a brief visit with friends in the city where his daring stunts and creative skill first won him fame. Unfortunately, in 1916 his departure had terminated that early era of motion picture production in Las Vegas.

Still the prosperity of earlier times had not been revived. For many citizens, the comedown was hard to take. They would continue their quest for a bonanza after a forced delay caused by the nationwide absorption in the crisis of World War I.

In 1922, as soon as water began filling a newly created reservoir back of Storrie Dam five miles north of the city, Thomas W. Conway, local manager of the project, filed a plat for a resort of 279 residential lots on the north side of the lake. For the several lots sold between 1924 and 1936, the deeds provided for a perpetual right of ingress and egress and for access to the waterfront for fishing and boating. Despite all promotional efforts, however, only one purchaser built a cottage at this proposed resort. The project then joined others shelved with great disappointment.

Simultaneously, beginning in 1923, a flurry of excitement about drilling for oil led townsmen to anticipate that the new wells, some of them expected to be "gushers," would make Las Vegas "the metropolis of the Southwest." For two years the *Optic* published a column of "Oil News," and petroleum companies hastily bought up mineral rights on most ranches in the county. This excitement, too, subsided.

Next, in 1927, members of the local Woman's Club, joined by others from Texas who were vacationing in Las Vegas, decided that the community would be a great place to conduct a Chautauqua program like those in some eastern cities. They obtained financial support from the Chamber of Commerce, elected Mrs. William Bacon of Fort Worth,

Texas, as president, and scheduled a series of lectures and musical performances for a program continuing through July and August. Mrs. Bacon anticipated that 750 club members would come from southwestern cities for the entire program and 2,000 others for brief visits, but the attendance did not come up to expectations.

A similar program called the Arts Festival was offered in 1928. Then, because several businessmen threatened to cease subscribing to the Chamber of Commerce if their membership fees, intended for the promotion of business, were to be applied again for promotion of things cultural, the Chamber withdrew its support. That blasted this endeavor, which had been undertaken with great promise.

The impression that everything turned out badly must be modified by recognition that a few other efforts yielded economic benefits of longer endurance, even though seasonally in most instances.

In 1897, the legislature had reorganized the territorial militia into the New Mexico National Guard, whose officers organized Company K of infantry and Company A of cavalry in Las Vegas in 1903. A year later, the Guard came for a territorial encampment at a site described as "on the mesa west of town," where a target range had already been prepared. Immediately Colonel R. E. Twitchell, an unattached officer, and the other members of the Fairground Association scheduled four days of horse racing and related events to entertain the guardsmen, but the commanding officer, General R. H. Whiteman, notified them that the soldiers would not appear there because they were "coming to work." However, on August 10, he decided that the troopers needed a practice march of about one mile in the direction of the racetrack.

The Guard went into camp in Texas in 1905 and returned to Las Vegas in 1906 and 1907 for drill and practice at what was described as "the finest National Guard Camp in America," commanded then by Major R. C. Rankin. This activity in Las Vegas resulted in the building of an armory on Douglas Avenue in 1908. When Las Vegas got the encampment again in 1909, the 2,000 visitors who went out to observe the maneuvers kept the streetcar line to the Insane Asylum, near the camp, crowded all day.

In 1910, the Guard went to Camp Atascadero in California, where it was so cold that a reporter said the New Mexicans "swore in three languages." A year later, about 500 came again to the local site, to which they returned in 1913, but then those encampments ceased temporarily.

Due to a lag in interest, there was no local company of guardsmen in March 1916, when Mexican revolutionaries, thought then to have been led by Doroteo Arango (Pancho Villa) made a raid on Columbus, New Mexico. Hastily, Major Ludwig Ilfeld and Sergeant Charles O'Malley enlisted forty men, who went to the border as support for the campaign of the regular army into Mexico. A year later, after Villa had eluded his pursuers, the campaign was called off. Then, as soon as the men returned home, all National Guard units were called into federal service for World War I.

After that war, when control of the National Guard was returned to the states, Company F of the 120th Engineers was formed in Las Vegas in 1923 as a step toward obtaining renewal of the encampments on the west mesa. Five other companies came a year later to reside in tents at the elevated site. Because the officers reported that they liked this location better than Fort Bliss, where camp had been held the previous year, this was designated the permanent site. Businessmen

A booster caravan headed for Texas *(Rex Studio)*

raised funds to purchase 668 acres from the Land Grant Board for $2.50 an acre, and M. M. Sundt of Las Vegas was low bidder for the contract to build a bathhouse, four mess halls, and sixty-two tent floors. In 1929, the 111th Cavalry Regiment began arriving for exercises for a period of two weeks following the encampment of the Engineers. In that year, Colonel N. L. King, commander of the cavalry, named the camp as a memorial to Maximiliano Luna, who had been captain of a company of the Rough Riders and who afterward had lost his life in the campaign against insurgents in the Philippines.

The encampment of the two regiments and of Battery A of the 158th Field Artillery brought hundreds of men to Las Vegas in each summer after 1929, and the townspeople became accustomed to hearing the rumble of artillery "peppering the mountain with shrapnel." In 1935, a grant from the Works Progress Administration, supplemented by funds contributed by businessmen, enabled the building of stone seats for 1,500 spectators in a natural arena at Camp Luna. It was named King Stadium as a memorial to the cavalry commander who had died in 1933.

The encampments from 1935 through 1939 were supplemented by horse shows which attracted a large attendance and some of the finest horses in the Southwest. These shows ceased when the 111th Cavalry was converted into the 200th Coastal Artillery. This well-trained regiment was rushed to the defense of the Philippines, where it engaged in a courageous effort to check the Japanese invasion. Outnumbered and overwhelmed, the survivors were incarcerated as Japanese prisoners of war for the duration.

Meanwhile, in May 1942, Camp Luna had been leased by the War Department, which hastily constructed 106 more buildings for the housing and training of 2,100 men of the Army Air Corps Ferrying Command. For three years the camp was a busy place and contributed significantly to ultimate victory in that national crisis. Afterward, although a small part of the camp again became the headquarters of the local National Guard, the greater part of it was vacated and therefore made available for other functions that would contribute in their own respective ways to improving the economy in Las Vegas and vicinity.

Another enterprise that endured for about one-half century was the promotion of local rodeos. There were early antecedents. In 1899, during the first reunion of Roosevelt's Rough Riders in Las Vegas, local cowboys had competed in horse races, steer roping, and a bronco riding contest. Six years later, at the first Northern New Mexico Fair, the events included bronco riding, a rope exhibition, bull riding, and a cowboy relay race.

A decade later, when many teachers were coming to summer sessions at the Normal University, the local Commercial Club proposed that a cowboy roundup be held so that the teachers and other visitors could see an exhibition of "real western life." That idea grew into a rodeo like those of some other western cities, only this one would be called "The Cowboys' Reunion." A "monster parade" on July 2, 1915, opened the three-day event for which the crowds filled the grandstand in the former fairgrounds in the afternoon and the opera house for western dances at night. A newly organized Reunion Association then purchased the idle fairgrounds, and groups of boosters drove caravans of cars to neighboring cities for promotion of a similar event in 1916, when an estimated 10,000 spectators enjoyed the four-day performance over the weekend of July 4.

As the annual rodeos continued, they rose into eminence as among the best in the West in the 1920s. Almost 100 cowboy athletes competed annually in bronco busting, bull riding, calf roping, and horse racing, while the large crowds also obtained entertainment from rodeo clowns, band music, trick ropers, fireworks, and western dances in town at night. In 1924, when a new arena had been built on the flats about a mile north of Old Town, the director, Tex Austin, began far-flung promotion. In that year and the next, he took the thirty-two-piece Cowboy Band, directed by B. J. Patterson, and a group of performers, including cowboys, Navajo Indians, and Spanish-American dancing girls, on tours to Denver, St. Paul, Minneapolis, Palm Beach, New York, and London.

Promotion of a successful rodeo after 1929 became more

and more difficult due to the worsening trend of business. Warren Shoemaker, a local rancher, Alvin Naylor, a perennial participant, and Dee Bibb, local world champion bulldogger, tried to give the event a shot in the arm by adding stock car races and polo contests, but attendance declined. After 1933, the rodeos were suspended. In 1939, a local post of the American Legion revived them in a new arena built two miles north of the city. At last Las Vegas had hit upon something that gave the local economy a shot in the arm for a few days seasonally, until interest declined in the 1960s and those big events were suspended again.

The location in the Gateway to Glorieta cast another opportunity in the direction of Las Vegas when automobiles came into common use, but capitalizing upon that natural advantage also required some local efforts. When venturesome citizens first bought gasoline buggies, curious people crowded around to look at them. By 1909, twenty-eight townsmen owned cars and five more had motorcycles. Driving one over the primitive roads between towns then was quite an ordeal. One carrying the territorial land commissioner as an emissary of good roads arrived in Las Vegas with springs broken and one wheel out of commission.

In 1910, the city council adopted the first traffic ordinance, which fixed speed limits of ten miles an hour in the business district and fifteen on residential streets, required that each car have a horn and two lamps, and levied a license fee of $2.50 for each car, to be paid only once upon acquisition of the car. Simultaneously, the county commissioners began making appropriations for rudimentary improvements on some of the local dirt roads. At that time, the Commercial Club and Daughters of the American Revolution were placing markers on those roads, and a pathfinder trip through Las Vegas led to the designation of the Old Santa Fe Trail as a cross-country highway. One day in 1911, two Mitchell cars arrived from Denver after having spent only three days on the road. In November two years later, a record was set when over fifty cars passed through Las Vegas.

After World War I, automobile traffic suddenly became heavy. An information agency estimated in 1921 that

510,000 cars, mostly Model T Fords, had traveled the Santa Fe Trail in that one year. Because previous dependence upon railroads had permitted neglect in road improvement, New Mexico was unprepared for that upsurge. On the deeply rutted dirt roads, a trip from Las Vegas to Albuquerque then required nearly a full day. Travelers carried extra cans of gasoline and oil on the running boards and a tow rope, baling wire, pliers, and a tire pump in the tool chest. One man recalled that after making the trip he had to replace brake linings that had burned out going down La Bajada hill. Milton C. Nahm wrote later that he tried to straddle the deep ruts and remain a mile behind the dust cloud raised by the car ahead. Once when he came to an arroyo filled with water, he and his companions piled up rocks and dirt in order to build a ramp. Then he hit it fast and jumped the car across.

Often when the little bridge at Tecolote washed out, villagers hitched their teams to stranded cars and pulled them across the river and up the muddy hill. A pioneer truck driver, Leroy S. Wicks, recalled later that he had to carry food and a sleeping bag to prepare for a camp-out when flash floods washed out the frail bridges. He also carried tools for rebuilding those bridges and added that a driver always had to be alert if he were to avoid hitting one of the many cows grazing along the unfenced roadways.

The service clubs in Las Vegas launched a road improvement campaign that they conducted by means of promotional caravans traveling to neighboring towns. They and the Santa Fe Trails Association obtained better marking of the highways and the provision of improved camping grounds. Those in Las Vegas filled with cars and tents on summer nights.

The heavy automobile traffic led to the founding of new types of business—service stations, supply stores, car dealers, and "stage," or bus, lines to neighboring towns. In 1926, the Fred Harvey System inaugurated "Indian Detour" trips for train travelers who took bus tours starting from the Hotel Castañeda for sightseeing in northern New Mexico.

Automobiles also created new public business. The municipalities adopted one traffic ordinance after another and

Lindbergh's visit, 1928 (*Las Vegas City Museum; Jo Anna Russel*)

required inspection of service stations. The city bought a car so that the police could run down speeders and required all operators to obtain city drivers' licenses in 1924, although in that first year only 350 of 800 complied. Moreover, as the state undertook road rebuilding, the Highway Department became the employer of specialized engineers and laborers. The rise of tourism had engendered for Las Vegas a new, continuing asset.

The "gateway principle" also became effective in the routing of travel by airplanes by way of Las Vegas and the pass over the mountains. Preliminaries were building up in the decade of the twenties, when "barnstorming" aviators began arriving to take people up for thrilling rides. In 1922, one aviator obtained contributions from merchants for the purchase of fireworks, which he displayed at night in spectacular "flaming loops in the air." A year later, another made aerial photographs for the Chamber of Commerce and Fox Films. In 1927, the Chamber obtained a lease on a farm field on the mesa a mile east of the city for use as a landing field.

In October 1929, Charles Lindbergh was greeted by thousands when he landed on Howell Field on the mesa in his Curtiss-Falcon airplane. At that time, as president of the Trans-Continental Air Transport Company, he was exploring a route to California. He announced that starting in January he would provide passengers with transcontinental service by conveying them on trains from New York to Columbus, Ohio, whence he would fly them in Ford trimotor airplanes to Dodge City for transfer there to trains owned by the Santa Fe Railroad. Near Las Vegas, his planes would pick them up for the flight to the west coast.

By the end of November, Lindbergh's company was obtaining bids for the building of a larger hangar and a two-story depot alongside the railroad tracks at Onava, ten miles north of Las Vegas, where an option to purchase 1,200 acres had been negotiated. Las Vegas came that near to the acquiring of a major terminal on the route of what ultimately was to become the successful Trans World Airlines, when suddenly Lindbergh announced a change in plans. The facilities at Onava would not be built. A local aviator said later that he

At dedication of the airport, 1933: *left to right* Les Aldridge, Alfred Rogers, Charles O'Malley, O. A. Larrazolo, Jr., Tom Truder, J. A. Cruikshank, Lorenzo Delgado, E. E. Marshall, L. R. McGehee (airmail pilot), Bill Jenks, Frank Delgado, Tom Conway (*Las Vegas City Museum*)

believed the reason for the decision to withdraw was the high altitude of the site and its proximity to the mountains. Instead, merely a small hangar was built on the landing field on the mesa.

In 1929, Mid-Continent Airlines leased a field for a new airport across the road and a little to the east of Howell Field for proposed commercial flights from Denver to El Paso, but that promise also failed to materialize. Then the Land Grant Board deeded that field to the City of Las Vegas, and local aviators made improvements. On November 11, 1933, a great procession of cars went out for the dedication of that airport and the celebration of the arrival of the first army plane bringing airmail. In 1934, the airmail contract was let to the Varney Speed Lines, but when that company began using large Lockheed craft, a federal inspector condemned the landing field as "unsuitable for the new fast equipment." The Varney line, which later became Continental Airlines, would bypass Las Vegas until a field with better runways could be provided.

In 1937, a federal inspector selected a suitable site five miles north of the city. By virtue of municipal bond issues and a federal grant, the city acquired the land, opened a highway to the field, built a hangar and radio building, and provided runways. In December 1940, it was ready for resumption of service by Continental Airlines. Immediately, after the United States was drawn into World War II, and a large airport became a prospective need for defense, the army spent $470,000 on more land, surfaced and lighted runways, a large hangar, and a brick office building, all completed in May 1942. The local university then obtained a contract to operate a wartime army airplane mechanics school and a navy flight school at the new airport, which continued only for the duration of the war.

The subsequent history of the airport is the story of one built too hastily to endure well and one too large for the city to maintain properly. Periodically, bond issues and federal grants made possible needed repairs. In 1948, Pioneer Airlines joined Continental in using the airport, but due to its poor condition and inadequate patronage, both ceased that local service in 1951.

All during the ordeals of the airport, a private flying service was operated successfully from first one field and another by Lloyd Bible, beginning in 1930. He gave instruction to candidates for licensing as pilots, and he flew a charter service to other cities for businessmen and an ambulance service to major hospitals for persons critically ill. In addition, other private craft made use of the airport.

Through the 1930s and 1940s, the federal government maintained flight control centers from which low-frequency radio beams were transmitted for reception in both private and commercial planes to keep them on their route. In addition, flight at night was facilitated by beacons installed along the route, so that from one the pilots could see the flashing of the next one. At Las Vegas, two major routes formed a junction for the crossing of the range by way of Glorieta Pass. In the flight service station at the airport, radio operators were in almost constant communication with pilots flying overhead. Thus, the "gateway principle" continued to be effective, but this later application of it required the employment of only relatively few technicians at the airport.

Las Vegans had entered the decade of the 1920s optimistically. The great war was over, and efforts to improve the economy looked promising. The optimism was reflected then in the construction of several new buildings for churches, schools, and business houses. Unfortunately, however, the Great Depression that hit the nation in the 1930s began in Las Vegas in the early twenties and was abetted by serious droughts. Few freight car loadings so seriously curtailed the income of the railroad that the Santa Fe laid off 150 local employees in May 1921. A year later, when the railroad unions went on strike, five trains were stranded in Las Vegas for two weeks. Several business firms went under, and between 1923 and 1925, bank failures reduced the number from six to only one.

On the other hand, some enterprises were able to contend against the lean years of the Depression. One, the retail clothing store of Joseph and Milton Taichert, founded in 1909, was augmented in the 1920s by a thriving trade in furs, hides, and wool for which two buyers traveled over New Mexico and into Arizona. Another was a new type of merchandising by chain stores, represented by J. C. Penney Company beginning in 1920 and by the opening of the branch outlets of Montgomery Ward and Company in 1929 and Safeway in 1930.

As already mentioned, several of the promising endeavors collapsed, and the few that were successful were not sufficiently fruitful to compensate for the steady downhill trend. Local cooperative efforts sometimes gave way to a "dog eat dog" scramble for survival, as was apparently observed by Dr. W. T. Brown, proprietor of the Valmora Sanitarium. When called upon to address the annual banquet of the Chamber of Commerce in 1927, he stunned the members by scolding them for their "hard feelings, suspicion, petty jealousy, disloyalty, hatchets, hammers, and any other factors acting as general detriments to the future prosperity and well being of the community." He exposed a fault that would persist as long as there were lean pickings.

As the Great Depression, worsened by additional devastating local droughts, plunged the community into greater depths, local charitable efforts were stepped up by the Salvation Army, the Associated Charities, the Sisters of Loretto, the Victory Missionary Sisters, the Sisters of Charity, and a case worker for the Charles Ilfeld Fund. The distress, however, grew beyond their ability to cope with it. Federal aid was needed. In 1933, the Civilian Conservation Corps, the Public Works Administration, and the Civil Works Act somewhat improved local employment by financing "made work" and building projects.

When direct relief to the destitute became available by the opening of the local State Charities Office in October 1933, it enrolled 700 applicants within a month. Because that office then had to depend upon only twelve volunteers to investigate cases, many of the needy had to wait a year before they obtained aid. Simultaneously, the burden became greater as many impoverished families moved into the city from neighboring villages in order to have access to either work projects or direct relief. From 1920 to 1940, several of those villages lost one-half of their population—the surging of a decline that later reduced some almost to ghost towns.

In the local welfare office, many of those case records opened in 1933 were not closed until the recipients of aid passed away in the 1960s. The report of a case worker about one family was typical of several:

> This family are badly in need of clothing and (especially) underclothing. Their food will not last until the next regular order. They obtain water from the well and complain that it hurts their stomachs and that it is no good even for washing purposes. They have no debts, no income, no insurance, and no compensation. They have no livestock. No garden.

People who had lost their means of subsistence and next their seasonal employment as a result of the Great Depression had become destitute.

Poverty long had been a way of life for many residents of Las Vegas, especially a large portion of the Hispanic population. It had begun due to the stringencies of their early subsistence economy, and it persisted among those *peones* who were obligated to a few wealthy *dons* under a debt servitude arrangement. James Meline, a visitor who had traveled extensively, wrote in 1866, in the era when the wealthy *dons* were dominant, that nowhere had he ever seen such a general prevalence of extreme poverty as in Las Vegas. Much of it continued into the era of the commercial boom, because so many townsmen were unable to engage in profitable activities which required fluency in English.

Through the years, little beyond the feeble efforts of private charities was done to alleviate the poverty. The prevailing American theory in that era was that once the poor were liberated from bondage and schools were made available to them, the rest would take care of itself. There was no place in that theory for legal prevention of discrimination and for federal antipoverty and economic development programs. Finally, in the 1930s, local poverty became a new kind of a way of life involving dependence upon the recommendations of case workers handling the dispensation of public assistance. When the annual reports of the State Welfare Department finally were subdivided into county figures in 1947, they revealed that 3,187 families in San Miguel County were dependent upon direct relief.

Following the hardships of the Great Depression, the community, along with the nation, had to endure the stresses of World War II. Thereafter it emerged with stabilization, accompanied by moderate growth in a new economic pattern. By that time, many citizens had become apathetic. They would enjoy the pleasurable aspects of life and work in Las Vegas while sluffing off with half efforts any ambitious proposals under the conviction that it was "of no use" because experience had taught that "nothing would succeed in Las Vegas." However, the appellation employed by one historian, "The Town That Wouldn't Gamble," is inapplicable, because this had been the town that had gambled upon everything conceivable only to become exhausted and frustrated by numerous failures and an economic depression entirely beyond local control.

Many innovations had not survived, as the community had gone through three cycles—subsistence economy, inflated commercial expansion, and transitional experimentation. From 1920 to 1940, while neighboring villages suffered a great decline in population, the two towns of Las Vegas had a gain of only about 800 persons. Nevertheless, in that era a foundation had been laid in the development of ranching, utility companies, small businesses, public schools, a university, a state hospital, services for tourists, highway maintenance, and government employment. The community by virtue of the strenuous endeavors of persistent leadership had entered upon its fourth cycle, in which sound growth was fostered with little change in that pattern through subsequent decades. Moreover, opportunities still were open for the application of ingenuity in capitalizing upon climatic, recreational, and historical assets.

Among the assets, one, which remained unappreciated by many residents but which appealed to visitors in recent times, was the presence of numerous, once elegant, business and residential buildings, mostly in the Victorian style. They had been built during the era of unbounded prosperity, but afterward some had begun deteriorating. As a result, a century later the community had many unique old buildings that no longer could be duplicated in materials and workmanship and that awaited restoration for utilization in the modern era.

Dress parade of the 200th Coastal Artillery *(State Records Center)*

Decorating the "hangmen's" windmill derrick *(Museum of New Mexico)*

III | Citizens Seek Order Amid Troubles

When the colony was founded at Las Vegas in 1835, the province of New Mexico had been a part of the independent Mexican nation for fourteen years, and Mexican hegemony was destined to continue for eleven years more. However, the great distance from Santa Fe in terms of difficulty of travel in those days rather isolated this community from the capital. Hence, the townsmen had few contacts there and little consciousness that they were citizens of Mexico. Instead, the pattern of life in the original community was much like that of a Spanish colony, and it continued to have that characteristic long after the change of allegiance to the United States.

Local administrative decisions were the responsibility of the *alcalde*, Juan de Dios Maese, and disputes were referred to the *juez de paz*, Hilario Gonzales. They were the government until a county was organized under American administration in 1852, when elected county commissioners became the administrators, the district judge presided over legal proceedings, and the elected sheriff and his deputies assumed responsibility for maintenance of order. At first the county seat was San Miguel del Bado, but in 1864, the legislature moved it to Las Vegas, against the remonstrances of people in distant Pecos. The editor of a Santa Fe newspaper observed that the "Las Vegas influence was too powerful," because the town by that time had "some very active wealthy and influential citizens." Then the former office of the *alcalde*, located a short block north of the Plaza, became the first courthouse. At that time, the eight million acres of San Miguel County made it the largest in New Mexico.

It was typical of the closely knit Spanish and Mexican

communities that controls were effectively maintained by the family and the church. In Las Vegas, however, located in a focal point, growth and social contacts introduced a degree of disorganization. In consequence, besides having to endure the crisis of the Civil War and the harassment by Indians, the citizens presently had to cope with social aberrations. As early as 1864, a grand jury was reported to have "found important indictments," and a decade later a Spanish-language newspaper in Santa Fe published the allegation that "Las Vegas is obtaining a reputation as the most disorderly place in the territory." In 1866, the hanging of Pablita Sandoval for murdering her lover created quite a sensation, according to information gleaned by W. J. Lucas in the 1920s, although the name was changed to Paula Angel in later published versions. Through the 1870s, an occasional murder made news in Santa Fe. In June 1879, two men accused of shooting two others were hanged from the windmill in the Plaza. It happened that on that very morning, visitors came in order to be present at the arrival of the first train; therefore, townsmen hastily removed the bodies and decorated the windmill with bunting and evergreens.

Immediately afterward, Las Vegas became notorious for its gambling rooms in the saloons. A visitor from Vermont counted two dozen in 1881. Each place, he wrote, had from two to four tables, and all were crowded. A local minister, Gabino Rendón, recalled many years later that gambling became such a mania that boys played at it, using buttons for chips. In his reminiscences, Miguel A. Otero, Jr. described the Exchange Hotel on the Plaza as having been a popular place for poker games at high stakes. It could have been called "the poker capital of New Mexico."

In 1881, J. H. Koogler, editor of the local *Gazette*, condemned gambling as "a disgrace to the town." On the other hand, Russell Kistler, editor of the rival *Optic*, condoned it as a natural human frailty and proposed that it be licensed and supervised. Nevertheless, in 1883, when the police raided the dens, the justice of the peace on the east side fined forty-five men for gambling and seven for operating gambling houses. After the east side became incorporated as a town in 1888, the

Buffalo Hall in the Exchange Hotel *(From* Illustrated Las Vegas, *1903)*

trustees chose to heed Kistler's advice. They adopted an ordinance assessing a license fee of $100 for operating one table and $60 for each additional table. However, the good church people soon became sufficiently influential to obtain local compliance with the law prohibiting gambling, but that merely drove it into hiding in back rooms of some of the saloons, where it continued secretly until after the turn of the century.

Five of the early saloons were called "halls," because they were large enough for promotion of public, commercialized dancing. One near the Plaza was maintained by Chata Baca, who, according to Otero, was a robust woman who enforced strict discipline. He recalled that she selected her girls for "beauty and neatness" and their "ability to drink lightly without intoxication." A visitor, however, described her hall as a "low, mud dance house thick with tobacco smoke, rum breath, fumes of perspiration, and adobe dust." Unattached Anglo males were paying fifty cents for two drinks and a dance with a "Mexican" girl, and all seemed to be "enjoying it immensely."

When Kistler of the *Optic* spent an evening in one of the halls in New Town, he found a mixed set of individuals there, including some "gray and baldheaded reprobates," and added that "all seem to enjoy themselves hugely with the bar girls, who dish out their 'lush' and play sweet on them, while they sip the nectar that sends them to their degradation and ruin." Those halls and the Exchange Hotel each had a small stage where periodically the girls presented skits. One night Kistler witnessed in one of them a play entitled "The Female Bathers," which he described as "one of the naughtiest acts we have ever seen."

In 1883, a crackdown by law officers put those places out of business. Then prostitution became segregated in red-light districts concentrated, of all places, in two localities having sanctimonious names, Church Street in Old Town and Zion Hill in New Town.

Kistler, who was a heavy tippler, probably took another swig and then proposed that a sign, "Public Prostitute," should be posted on every bawdy house, that each girl when on the street should be required to wear a distinguishing garb, that only policemen should be allowed to speak to them, and that the police should report at each council meeting the number and location of all houses. Although in 1882 an ordinance did outlaw bawdy houses, apparently it was not well enforced, because a complaint arose in 1884 that at those on Zion Hill "A number of courtesans make public exhibition of themselves in broad daylight, and the nights are becoming hideously notorious."

When police officers finally did obliterate that nuisance, prostitution went "underground." Thenceforth, like gambling, it was known to be continuing surreptitiously. Toleration of those practices in seclusion was acceptable by the social standards prevailing in that era in Las Vegas and in many other cities. When the standards were set higher in the 1920s, an aroused citizenry would assault those vices again.

Even worse was the local scourge of crime in the early 1880s. Numerous outlaws came, as recalled later by Miguel A. Otero, Jr., as a "backwash from Texas, Colorado, California, and Arizona," and then New Town "fell under the control of as vicious and corrupt set of scoundrels as could be found anywhere in the west." When the district court convened in August 1879, a Santa Fe newspaper reported that the calendar was crowded with 100 criminal cases and 150 civil actions and that Judge L. Bradford Prince blamed the "peculiar condition of affairs" upon the coming of the railroad, which, he said, had brought in a "crowd of rough characters."

Late in October 1879, five masked men robbed a railroad baggage car, but when Dave Mather and Dave Rudabaugh, the latter of whom had attempted a train robbery in Kansas, were taken before a justice of the peace, the prosecution failed to appear. A year later, Rudabaugh confessed that he had been one of the robbers, and William Mullen, convicted for his part in it, said that three of the others were Joe Carson, Frank McCoy, and Joe Martin.

In November, Dave Mather and Joshua J. Webb, a crony of Rudabaugh, were employed as policemen and Joe Carson as a deputy sheriff, and another shady character, H. G. Neill, known as "Hoodoo Brown," had become a justice of the peace. Later that month, when three men robbed the Monarch Billiard Hall, the proprietor shot one of them, Tomás Suazo of Trinidad.

One day in January 1880, as Joe Carson sought to disarm four Texans, he was riddled with bullets. In the shootout that followed, Dave Mather killed William Randall and wounded James West, who then was jailed. The other two fled. Immediately afterward, a freighter, Theodore Caston, was murdered brutally near Bernal and robbed of his money, said to have been about $1,500. Almost simultaneously, when policeman Dave Mather sought to break up a fight in a restaurant, Joseph Castello, a railroad foreman, drew his gun, and Mather killed him with one bullet. A week later, J. J. Webb formed a posse of five others, including Rudabaugh, and went after two of the cowboys who had murdered Carson. Near Sapelló, the posse captured Tom Henry and John Dorsey and returned them to Las Vegas. On February 8, a mob of vigilantes removed them and West from the jail, strung all three up on the windmill derrick, and peppered

J. J. Webb in jail, 1880 *(Highlands University Collection)*

their writhing bodies with bullets.

On March 2, 1880, a cattle buyer, Michael Kelliher, and his companion apparently were "set up" by "Sport" Boyle, who lured them into a saloon and quarreled with them about who was going to pay for the drinks. Policeman J. J. Webb then entered and shot Kelliher. "Hoodoo Brown," justice of the peace, conducted an inquiry on the spot, exonerated Webb, and took possession of Kelliher's $1,900. On that same day, James Morehead, a salesman from St. Louis, ordered poached eggs in a restaurant at a later hour than the waiter, James Allen, would serve eggs. As their quarrel over this turned into a fistfight, Allen went for his gun and murdered Morehead. When Webb and Allen were jailed by the sheriff for these two killings, $500 of Kelliher's money was found in Webb's pocket.

As the vigilantes assembled that night, they received a warning that the jail was heavily guarded, so they dispersed. Nevertheless, that threat was ominous, and besides, a grand jury was conducting an investigation. Mather resigned his job as policeman, and on March 5, "Hoodoo Brown," "Dutchy" Borne, and the widow of Joe Carson hastily left town, taking with them most of Kelliher's money. The governor offered a reward of $300 for the apprehension of "Hoodoo," and on April 1, the *Las Vegas Daily Optic* published a lengthy description of his capture—but that turned out to be an "April fool" story.

On April 2, 1880, Dave Rudabaugh and James Allen, who had been released, killed the jailer, Antonio Váldez, to free their friend, J. J. Webb, but Webb chose to stay there and await the outcome of an appeal of his death sentence. Three other prisoners fled, along with their liberators. A posse found their abandoned, stolen hack twenty-five miles east of town. All had escaped, and Rudabaugh joined Billy the Kid, notorious for his deeds in the Lincoln County War. Thus, most of the outlaws were on the run; but even so, George Davidson murdered Nelson Starbird, a genial hack driver, at 3:00 A.M. on April 8. On that day, R. A. Kistler received this card for publication in the evening paper.

To Murderers, Confidence Men, Thieves: The citizens of Las Vegas have tired of the robbery, murder, and other crimes, that have made this town a by-word in every civilized community. They have resolved to put a stop to crime, if in attaining that end they have to forget the law, and resort to speedier justice than it will afford. All such characters are therefore hereby notified, that they must either leave this town or conform themselves to the requirements of the law, or they will be summarily dealt with. The flow of blood must and shall be stopped in this community, and the good citizens of both old and the new towns have determined to stop it, if they have to H A N G by the strong arm of force every violator of the law in this country—VIGILANTES

The community had a breathing spell for almost two months, and then when a murder did occur, it was not the deed of outlaws. A quarrel over a girl in Occidental Hall resulted in the killing of J. J. Tuttle, but the murderer escaped. Then "Doc" Holliday, one of the cronies of J. J. Webb, came to join Webb in Las Vegas, only to find him still in jail. Holliday hunted up Charlie White, against whom he had a grudge, and wounded him. White recovered and skipped out. Holliday opened a dental office on Center Street (now Lincoln Street), and then another of his previous antagonists, Mike Gordon, appeared in town, and Holliday killed him. A townsman filed a complaint, but before the officers could find "Doc," he had fled back to Dodge City, whence he moved to Arizona.

Peace then prevailed until November 7, 1880, when three murderers, two train robbers, and a mule thief escaped from the county jail. Among them were George Davis, the mule stealer, and Webb, who had had a second thought about awaiting the appeal of his death sentence. "Pat" Garrett, then sheriff of Lincoln County, soon captured those two and returned them to Las Vegas. The vigilantes overtook the other four near Chaperito and killed all of them. They brought in the four bodies and laid them on the platform of the windmill as a ghastly warning to others. Among them were the murderers of Morehead and Starbird.

Garrett and a posse rounded up four more outlaws at Stinking Springs and on December 27 brought to the jail in

Las Vegas Billy Wilson, Dave Rudabaugh, Tom Pickett, and Billy the Kid. Before Billy the Kid was transferred to the jail in Santa Fe, he told a *Gazette* reporter, "I don't blame you for writing of me as you have. You had to believe other's stories; but then I don't know as anyone would believe anything good of me anyway." Jubilant citizens raised $695 as a gift for "Pat" Garrett, whom they honored at a New Year's party for his capture of Billy the Kid. The defendant, however, was transferred later to the jail in Lincoln, whence he escaped. Soon afterward, Garrett ambushed him in his hiding place at Fort Sumner and killed him.

On December 3, 1881, Rudabaugh and Webb, along with six others, picked a hole through the wall of the old jail in Las Vegas, crawled out, and scattered to distant localities. Webb was reported to have died of smallpox in Arkansas in 1882, and Rudabaugh was recognized while working on a ranch in Montana in 1892 and again in 1927 when he was an old, destitute drunkard.

A man was shot by the bartender in Bertha's Parlor one day in March 1881, but during the remainder of that year, news about violence was meager. Instead, the court of William Steele, justice of the peace on the east side, was busy with cases involving mostly minor assaults and disputes about debts. Sentences for misdemeanors so filled the jail that the cost of feeding the prisoners grew burdensome. The vigilantes, lacking more serous business, hit upon an ingenious procedure for relieving the county of that expense. On January 19, 1882, they forced the jailer to turn over a prisoner. They took him to the roundhouse, where they had a rope strung over a beam. When the frightened prisoner begged for mercy, they told him that they would spare his life if he would leave town in five minutes. He did. Then they returned to the jail for another, and another, until they had it emptied.

After the ensuing period of inactivity, on March 24, 1882, a printed placard was posted at several places around town. It read

> Notice to thieves, thugs, fakirs and bunko-steerers among whom are J. J. Martin alias "off Wheeler," Saw Dust Charlie,

William Hedges, Billy the Kid, Billy Mullin, Little Jack the Cutter, Pockmarked Kid and about twenty others; if found within the limits of this city after ten o'clock P.M. this night you will be invited to attend a grand necktie party, the expense of which will be borne by 100 substantial citizens.

The next day, the *Optic* carried the observation, "Yesterday's notice warning the thug outfits to leave the city packed off nine of the ilk in one bunch." The inclusion of Billy the Kid, who was known to be deceased, could be taken as lending credence to the myths about his survival if it were not for the fact that the other names were not those of any ruffians known to be lurking about Las Vegas then. In fact, the community had been rather effectively purged of its vicious characters, so that the report of the grand jury released two days prior to that warning included no mention of rampant crime. That notice can well be attributed to Miguel A. Otero, Jr. and Jacob Gross, both of whom had been leaders of the vigilantes, and the original draft of it is in the handwriting of Jacob Gross. Since both also were well known for their comic stunts, the posting of that placard has all the earmarks of another of their pranks, in which the editor of the *Optic* joined with a few witty words on the following day. This conclusion seems to be verified by the fact that Otero said nothing about this incident in his reminiscences, whereas he did attest to the authenticity of the notice published by the vigilantes a year earlier.

The ensuing summer, 1882, did witness one, but only one, outbreak of violence. When a man known as Navajo Frank lassoed and dragged to death an unsuspecting, respected citizen, R. H. Hunter, a posse caught up with the culprit at Sapelló and returned him to the county jail. That night a mob of 200 removed him forcibly and hanged him on a telegraph pole on Railroad Avenue. Although the names of the lynchers were known, no attorney would agree to conduct the prosecution for the county.

A full year passed peaceably, and then, in July 1883, H. C. Brown, who had been caught stealing from his employer and had been released after serving his sentence, returned to the butcher shop and pistol-whipped to death his accuser, Frank Maier. This time when a mob tried to lynch Brown, Sheriff Hilario Romero had fifteen armed deputies waiting on the roof of the jail. They dispersed the mob by firing into it and wounding four.

Certainly, conditions were improving. Although in the next two years some thievery and occasional stabbings were reported, as well as a few fires that appeared to have been of incendiary origin, thieves were pursued relentlessly by deputy sheriffs, and the courts were functioning more effectively. In fact, when Robert "Bob" Ford, formerly a member of the outlaw band led by Jesse James, opened a saloon in Las Vegas in the autumn of 1884, the townsmen ridiculed him as a braggert. After he had missed the target when challenged to a shooting contest, he packed up and moved to Creede, Colorado. Moreover, two years later, Clay Allison visited Las Vegas, but, a reformed desperado, he came as a cattle dealer.

A visitor then expressed surprise to find no "rowdyism, nor gun and pistol shooting" but rather "orderly, well-dressed people." In 1888, Dr. Francis A. Atkins, town physician, reported that there had been only one death resulting from a gunshot. An article in *Harper's Weekly* said of Las Vegas, "it would be hard to find a more quiet and law-abiding community in the far West."

For harboring evil characters in the early years, it appeared that Las Vegas was chastised by fires and plagues. The first serious fire burned out the south side of the Plaza, including the Rosenwald and Friedman stores, on June 8, 1877. The losses were estimated at $100,000. The next conflagration took out the entire city block on Railroad Avenue across from the first depot on September 18, 1880. As a high breeze spread it rapidly, the townsmen tried to fight it with fire extinguishers, bucket brigades, salt, and dynamite, but to no avail. In the ruins of the twenty-seven business places, vandals stole all the valuables they could find, until the townsmen posted guards and put a stop to that. The proprietors rebuilt their stores, only to be threatened by another serious fire in November a year later. By that time, a company of volunteer firemen had a hook and ladder cart, but no hose cart. This time they were able to stop the fire from

The south side of the Plaza before the fire of 1877 *(Museum of New Mexico)*

spreading after it had destroyed only three buildings on Center Street.

Another fire, which started in a store on the corner of Railroad and Tilden in May 1882, damaged nine other properties, mostly residential, before it was checked. At that time, the volunteers had ordered a hose cart, but it had not yet arrived. The new cart, which came in June, helped the firemen to control two big blazes in November and December of that year, after one had destroyed a wholesale house and the other a saloon. As the two companies of volunteers acquired experience and equipment, they became more effective, so that time and time again they were able to extinguish fires that might have been disastrous—that is, until December 1891 and June 1892, when two more blazes, fanned by high winds, did serious damage in the same neighborhood.

The "plagues" were epidemics of smallpox. The first of record occurred in 1877, when the known deaths numbered eighty-two. All work in Old Town came to a halt, and a boy of that era recalled years later that his father had used his wagon to haul the dead to the graveyard—thirty of them in one day. The next scourge hit in 1882—the first year of the temporarily incorporated city. In August, the governing body immediately adopted an ordinance to quarantine the sick, and the county commissioners did likewise in October.

Leaving town during the smallpox scare of 1898 *(Rex Studio)*

The city also ordered all dance halls closed and established a "pest house" out in the country. No record was made of the number of cases quarantined, but at the pest house, the city physician and special nurse cared for seventy-seven patients, of whom twenty-eight died. Municipal expenditures for those emergency services amounted to $5,330.44. By the time of the next scare, in 1886 (and again in 1889 and 1898), many citizens had been vaccinated, and the few cases were so promptly segregated that the disease was effectively checked.

Amid the troubles of those years, citizens were obtaining services from local units of government set up in the American pattern, and the operation of those governments had the by-product of provoking more troubles.

Wealthy, well-educated *dons* quickly adapted to the new system by acquiring control over many voters under the *patrón* system. Years later, a pioneer described how a *don* who owned much of the land around San Gerónimo employed many of the men seasonally in his freighting business, remunerated them with goods charged out of his store at high prices, and then from his profits paid for their weddings and funerals and even sent some of their children to school in town. One can imagine how all of his part-time employees humbly cultivated his favor even to the extent of casting their votes as requested by him.

By 1880, the sons of Miguel Romero, founders of a flourishing mercantile business and owners of extensive properties, had commanded control of the Republican Party in San Miguel County. When Lorenzo López challenged their leadership, beginning in 1882, great contests occurred in the county conventions between him and Eugenio Romero, his brother-in-law. Either Romero or his brother Hilario came off with the party nomination for the office of sheriff, which then was tantamount to victory, until in 1890, when López finally stormed his way to election to that office, which in those days was the one reserved for the county "boss." Two years later, a new Peoples' Party, or Populists, temporarily broke the control of the Republican *dons* and merchants in a bitter campaign in which the candidates of that party were supported by a new newspaper, *La Voz del Pueblo*.

In Old Town, the maintenance of order in the early 1880s was the duty of two deputy sheriffs, one of whom was designated as *jefe de policía* by the county commissioners. In 1881, police regulations provided that each deputy would get, besides his salary of $35.00 a month, one *peso* for each arrest and fifty *centavos* for each conviction. On the east side, the businessmen raised a fund by subscription to employ two merchant policemen, who held appointments made by the probate judge. Sometimes they and the deputies had nasty conflicts over the question of the realm of their jurisdictions.

The need for many improvements during the great boom led immediately to discussion about the possibility of incorporating a municipal government that would serve both communities. The editor of the *Gazette* on the west side, J. H. Koogler, favored it, whereas the editor of the *Optic*, Russell A. Kistler, opposed it, because the east side, "full of activity and enterprise" should be governed "by Americans only," as he put it. However, in 1882, when a group of citizens presented a petition for the incorporation of one city, he changed his tune, because, he claimed, "the best classes of people are for it."

It came about, therefore, that in July, 1,097 men cast their votes in an election in a consolidated city in which Eugenio Romero won the office of mayor. That outcome did not please his rival, Lorenzo López, who challenged him in a poorly conducted, farcical election in December of that same year—1882. Election clerks chosen by those who arrived first at each polling place had no registration lists for determining the eligibility of voters. When some young men heard that the two polling places on the west side were running up a total of 1,800 votes, whereas there were approximately only that many eligible in the entire city, they voted all of the names in a city directory. The partisans of Romero then claimed that legally no election had been held and therefore the incumbents should continue in office, while López sought to unseat them by protracted court action in which he contended that the municipal government had been founded illegally in the first place. That was a strange reversal on his part, because he had been a member of the committee that had presented the petition for consolidation to the county commissioners.

Under a cloud of legal uncertainty, the city fathers did improve the streets and did crack down on gambling and prostitution, but the smallpox epidemic in 1882 called for such unanticipated expenditures that they bankrupted the young city. Next, while a decision in court was still pending, in 1884, the legislature adopted a new municipal code by which all municipalities were disincorporated so that they could reincorporate under the new rules. All were expected to do so immediately, but in Las Vegas, the previously troubled government folded up without any effort to reincorporate.

In the interval when all of Las Vegas was again under county administration, the county commissioners had a new stone courthouse built on the west side in 1886 and had a new iron bridge constructed across the Gallinas River a year later.

Citizens Seek Order Amid Troubles

By 1888, when the need for municipal services was becoming obviously urgent, the question of reincorporation again provoked a lively discussion. This time reluctance had arisen among many on the west side, where the *Gazette* had changed its tune and expressed opposition. On the other hand, the *Optic* again advocated consolidation and published many letters in support of unity. That effort was fruitless. Instead, when a petition was presented to the county commissioners by representatives of the east side, it requested the incorporation of a town for only their community, which was done. In 1895, when the population of New Town had passed the 3,000 mark, the town was reincorporated as a city.

In the 1890s, the municipality fostered remarkable improvements of the streets, sidewalks, parks, and schools of the city—actually of County District Number Two. In addition, an issue of bonds was floated in 1891 for the building of a new stone town hall and fire station. Typical of those times, it, too, encountered troubles. First, the original bond issue turned out to be inadequate, so that another one had to be approved and floated. Then the contractor got into difficulties and turned over his payments from the town to his bondsmen. They sought to buy up the laborers' claims for wages at five cents an hour, whereupon the workmen went on strike. The upshot was that the governing body had to engage another contractor. The building was completed enough to allow its dedication as a part of the Fourth of July celebration in 1893.

While the two successive municipalities were having their troubles, those incidents were overshadowed by a rural rebellion of "White Caps" in 1889 to 1892, which arose from problems related to the Land Grant. (This topic comes up for analysis in the chapter on the land grants.) Next came the Panic of 1893 and simultaneously the activities of a gang of bandits on the west side from 1892 to 1894. Ironically, the resort to violence occurred immediately after Las Vegas had won premature praise for its achievement of good order.

The gang of bandits had as its head the proprietor of the Imperial Bar on the Plaza, the robust, redheaded Vicente Silva, who had arrived in Las Vegas in 1875 and had become a respected businessman. As he turned greedy, he enlisted a band of similarly motivated *compadres,* whose indulgence in robberies and in cattle rustling soon led them to the next step—murder. A few members of his gang were identified later as having been White Caps; therefore, some averred that Silva had secretly been the leader in their depredations. Likewise, because three of Silva's band were identified later as having been deputies of Sheriff López, it became convenient for stalwart Republicans, who disliked the disruptive tactics of Don Lorenzo, to smear his name by alleging that he had been the secret leader not only of the White Caps but also of Silva's bandits. The evidence indicates that Don Lorenzo was guilty only of being rather helpless at first in his contention against the secret planning and sudden strokes of both groups. Ultimately, he did apprehend several of Silva's bandits.

Silva's men sought to cover up their meetings by claiming that they were members of the People's Party. In late October 1892, when Patricio Maes gave notice that he was resigning from that party to join the opposing Knights of Mutual Protection, Silva arraigned him in a mock trial conducted by the gang in an upstairs gambling room. Because they feared that Maes' effort to resign meant that he was going to betray their involvement in crime, they hanged him from the frame of the iron bridge. That and other crimes even brought Governor William T. Thornton to Las Vegas to conduct an investigation.

The several misdeeds were climaxed in April 1894 by the execution of Gabriel Sandoval, brother of Silva's wife, Telésfora, because he, too, was suspected of betraying them. By that time, because Silva's complicity was becoming known, the deputies sought to arrest him; but he went into hiding near the village of Los Alamos, north of Las Vegas. Fearful then that his wife might turn informant, he had their adopted daughter Emma kidnapped in order to induce Telésfora to confer with him at Los Alamos. There he murdered her. By that time, his henchmen were fed up with all the bloodletting. As Silva was burying his wife's body, one of the gang murdered the leader and buried him in the same grave.

Accumulating evidence against twelve of the bandits convinced Sheriff López that they should be rounded up and brought to trial. Several were found guilty and sent to the penitentiary. The roundup, however, had failed to catch Silva. Where was he? Police in other cities were alerted. In Flagstaff, Arizona, local officers in May 1894 arrested a couple thought to be Silva and his wife, but they had the wrong couple. Soon came news of the arrest of Silva in Pueblo, Colorado, but that, too, turned out to be a case of mistaken identity. Almost simultaneously, when one of the bandits was convicted of murder and hanged, a Santa Fe newspaper named the wrong man as the one who had tripped the trapdoor. Sheriff López immediately wrote a letter to the newspaper in order to let everybody know that he had done it. He wanted credit for that hanging. Herman Maestas, the culprit, had informed the deputies that he believed they could find the bodies of Silva and his wife buried in an *arroyo* near Los Alamos.

After a month-long search, Cleofes Romero, Rafael Gallegos, and Manual C. de Baca found the badly decomposed bodies. It was the latter, then, who wrote a history of Silva's bandits, which has been the principal source of all subsequent narratives on the subject. As for Emma, friends sent her to the Presbyterian school near Taos, where a teacher from Kansas adopted her. The publications about this sordid affair describe the subsequent careers of the members of the gang who did not disappear entirely. Most of them fell afoul of the law sooner or later. In 1938, one survivor was incarcerated in the State Hospital.

An affair involving young Billy Green occurred as an aftermath of Silva's banditry. Because he had acquired a reputation for being handy with his gun, a justice of the peace on the east side made him a deputy and urged him to help stop the depredations. When he crossed to the west side once in 1894 and shot a suspect who resisted arrest, it aroused his former friends there. Fifty of them pursued him to the Green ranch house, and, as they attempted to storm it, he fired into the crowd, killing four. He refused to heed the order of

Sheriff López to surrender, and the sheriff called upon the Territorial Guard, which had a company posted in Las Vegas to protect railroad property during a strike. The Guardsmen took him into custody, and in his trial he was acquitted of guilt for both killings, because both times he had fired in self-defense. Within a year, Billy himself was murdered by a former member of Silva's gang

The next local alarm arose in response to a national emergency. Since 1895, citizens of the United States had been sympathetic toward the Cubans in their revolt against Spanish rule. The yellow press and imperialists pushed the United States into that war on April 11, 1898, in order to help the Cubans win their independence. For the United States, a crisis loomed, because the new battleships had not been tested, the military establishment was at low ebb, and the response of European powers was uncertain. For New Mexicans, the crisis was local and real, because in view of the slander directed at Spanish Americans by easterners in the early nineties, they might be suspected of disloyalty in this war with their mother country, removed by a few generations.

Governor Miguel A. Otero, Jr. sought to allay suspicion by sending to the Secretary of War this message: "Have full squadron of cavalry ready for service, . . . and can raise batallion of mounted riflemen in about a week." He was referring to the Otero Guard, but his offer merely planted an idea in Washington. The War Department would enlist a regiment of cavalry from among "the wild riders and riflemen of the Rockies and the Great Plains." It would be commanded by Colonel Leonard Wood and by the inexperienced, impulsive Theodore Roosevelt, who would be commissioned as lieutenant colonel.

At a patriotic rally in Las Vegas, only twenty-one local applicants gained acceptance. The recruiters said that the quota for Las Vegas was twenty. On April 30, as the young men left by train to be mustered into the First Regiment of United States Volunteer Cavalry, almost the whole town was there to send them off. In the training camp near San Antonio, Texas, Theodore Roosevelt marveled at the skillful riding of these western men. So did newspaper reporters, who dubbed the regiment "Roosevelt's Rough Riders." In Florida, however, the lack of adequate shipping required that the horses be left behind, so that these cavalrymen had to charge on foot into the battles in Cuba.

Soon that war surprisingly turned out to be a pushover, and in August, the regiment was mustered out in New York, with Roosevelt promoted to commanding colonel. The troopers agreed that because the largest contingent, 400, had come from New Mexico, they would have a reunion there the following June.

The announcement left it up to cities in New Mexico to bid for selection as the site of the reunion. Because Las Vegas raised more money and had better hotel facilities than any of the rivals, this city emerged as the winner. When the young veterans began arriving on June 23, they went to a camp prepared for them in Lincoln Park by the Otero Guard. Due to a heavy rain the next day, the crowd got soaked before Roosevelt swung off the train for meetings first in the Hotel Castañeda. Then he, too, encamped with his "boys" in Lincoln Park.

On Saturday morning, "Teddy" borrowed a horse from Ludwig Ilfeld so that he could lead the immense parade. There followed a program of activities on through Sunday and Monday, including contests similar to those of later rodeos. Afterward, the veterans held their reunions in other cities until 1949, when fond memories of the first such event brought them back to Las Vegas for their fiftieth anniversary. When they came again in 1952, they designated this city as their permanent reunion headquarters "to the last man," who came alone in 1967 and 1968. That war with Spain was one crisis that had resulted in a great celebration in Las Vegas.

Soon afterward, no joy was derived from the scandal which shook the foundations of the Insane Asylum in 1903 (as previously described), and from a jolt which nearly sank the Normal University in that same year (this story is reserved for narration in a subsequent chapter).

Simultaneously, an unusual runoff raised the Gallinas River to the floor of the bridge in May 1903, and other streams washed out railroad bridges. While they were being repaired, 700 passengers were stranded in Las Vegas and had to be housed and fed by the Santa Fe. Usually through the years, the community had suffered more from droughts than from floods, but the Gallinas had gone on damaging rampages in 1855, 1886, and 1888. The flood of 1903 was only the forerunner of another which was caused by a cloud-burst in September of the following year. It flooded homes in the lowlands and drowned four horses in a livery stable.

Pueblo Indians greeting "Teddy" *(Las Vegas City Museum; Rough Riders' Collection)*

Again, passengers, 250 of them, were marooned for two weeks. Fortunately, no lives were lost in Las Vegas, but eight were drowned in Springer, eight in Watrous, and four in Chaperito. This was remembered as the worst flood in local history.

Meanwhile, strife had been stirring up animosities. It was caused in part by conflicts between the police officers of the two jurisdictions, county and city, and by the bitter rivalry of the two fire companies in their annual public races. The latter cannot be set forth as "racial," however, because in those years both teams were nearly 100 percent Anglo.

After joint celebrations of the Fourth of July had been held successfully, beginning in 1882, the planning committee in 1888 split over misunderstandings and conducted two celebrations. The great one on the west side was the first in the series of annual *fiestas*. However, in each of the next three years, politicians converted that event into Populist rallies against "Republican oppression" which were said to have attracted an attendance of up to 4,000 people.

After the turn of the century, when the Post Office Department closed the office on Bridge Street in order to maintain one consolidated office far to the east in the Crockett Building, west siders felt that they had been double-crossed by the Commercial Club. Then Margarito Romero instituted a law suit that led ultimately to the reopening of a post office on the west side. Simultaneously, when the city council made plans to build a library in Hillsite Park, Romero and others went to court in an unsuccessful effort to halt that in favor of a central location between the two communities.

Those disputes were crowned by one even more serious over the management of the Las Vegas Land Grant, which will be reviewed in a subsequent chapter. Suffice it to say here that again it was principally Don Margarito who aroused the hopes of the townsmen on the west side that, if they would incorporate as a separate municipality, it could win the profitable possession of the unoccupied lands. This was the foremost of several reasons why they incorporated their town in 1903, and it comes as no surprise that they elected Don Margarito, who was then proprietor of a resort hotel at El

Porvenir, as their first mayor. Immediately afterward, he sought an injunction to stop the city from condemning property in the southern part of the new town for a road to connect Grand Avenue with the highway to Romeroville. After it was finally granted in 1909, for several decades persons traveling from the city to Santa Fe had to cross through the town to get to the highway.

As can well be surmised, the Romero Republican "machine" had recovered control in the county under the leadership of young Romeros. One, Cleofes, while serving as deputy sheriff, was alleged to have won election to that office on his own in 1900 in part by releasing numerous men from jail on their promise that they would campaign for him. Later, as Secundino Romero was rising to eminence, another newcomer in politics, Lorenzo Delgado, began challenging the Romero dynasty, just as Lorenzo López had done previously. Hotly contested elections ensued in the county and town.

In the city, on the other hand, rival factions, supported by the *Optic,* agreed in 1906 to divide offices between them in fusion tickets. The publisher of *La Voz del Pueblo* did not like this, because agitation published in that paper could have no effect upon the outcome of listless elections in which only one ticket appeared on the ballots.

From 1909 to 1910, the county commissioners had a new concrete bridge built across the Gallinas River, but failure otherwise attended efforts to unite the two sides. The *Optic* was advocating consolidation of the two municipalities, and even *La Voz* swung over to support consolidation. However, the joint commission that was appointed came up with a plan in which the town would constitute one ward, whereas there would be two wards on the east side. Rebellion of the west side against this proposal brought the movement to an abrupt termination.

By that time, an intense campaign for statehood had become an absorbing local issue, and as easterners, too, divided into pros and cons, the literate public in Las Vegas became furious about the slandering of New Mexicans by some of the easterners as "Unamericanized greasers," who were "ignorant, superstitious, and dominated by the priests." The best that the factions in Congress could come up with then was a compromise plan, called "jointure," by which Arizona and New Mexico would become one state. In the referendum conducted on that question in 1906, voters in San Miguel County joined with others in the territory in lukewarm support of the measure, largely because New Mexico had so long been frustrated in previous efforts to gain statehood. However, when Arizona voted it down, the proposal was killed.

Finally, in 1910, Congress passed an act enabling New Mexico to adopt a constitution and prepare for admission. As delegates to the convention from San Miguel County, all nine of the Republican slate won election in September. Among them were five eminent Hispanos, including, of course, Margarito and Eugenio Romero; but it was a local Anglo and eminent lawyer, Charles A. Spiess, who was chosen to serve as chairman of the proceedings. In January 1911, the adoption of the conservative document by New Mexicans was abetted by a large, favorable margin in San Miguel County.

Next would come the election of officers for the new state. Previously, local Republicans had been in an enviable position of leadership. They had produced two of the territorial delegates in the Congress, Trinidad Romero and F. A. Manzanares, and two territorial governors, Miguel A. Otero, Jr. and William J. Mills. Thrice, Octaviano A. Larrazolo, a native of Mexico who had practiced law in Las Vegas since 1895, had run as a Democrat for election as the delegate in Congress, but his silver-tongued oratory about mostly "racial" issues had failed to win his election. Now he switched his affiliation to the Republican Party, but the county organization let him sit on the sidelines for a while and backed Secundino Romero for election as governor. The territorial convention, however, nominated Holm A. Bursom for that office and Romero for the office of secretary of state.

For governor, local Democrats proposed Don Ezekiel C. de Baca, associate editor of *La Voz del Pueblo,* and for secretary of state Antonio Lucero, formerly an editor of that paper but lately a member of the faculty of the Normal University.

Governor Ezekiel C. de Baca *(Donaldo A. Martinez)*

The convention selected W. C. McDonald as candidate for governor, with C. de Baca as lieutenant governor and Lucero as secretary of state. A schism which weakened the regular Republicans nationally then had a local counterpart which contributed to a surprise victory by McDonald, C. de Baca, and Lucero.

Four years later, Don Ezekiel won election as the first Spanish-American governor of the state, but his untimely death in 1917 cut short his term in office. In 1916, too, a local Democrat, Andreius A. Jones, went to Washington to represent New Mexico in the United States Senate, where he served until his death in 1927. Meanwhile, as the Democrats were losing favor, in 1918, Larrazolo gained the Republican nomination for governor, and his brilliant oratory won his election—not against an Anglo, but against Félix García, the Democratic nominee. The achievement of statehood, therefore, had continued the eminence of Las Vegas, but at first by a temporary shift in leadership.

The foregoing review of the fortunes and misfortunes of contending politicians carries over into the time when this community, and all others in the nation, were plunged into the crisis created by the entry of the United States into World War I. Then all local people joined in a common effort, as typified by the appeal of the editor of the usually recalcitrant *La Voz del Pueblo,* who wrote, "We are all a people united. Blacks and whites, saxons and hispanos, . . . all are Americans." Immediately local young men, selected by the drawing of numbers in Washington, were drafted into military service.

On the home front, Secundino Romero served on the State Council of Defense, which sought to muster all resources, and Mrs. W. E. Gortner was the local representative on the Women's Auxiliary. The county agent labored for improvement of agricultural production, and the Y.M.C.A. and the Knights of Columbus spearheaded the campaigns to sell war bonds. Moreover, concerned townsmen organized a Loyalty League and elected Jefferson Raynolds as president. In order to suppress "Pro-Germanism," the members took a loyalty oath and went forth to administer it to others, especially to local teachers.

All of the community read with anxiety reports about the battles in Europe and celebrated the final victory on November 11, 1918. Joy was subdued, however, by sympathy for the families of these twelve young men who had made the supreme sacrifice: Antonio Archebeque, Federico Baca, John W. Barr, Manuel Chávez, Charles A. Garner, Leonard C. Hoskins, Arturo López, Alejandro Martínez, Gregorio Martínez, Philip B. Montoya, Stanley C. Price, and Procopio Valerio. When they came home in coffins, the newly organized posts of the American Legion conducted memorial services. Joy was dampened, too, by a serious epidemic of Spanish influenza in the autumn of 1918.

Soon afterward, the onslaught of economic depression caused local distress, but it did not hamper at all the contentious activity of local politicians. In fact, it seemed to stimulate them, because when other jobs became scarce, those offered by political patronage became critically desirable.

On the west side, the town had a one-sided contest in 1920, when Lorenzo Delgado as the Republican candidate easily defeated Antonio Lucero, Democrat. After he had won again in 1922, the Republican kingpins, Secundino Romero (Lorenzo's cousin) and Judge David J. Leahy refused to endorse his candidacy in 1924 and backed Cleofes Romero instead. Delgado then made an alliance with another Republican, Luis Armijo, and headed a "fusion" ticket. Romero, the victor in a close contest, had an audit made of town finances. It revealed a shortage of almost $6,000, which opponents alleged Delgado had pocketed. He was county sheriff then, too, and a county audit also showed a considerable sum missing. In district court, he refused to submit his financial records and lost in the suit filed to remove him as sheriff, but in his appeal to the State Supreme Court, he obtained an "alternate writ of prohibition" and remained in office. Again he headed a fusion ticket in contests for city offices and won regularly on into the succeeding decade.

Just as the Populists had been coalesced back in the 1890s by vigorous journalism, now the Republicans had a popular, influential Spanish language newspaper, *El Independiente*. It helped sustain the county Romero organization, because Secundino was the principal shareholder in the publishing company and president of its board.

The politics of town elections were closely linked with the contest for control of county offices, for which the elections were dominated early in the decade by Secundino Romero and Judge Leahy. Soon a legal hassle initiated outside of this county came before Judge Leahy. Carl C. Magee, the crusading editor of the *Albuquerque Morning Journal* and the *New Mexico State Tribune,* wrote editorial allegations ranging far and wide. A statement about a banking incident in the past of Joshua M. Raynolds, president of the First National Bank of Albuquerque, was answered by the filing of a $50,000 libel suit against him, and revelations about financial mismanagement at Normal University by President Jonathan Wagner contributed to Wagner's dismissal and his filing of a suit for $100,000 in damages. Moreover, Magee's testimony in Washington about Albert B. Fall, Secretary of the Interior, contributed to the conviction of Fall for alleged bribery.

In Magee's digging up of dirt about affairs in San Miguel County, he alleged that the Republican "boss," Secundino Romero, as a board member of the State Hospital, had diverted its funds to other uses. He claimed, too, that President Wagner had made Normal University a financial and vote-delivering unit in "Sec's" machine. Next, when he alleged that the clerk of the State Supreme Court was pocketing court funds with sanction by Supreme Court Justice Frank W. Parker, that justice indicted Magee for "defamation and criminal libel," for which he was to be tried before Judge David J. Leahy of the Fourth Judicial District. Judge Leahy was a big, powerful man who had a reputation not only for his Republican loyalty but also for his ill-tempered threats to knock flat anyone who might contradict him. That case in this court, therefore, should be disposed of promptly by a verdict that would make an object lesson of the upstart Magee. However, Magee refused to be cowed. When Sheriff Delgado brought him into court for trial before Judge Leahy, Magee said, "I deny that this is a court." Then Judge Leahy arraigned him for contempt of court; but Magee kept on writing and making speeches until he had incurred three more citations for contempt, for which Judge Leahy sentenced him to one year at hard labor in the state penitentiary. However, Governor J. F. Hinkle granted Magee a full pardon on the supposition that he had been "persecuted."

Next came Magee's jury trial on the charges filed by Justice Parker. In the course of it, the shouting lawyers had to be restrained by the bailiffs, and one of Magee's defense attorneys, Richard H. Hanna, also made unkind remarks about Judge Leahy's court, whereupon the judge suspended him from further practice in the Fourth Judicial District. The chief defense attorney, George Hunker, also state Democratic chairman, subpoenaed local Republicans and asked embarrassing questions, a reporter for a Denver newspaper wrote accusations even more critical than those of Magee, and Judge Leahy once lost his temper and promised Magee that he would punish him later by "physical chastisement." The cumulative effect was that the tables had been turned—Judge Leahy's court had been placed on trial and the Romero machine was being torn asunder.

When again Magee was relieved of his conviction by another pardon granted by Governor Hinkle, the prosecution challenged the governor's power to do that in a hearing conducted by the State Supreme Court, which upheld the governor. For the appearance of Magee there, Sheriff Delgado had refused to recognize the governor's pardon of Magee and at first would not release him. An angry mob in Las Vegas demonstrated in behalf of Magee, and the governor sent over two more pardons, which finally persuaded the sheriff to take Magee to Santa Fe. When released again, Magee continued his condemnation of the "Leahy-Romero imperialism" and "the political domination of the courts."

The ultimate effect of this protracted affair was that the faction headed by Lorenzo Delgado and Luis Armijo emerged victorious, especially after the death of "Sec" Romero in 1929. They returned then to regular Republican affiliation; Delgado reigned supreme as town mayor and county sheriff, and Armijo won election and reelection as district judge. Incidentally, thrice during all the turmoil, in

1924, in 1930, and again in 1932, the governor sent National Guardsmen to Las Vegas to supervise the elections. Finally, in 1932, when Democrats returned to power in the state and nation, they were victorious in the county contests, but Delgado won reelection as town mayor by a large majority.

The Magee trial had a tragic sequence. When Judge Leahy entered the Meadows Hotel on August 21, 1925 and saw Magee there, he knocked him down and kicked him. Magee fired twice at Leahy with an automatic pistol, but the judge dodged, and one of the bullets killed an innocent bystander. When Magee was brought to trial for manslaughter, his lawyer presented testimony that he had fired in self-defense. The jury agreed, and the charges were dismissed. Subsequently, Magee moved to Oklahoma City, where he made a fortune as the inventor of the parking meter.

In the city on the east side in 1921, the mayor ordered a crackdown on gambling, which was followed by the campaign of a host of "feds" in their efforts to enforce the prohibition laws. In 1926, they arrested eight local men for operating stills and a year later four more, including the town marshal, for operating "speak-easy joints." A local newspaper reporter of that era, Milton C. Nahm, wrote later about having seen a constable arrest a bootlegger for possession of a barrel of booze, and then in the office of the justice of the peace the policemen, firemen, and town trustees helped themselves until only two quarts were left in the barrel for evidence in court.

In the spring of 1928, the prevalence of vice in the city prompted a community-wide protest to the council, but the police were able to do little beyond arresting more men for public intoxication. Federal agents, however, did round up eight bootleggers that summer and twenty-three more the next spring. Finally, in the 1930s, the repeal of the prohibition amendment permitted the reopening of local saloons.

In the city, too, negotiations with the Agua Pura Company stirred up acrimony and filled the time of council meetings off and on in the twenties. The shortage of water and the rates charged for it were the bases of complaints which led to rejection of franchises, obtaining of injunctions, advocacy of municipal ownership, appraisals by engineers, and the calling of public meetings. The controversy precipitated a conflict between Mayor Thomas V. Truder and the council in 1930. He assumed to represent the consumers against a council which he thought had been bought up by lavish entertainment by water company officers. He vetoed a franchise approved by the council, which carried it over his veto.

Truder had headed a "fusion ticket," but in 1932, when the Democrats defected and ran Thomas Doran against him, Truder named the election officials without confirmation by the council, whereupon that body obtained an injunction preventing the use of his list. Then the registration books disappeared, and Truder filed charges of "felony" against D. A. Sulier, councilman, for "stealing" them; but at the last minute, they were found in the office of the clerk. In a hectic election, Truder won by a narrow margin. Next, when he made two appointments to fill vacancies on the council, without obtaining confirmation, the majority of that body obtained a court decision declaring those appointments illegal.

Finally this turmoil subsided. Amid it, it is a wonder that the city council made any progress, but that body did manage to get many streets paved, and it did experiment briefly with an innovation, the employment of Mrs. James D. Gibbons as a social worker in 1928 and 1929. Her function was to seek the causes of social ills so that remedial efforts could be applied, but with no funds, there was no point in continuing the investigation.

Municipal funds, derived then largely from property taxes, permitted few frills in the 1920s and became inadequate even for provision of essentials in the 1930s. Especially was this true of the town, which had an appraised property valuation of only $1.5 million against over $4 million in the city—a differential created by a shift of large businesses to the east side.

An earlier generation in the town twice had rejected overtures for consolidation, but desperate financial straits caused a reversal of opinion. In 1932, it was the Town Commercial Club which made a plea for union, but the

A political rally in the Opera House, 1932 (*Father James T. Burke*)

officers of the Chamber of Commerce merely praised the idea. They balked at going further, because such a step would have to have, in the words of A. T. Rogers, an equitable base on "taxation and financial responsibility."

As Las Vegas rounded out its first century, there had been troubles in a great variety, but the citizens had surmounted them one by one, even though some had been scarred in the process. Subsequently, although some politicians continued their provocation of strife in their competitive efforts to become the modern equivalent of *dons,* the elections, and the community at large, steadily became more orderly.

Throughout the first century, an evolution in the nature of the troubles had paralleled the changes occurring in the status of Las Vegas. In early times, they had arisen largely from disorganization attending the meeting of two frontiers at a focal point in the Gateway to Glorieta. Next, during the great boom, most disorders were the result of the recklessness, lawlessness, and aggrandizement existing during those "wild times." Starting at the turn of the century, most of the serious sources of distress were political and institutional upheavals along with local effects of international crises—the types of affliction associated with a more sophisticated society.

Stripping the canyon of timber *(Rex Studio)*

IV | Much Land and Little Water Require Action

On March 20, 1835, four citizens of the populous town of San Miguel del Bado applied to the local *ayuntamiento,* or town council, in behalf of themselves and twenty-five others for a grant of land at Las Vegas for grazing and farming. They proposed boundaries almost identical to those of the previous grant made to (but no longer occupied by) Luis María C. de Baca and his seventeen children, as follows: On the north the Sapelló River, on the east the Watering Place of the Mare, on the south the boundary of the grant of Antonio Ortiz, and on the west the boundary of the San Miguel del Bado Grant.

This application the *ayuntamiento* transmitted to the *Diputación* in Santa Fe, with the recommendation that it be adopted. That body granted approval on March 23 but changed the western boundary to that of the Tecolote Land Grant, which had been awarded in 1824, after Don Luis had filed his application. The next day the governor dispatched an order to the *alcalde* in San Miguel to place the applicants in possession.

The act of approval included the reservation that the lands were conceded not only to the applicants but to "others who may be unaccommodated with lands for farming and with notice that the grant of these lands is made without detriment to the common grazing lands and watering places." Significant also is the change in the boundary in order to give recognition to the prior grant of land at Tecolote to Salvador Montoya and others. Subsequent documents and secondary works consistently quote the boundaries as proposed in the application, with San Miguel del Bado on the west, even the patent issued by the Land Office in 1903 and local abstracts of title. Yet, on the map based on the survey by Frank M. Johnson from 1899 to 1900 in preparation for the patent, and only there, do the boundaries appear correctly, with an indentation in the southwestern corner allowing for the Tecolote Grant. This discrepancy accounts for the fact that the original survey of 1860 embodied 496,446.96 acres. This acreage was reduced to 431,653.65 after Johnson surveyed the boundaries in 1900. Years later, the Land Grant Board and local attorneys regarded that loss of 65,000 acres as mysterious and unjustified.

In his report, José de Jesús Ulibarrí y Durán, *alcalde* of San Miguel del Bado, wrote that in making the allocation on April 6 he had followed the instructions of the governor that all should promise not to leave the land uncultivated and that he should indicate a place for a *plaza* around which the colonists should locate their houses, with precautions for their security. Then he helped the applicants and others who had accompanied them select tracts that he considered in fair proportion to their needs and measured them in *varas* (thirty-three and one-half inches) "from north to south" with observance of "the requirements of the Law for Colonization." He specified that all the men must be equipped with arms and present themselves for review before the police lieutenant every eighth day. Moreover, he warned that nobody could sell his land until he had received his title for the specific tract. Then he gave each formal notice of his exact allotment and made a record of it for his own *archivo*.

For those colonists, the justice measured off divisions of land ranging from 100 to 200 *varas* in width, which when added together would have extended for two and one-half miles along the river front. He also designated 125 *varas* on the north side as a public garden and seventy-five *varas* as a roadway from one side of the river and the other side to the common watering place (that would be the present Bridge Street, including the row of building lots laid out later on each side of it).

Because the land was divided into strips measured from north to south according to the laws on colonization, the pattern can be identified as that which was common in Spanish villages on the northern frontier. Those original tracts, therefore, extended west from the river front to the contour line where the settlers planned to locate their *Acequia Madre,* which they would dig soon to irrigate their fields that summer. According to custom, then, the Plaza was laid out on ground higher than the ditch, but near it. Around the Plaza and along the approaching roads, the colonists selected lots for their houses. All had access to the outlying common pastures and forests, as did those who arrived later to acquire their free tracts along the stream and along ditches on both sides of it.

Various figures from twenty-five to thirty-four have been given for the number of colonists accommodated west of the river on that first day, but according to the *alcalde's* recorded list, the number should be thirty-seven. They included seven Martíns, five Ulibarrís, five Bacas, three Duráns, three Rendóns, two Crespíns, and one each of other surnames—Archuleta, Benavides, Blea, Griego, López, Lucero, Maese, Ortega, Romero, Romo, Segura, and Tafoya.

Following the list of those first allocations, the *alcalde* added 113 names of others accommodated soon afterward, many east of the river and several to the west beyond the *Crestón* and near the *Puertocito*. In 1841, he awarded tracts to five more settlers south of the church, to eight who were founding the "Upper Plaza," and "at the Hot Springs to the foreigners, Julian and Antonio Donaldson." Subsequently, additional grants were made by the local *alcalde,* Juan de Dios Maese, and by the *jues de paz,* Hilario Gonzales, both of whom gave the recipients certificates called *hijuelas*. Altogether, by 1846, close to 6,000 acres had been distributed as "homesteads" in this large grant, and the population had grown to 1,550.

After 1848, titles to land had to be reestablished under procedures followed in the United States. The Treaty of Guadalupe Hidalgo was interpreted to provide that Mexicans who remained in their homes under the new jurisdiction should be protected in the ownership of their property. Six years passed, however, before the Congress created the office of surveyor-general. The appointee was authorized "to ascertain the origin, nature, and character and extent of claims to all lands in New Mexico, under grants extended by Spain and Mexico." To that end, he would take testimony, examine documents, and recommend to Congress which claims should be accepted.

In 1855, after the surveyor-general had issued a call for the filing of claims, only fifteen came in during the ensuing nine months. Most persons apparently thought that all they had to do was to sit tight in possession of whatever they claimed; moreover, many could not find all of the required documents and could not afford a surveyor and lawyer to prepare the claim. They were also handicapped by their inability to understand procedures involving the use of the English language.

As citizens in Las Vegas applied for confirmation of the Las Vegas Land Grant awarded in 1835, to their consternation the heirs of Luis María C. de Baca also filed a claim for possession of the same tract as granted to that family in 1821. The surveyor-general, in his report of December 18, 1858, concluded that both claims seemed valid. If the Congress were to confirm only the prior grant, then the thousands of residents in Las Vegas and vicinity would have to evacuate their lands and homes and turn them over to the numerous heirs of Don Luis. Instead, the Congress awarded the latter an equivalent land grant to be selected in five tracts of 100,000 acres each in locations where the lands were as yet unoccupied.

With provision made for the Bacas, the Congress was freed of that complication but inadvertently introduced another. Application for the Las Vegas Grant had been made originally by three land owners, Dr. Henry Connelly, Francisco López, and Hilario Gonzales, in behalf of themselves and "others," meaning in behalf of all of the settlers on the grant. Somewhere along the line in the review of that by a congressional committee, the designation of the applicants was abbreviated to merely "the Town of Las Vegas." It was in that form, then, that the Congress approved the claim as number twenty in an act which confirmed thirty-two claims on June 21, 1860. That approval, however, left some problems unsolved. In the first place, because there was at that time no incorporated body known as "the Town of Las Vegas" authorized to receive the patent and to act in behalf of the grantees, forty years of uncertainty as to the ownership were destined to ensue. Second, the survey of the boundaries, which at the time encompassed 496,446.96 acres, proved later to be inaccurate, and that discrepancy caused additional confusion and dissension. Third, the confirmation did give authenticity to the titles to many small tracts granted by the *alcaldes* of San Miguel del Bado and Las Vegas, but those properties had not been surveyed. Town tracts were described usually in terms of so many *varas* (thirty-three and one-half inches), bounded on each side by landmarks or by the tracts owned by neighbors, and soon the word *pies* (feet) began to appear instead of *varas*. Those outside of the town also were described in terms of landmarks recognizable then but subject to alteration by a cantankerous neighbor, or even to ultimate disappearance. As an example, one can well imagine the difficulty in locating, and in holding uncontested, this tract of land southeast of Las Vegas, as claimed by Alexander Hatch in 1860:

> All of the tilable [sic] land lying on both sides of said river of Pecos above a certain furrow running nearly east, and West a little above the Canon where the men were killed, as well as all the tilable land laying [sic] on the Gallinas Creek of any kind whatsoever.

Through forty-three years following the confirmation of the grant, nobody had undisputed authority to make grants out on the unoccupied lands, yet numerous titles were claimed, some by presumably legal means and others by devious devices. To make matters worse, some early settlers, notably *dons* whose actions could go unchallenged, expanded the boundaries of their claims so that they overlapped lands of neighbors. This resulted in a crisscrossing of boundary descriptions that would make it difficult ever to clarify the titles to many properties. Meanwhile, in the 1860s, probate judges had assumed that they were successors to the *alcalde* and therefore issued confirmations of occupancy.

In 1873 persons interested in the land grant convened in the old courthouse and elected Trinidad Romero chairman. The surviving original settlers and their heirs, who assumed that they owned the undivided lands, walked out when they saw that they were being outvoted by the numerous newcomers. Those remaining, acting on the principle that the undistributed lands belonged jointly to all persons residing within the grant boundaries, elected May Hays, Juan Romero, and Miguel García as a committee with authority to issue titles to tracts of forty to eighty acres each to all residents, especially to those who lacked lands, in order to save them from becoming "idlerers." By formal petition, the original grantees asked for a restraining order to stop that procedure on the ground that it was dispossessing them of surrounding lands for grazing to which they were entitled, and the district judge granted the injunction. Thirty years later, Eugenio Romero submitted a bill to the Land Grant Board for $800 which his deceased father, Don Miguel, had spent in 1873 in saving the land from being all divided up and disposed of at that time. With interest, the total amount due, he claimed, was $2,248. Finally, in 1906, the board recognized his claim but reduced the amount to $1,880 and awarded him, as an equivalent, three sections of grazing land that he could select at a distance beyond ten miles from town.

The original grantees and their heirs, of whom about eighty acted in behalf of an estimated 800, pressed a countermovement in the 1880s. Some of them held meetings and employed lawyers to defend their claims. Before the end of the decade, however, that contention became subverted. Somebody calculated that 400,000 acres divided by 800 gave each of the heirs an interest in about 500 acres, and then others bought up many of those shares. A few of the latter even went forth and staked out their tracts of 500 acres. In four years, taken as a sample period, sales of forty imaginary undivided shares in the common lands for ten to thirty *pesos* each, by original settlers or their heirs, were entered in the county records, and probably more sales went unrecorded.

The speculators, not all Anglos, who made two or more

of those purchases between 1879 and 1883, were Benigno Jaramillo, Lorenzo López, Trinidad Romero, F. A. Manzanares, Arthur Morrison, O. Geoffrion, James G. Whitney, and Louis Sulzbacher. Thus, by 1890, when advocates of the claims of the original grantees spoke in their behalf, it was not always what it seemed to be, because they represented, instead, the speculators who hoped to reap large profits from the slips of paper in their possession. In opposition to that contention, the newcomers also held meetings and circulated petitions claiming ownership for "the whole people."

Meanwhile, the county commissioners were assuming that the county owned the undivided land and that they, as the successors of the earlier *alcaldes,* had authority to manage it. They claimed ownership of the Plaza, disposed of vacant unclaimed town lots, ordered transgressors to cease occupying the "common pastures" out in the county, and opened roads on unclaimed land.

The Homestead Act, adopted in 1862, was referred to infrequently by local residents in the 1870s, because there had been no suggestion yet that the federal government owned any of this land. Rather, those who recorded claims were more likely to base them merely on a long period of occupancy of the respective tracts. In the 1880s, newcomers became receptive to the theory that because under Mexico this grant had been ordered to be kept open for colonization, the undistributed portion of it therefore had been in effect part of the public domain of that nation, to which the United States became the successor after 1848. Then the number of homestead certificates issued by the United States Land Office in Santa Fe for the northern part of the territory, including San Miguel County, jumped from three in 1879 to 263 in 1882.

As announced by the territorial surveyor-general in August 1888, the secretary of the Department of the Interior then adopted as official policy the conclusion that all open lands in the local grant were public domain, whereupon the number of entries in the Santa Fe office rose to 736 for the succeeding five years.

Exactly what land was available still remained undetermined. So as to be certain, in 1889 the surveyor-general employed R. B. Rice to survey the boundaries of the small claims. Evidence of the validity of those claims also had to be gathered. Because he found the records in the courthouse then to be in a "confused state," his task was so formidable that the funds provided soon ran out and the survey remained unfinished.

The lack of a survey of the small tracts was no impediment to homesteading at a distance from the populous localities, and there the cattlemen made entries, of which forty percent were later found to be illegal. In fact, Victor Westphall found that in this county one cattle company, alone, had filed for eighty-four homesteads. Wilson Waddingham, when he was consolidating several holdings into the mammoth Bell Ranch, recorded sixty-nine tracts of forty to 360 acres each that he had bought from the government. Previously, an agent of the Land Office had warned the several Spanish-American occupants that they should get titles to their claims, but they failed to do that, and Waddingham evicted them. Others made fraudulent acquisitions by purchasing from an agent for a small sum tracts of land for which he had had witnesses file false affidavits of occupancy dating back several years. Still others did not bother to file anything but simply fenced illegally large areas of the common lands in the expectation that they could frighten away anyone who might challenge them.

In the mountains, the aggrandizers were mostly the "new *dons*," who established camps of tie cutters to exploit large areas of virgin timber for their personal profit. When complaints about a number of fraudulent land entries were submitted to a federal grand jury in Las Vegas in 1888, the foreman reported that the jury was unable to act on them "owing to want of data necessary in such cases." Moreover, when the surveyor-general gathered evidence and filed 149 cases allegedly involving fraud in the Fourth Judicial District, which included San Miguel County, he could not obtain convictions.

In 1887, Pablo and José León Padilla, who were squatters out on the common land, filed for homesteads, which would be larger in acreage than their existing tracts. As they expanded their area to cut hay and graze sheep, Philip Milheiser, on behalf of himself and the Las Vegas Land and Cattle Company, applied for a court order to restrain the Padilla brothers. The Chief Justice of the Territorial Supreme Court, Elisha V. Long, who resided in Las Vegas and presided over the district court while "riding circuit," appointed a master in chancery, who made a thorough study and rendered his report a year later. On the basis of it, the judge rendered an opinion in which he disposed of the heirs of original grantees by finding that the Mexican government never intended that they "should have the exclusive right to appropriate to themselves the whole of the said land to the exclusion of actual settlers coming later. . . ." Because this was a colonization grant, the Padillas had acquired a valid claim, he concluded, and, further, the open lands belonged to a community, or "the Town of Las Vegas," exactly as had been stated in the congressional act of confirmation.

While a decision in that case was pending, seventy persons, including Lorenzo López and Félix Martínez, signed a petition proposing a compromise by which the mountain lands would be reserved "in trust for public use under the supervision of the county commissioners," while the unoccupied grasslands would be granted to the assignees or heirs of original settlers. Soon the flaws in it became apparent. "Public use" of the mountain lands meant continued rampant exploitation of the timber resources by *dons*, while the "assignees" of the original settlers meant those speculators who had bought up the shares.

The legal opinion in the Milheiser case scotched any further discussion of the compromise and aroused anticipation that East Las Vegas, which then was incorporated as a town, was entitled to possession of the unoccupied lands. The editor of the *Courier* speculated that 400,000 acres sold at one dollar an acre would produce an endowment which would yield $40,000 annually for the creation of a "beautiful and adorned city" without any taxes.

Because the Secretary of the Interior persisted in his

opinion that the undivided lands had become part of the public domain, an effort was made to get the Congress to issue a patent to the Town of Las Vegas, and Judge Long proposed that it be held in trust by the county commissioners until the east and west sides could effect consolidation into one town. Then the Commercial Club on the east side suggested that a commission be elected to administer the grant, while simultaneously Philip Milheiser was petitioning the Secretary of the Interior to issue the patent to the original grantees; but the Secretary of the Interior still held that the lands were public domain.

Amid the frustrating legal confusion, desperate villagers arose in rebellion. One night in April 1889, at a ranch acquired by two Englishmen, night riders cut four miles of new barbed wire fence and chopped down the posts. Much more followed at ranch after ranch. When a local man, Juan José Herrera, became an organizer in 1889 for a radical new union, the Knights of Labor, its members expressed alarm. Wherever Herrera set up local units, the cutting of ranchers' fences at night began in that vicinity.

A grand jury indicted twenty-six rural residents whom Sheriff López rounded up, but after a jury found the first one tried "not guilty," the district attorney dropped the charges against the others.

When another grand jury began investigations in October 1889, sixty-three men on horseback wearing long white masks rode around the courthouse and on past the home of the prosecuting attorney. The participants thenceforth were called *Las Gorras Blancas,* or "White Caps." Well-informed witnesses who could identify some of the men were afraid to talk; nevertheless, the jury did obtain the names of forty suspects, and ten of them were arrested by the sheriff. Among them were Juan José Herrera and his brothers, Pablo and Nicanor. Then a mob of White Caps made a demonstration, shot guns in the air, and broke windows in the new courthouse. As soon as an attorney filed a writ of *habeas corpus* and got the ten out on bail, 300 sympathizers paraded around the Plaza singing *John Brown's Body.*

Editors and judges appealed in vain to the White Caps to

resort to legal recourse. In response, about 200 of them paraded in New Town one night in March. They distributed handbills in which they claimed that they stood for a "free ballot and a free count. Be fair, or take the consequences." When the editor of the *Optic* named Juan José Herrera as the leader of the White Caps, Herrera called at the newspaper office and denied it. He said that he was a loyal supporter of American institutions, and as a member of the Knights of Labor he had never heard at their meetings "the least mention of resort to brutal acts." The editor of *La Voz del Pueblo* came out in defense of the Knights of Labor and contended that the real causes of the continued depredations were the outrages committed by Republican politicians.

Conditions were so bad that Jefferson Raynolds called a meeting of citizens on August 17, 1890, to discuss a solution. Governor L. Bradford Prince came and begged those present to identify the White Caps so that the participants could be apprehended. To that end, Raynolds proposed the appointment of a Committee on Safety. When representatives of the "poor people" demanded that such a committee be elected, the row over that issue caused the meeting to break up "amid the wildest confusion," according to the press report.

During the uproar that night, Félix Martínez gave Philip Milheiser a tongue lashing, calling him a "landgrabber," and an altercation ensued the next day. Milheiser threatened to thrash Martínez, but Martínez deterred him by rapping him on the head with the butt of his pistol.

In a bitterly contested election that fall, the Populists, supported vigorously by *La Voz del Pueblo,* wrested hundreds of votes away from the Republican Ring, or, to put it another way, they broke the control of *dons* over their *peones* under the traditional *patrón* system. Among the victors were Félix Martínez, as a member of the Territorial Council, and Pablo Herrera, a suspected White Cap, as a representative in the Assembly. Nevertheless, the fence cutting continued.

While in the legislature, Herrera apparently became disillusioned. He was reported to have said in a closing speech that his term in the penitentiary had been more enjoyable, because "there is more honor, truth, and honesty within the walls of the penitentiary than there is here." After he returned, he quarreled with an opponent of the White Caps, Doroteo Sandoval, and murdered him. For that he was convicted, but while awaiting his sentence, a friendly jailor allowed him to escape. Finally, just before Christmas in 1894, a posse led by Sheriff López found him, and when he resisted arrest, López shot him dead.

López was also a Populist, like his victim. He had astutely changed his affiliation to that party, which had been victorious again in the election of 1892. After López deserted the Republicians, the organization politicians condemned him. For years he had been a thorn in their side, and now they sought to derogate him by alleging that secretly he had been the leader of the White Caps. He was furious about the allegations. He reminded everyone how he had once arrested ten of the suspects and how the White Caps had burned his hay, had written him threatening letters, and had conducted demonstrations outside of his office in efforts to intimidate him.

Through those years, when the depredations made news, the names of the victims included about as many Hispanic names as Anglo. Among the former were Eugenio and Cleofes Romero, both of whom had had stacks of thousands of freshly cut railroad ties destroyed at night by the White Caps.

The revolt of the White Caps did not cease in 1890, because then "all of the fences were down," as one historian has written. As late as March 1892, the *Optic* was deploring the continuation of such depredations, and then they ceased. The agitation had at least helped the Populists to put into office men who were sympathetic. But even after those victories, troubles continued. Finally, the uprising tapered off without gaining any land for *los pobres,* without putting a stop to the cutting of timber and the fencing of grasslands, and without securing immediately any authority to manage the land grant.

In contemporary accounts, the causes were attributed about half and half to "landgrabbing" and "Republican oppression," and "Republican" then meant the Romeros along with their affiliated *dons,* merchants, and lawyers.

There was a significant correlation in that the beginning of the depredations coincided with the launching of fiery anti-Republican agitation in *La Voz del Pueblo* in 1889—depredations that subsided after they had been condemned by respected Jesuits in editorials published in *Revista Católica* in 1891. Yet, there were other factors more deeply rooted.

Originally, the Mexican families had subsisted by farming their small tracts, by grazing sheep on the common grasslands, and by hunting game and cutting wood in the mountains. They had little money, because the *dons* garnered the monetary profits from sheep raising under the *partido* system; but in those days they had little need for money. Presently, the Anglos introduced a capitalistic economy, which created new wants and called for acquisition of money to satisfy those wants. One of the innovations was a property tax, which offered an opportunity for "landgrabbers" to buy up the land of the poor at tax sales. No doubt it also induced many heirs to sell their claims to undivided shares in the common lands, which, according to a report by Governor Prince, had caused the heirs of the original settlers to contribute to their own undoing.

Against the oppressive turn of affairs, the revolt was an expression of resentment with only short-term objectives and no clear realization of the involvement in complexities. The only real gain had been measures in behalf of the long-neglected improvement of public education contributed by the Populists who were elected to the legislature. Otherwise, the resort to violence undoubtedly helped retard Las Vegas in that critical decade of its history.

In 1893, after the rural rebellion had subsided, Jefferson Raynolds, town banker, enlisted a battery of lawyers who spent a year preparing information for legal action against the claim of the Department of the Interior that the common lands were public domain. In the district court in Washington they won a decision that the "Town of Las Vegas" had "good and indefeasible title" to them. In 1897, therefore, the secretary announced that he would issue the patent to the "Town of Las Vegas" as soon as that recipient would have the boundaries surveyed.

A view across the valley in 1900 (*Rex Studio*)

While the survey was being made, attorneys representing Herman Maes and other heirs and assignees of original settlers, also went to Washington and petitioned for an order to reverse the decision. In 1902, the Supreme Court denied that request because the grant had been made by Mexico in 1835 "as much to a community as to individuals" and the patent must be issued to "the confirmee of Congress, the Town of Las Vegas."

What was "the Town of Las Vegas"? By 1902, the east side could not advance a claim because it had become a city; therefore, there was no incorporated body by that name that could act as agent for management of the lands. The attorneys mustered by Raynolds had said that the name really meant a community of all of the persons occupying the land grant. Obviously, if one town were to get all of that land, possession of it would be a discrimination against persons who happened to reside in other localities. Therefore, at public meetings in 1902, discussion centered on a proposal to have the Congress pass an act authorizing the district judge to appoint a commission to act in behalf of all residents. Opponents contended that such a commission should be elected, like in other community land grants in New Mexico. Some proposed that if the west side should incorporate as a town, then its elected trustees would constitute that commission.

An eminent Democrat, Ezekiel C. de Baca, developed a plan for the proposed town trustees to have precinct representatives elected to join with them to form a large board for management of the land grant. His proposal, of course, had little chance of adoption in a community that was then predominantly Republican. Long afterward, partisans of Don Ezekiel continued to lament that, because his plan was not adopted, the appointed board sold all of the "people's land"; but his plan also contemplated management of "profits from the sales of land." With partisan politics involved, it seems to boil down largely to the issue of which side would get to do the selling.

The proposal for appointment of an independent commission became embodied in a petition sponsored by Charles A. Spiess, a Republican attorney but not a partisan of the

Romeros. After it had been presented to the district judge, William J. Mills, he responded in December 1902 by appointing such a commission. In order for it to qualify as recipient of the patent, he named it "the Board of Trustees of the Town of Las Vegas" and specified that the board should represent all occupants of the land grant. As members he named seven prominent citizens—Jefferson Raynolds, banker; Charles Ilfeld, merchant; Elisha V. Long, previously the chief justice; F. H. Pierce, president of the water works; Félix Esquibel, a wealthy, respected rancher; Isador V. Gallegos, a dealer in land and livestock; and Eugenio Romero, retired timber-cutting contractor and erstwhile political "boss." All of them served through the critical, formative years to 1909, when Ilfeld and Gallegos resigned. The remaining five continued until Raynolds and Pierce resigned in 1911. Romero and Esquibel continued to serve, along with other appointees, through most of that decade.

The principal timber cutter at that time was Margarito Romero, a brother of Don Eugenio. He was arrested in 1903 but acquitted for cutting timber for railroad ties on the Pecos Forest Reserve, and simultaneously the board had him arrested for cutting timber in Gallinas Canyon on what the members claimed to be grant land. He answered that arrest with a counter-complaint alleging that the board should be abolished because it had been created illegally. Then Spiess, who was a member of the territorial legislature, obtained hasty enactment of a statute on March 12, 1903, authorizing the district judge to appoint a board for management of this land grant, thereby legalizing an act already done. In Romero's subsequent complaint, he contended that that statute was "special legislation" of the type forbidden by a federal act of 1886, but the courts did not sustain his interpretation.

At protest meetings in the Exchange Hotel in May 1903, Don Margarito spoke bitterly about his threatened loss of hundreds of acres of timberland, which he claimed, without submitting evidence, had been in the possession of his family for years. He advocated that the west side should incorporate as a town in order yet to obtain the land grant. His motive was apparent, but he did not mention that by winning election as mayor he could persuade the town trustees to recognize his claim to a large private estate in the mountains. Eusebio Chacon, Ezekiel C. de Baca, and Eugenio Romero also spoke in favor of separate incorporation to escape other alleged injustices attributed to the Anglo citizens of the city.

Despite the advice of an attorney, John D. W. Veeder, that legally the proposed town never could acquire the land grant, despite the warning of Spiess that such a town would have an inadequate tax base for sustaining municipal services, and despite an eloquent, impassioned plea by O. A. Larrazolo for a merger with the city, those present enthusiastically approved a motion for separate incorporation, which was effected immediately.

The Land Grant Board borrowed $2,400 from two local banks to pay Frank M. Johnson for making the survey of the boundaries of the grant and then became the recipient of the patent issued on June 27, 1903. As soon as Don Margarito was elected mayor of the town, he demanded that the board turn the patent over to the town, only to meet with a blunt refusal. He responded by writing a long, vitriolic letter to the Spanish-language newspaper condemning that alleged violation of an edict of the Supreme Court.

He had so thoroughly aroused the hope of townsmen on the west side that they could get possession of the land grant, and then he so bitterly condemned the outcome, that for long afterward the conviction prevailed among many that an "Anglo" board, which it was not entirely, had been set up hastily in a scheme to "steal" the land grant from them. However, the claim of the town was entangled with that of an eminent *don* and was clouded, too, by the conflicting claims of others.

That board had more clashes with Romero on up to 1909, when an injunction again prevented his destructive cutting of timber. By that time, too, he had failed in his effort to get Judge Mills to abolish the board created by that judge.

Although Raynolds was elected president and Ilfeld treasurer, it was "Judge" Long, the secretary, who emerged as the guiding spirit, and spokesman, of the board as it sought

Early farmers display their fabulous produce *(Our Lady of Sorrows Collection)*

to develop and apply policies. First, that body had to contend against numerous transgressors on grant land. Time and again, the board sent orders to residents to cease unauthorized commercial cutting of timber and illegal fencing of large tracts for which they could not show titles, as well as to nonresidents to withdraw from grazing cattle and sheep on the commons. In a few instances, the board had to resort to court action in order to halt the building of fences by ambitious ranchers. Surprisingly, among them were more Hispanos than Anglos, and hardly could that be said to have been prejudicial in view of the influential Hispanic representation on the board. Altogether, the difficulties in the breaking up of help-yourself practices affirm that certainly the White Caps had been animated by a real aggravation back in the years from 1889 to 1892.

Simultaneously, from 1904 to 1906, the board demonstrated concern for the welfare of the Hispanic villagers. Resolutions were enforced to reserve all of the unoccupied grazing lands for use by residents as of 1903, and one person could graze on them no more than 4,000 sheep and 400 cattle.

In addition, all common watering places were required to be kept open and accessible to them.

Meanwhile, puzzled about the aforementioned reduction in total acreage, the board had immediately protested to the Department of the Interior and then, in 1905, employed John L. Zimmerman to resurvey the boundaries, for which he was paid by a grant of two sections of land. Next, the board retained an attorney to try to recover the "lost" 65,000 acres, but obviously that could not be done without dispossessing the Tecolote settlers of their land grant.

Because the board had no funds at first, the members approved the meeting of obligations by granting land, valued at $1.00 an acre. To three attorneys, who had obtained the court action in Washington that brought forth the awarding of the patent, the board deeded each from four to eight sections (640 acres). In 1906, it also paid John D. W. Veeder with eight sections for representing it in crucial cases in the district court. Presently, the members decided that the laborious services of the secretary merited a salary, which they paid by awarding him four sections in 1905.

In the beginning, and later too, when the board did have cash to pay bills, the members quibbled with lawyers about the amount of their fees. For example, in 1910, when five submitted bills amounting to $4,000, the board offered them $500, which they refused. However, Judge Mills advised that the board pay those requested fees, because the cases in court had been "very important," which indeed they were.

Once before, in 1906, the board received another kind of a bill to which the members objected. The county treasurer computed a charge for taxes at thirty cents an acre on 486,706 acres, which was more than the land grant had contained originally. Meanwhile, much acreage had also been disposed of. The bill came to over $17,000, with a penalty of $800 tacked on. The members protested and finally negotiated a compromise payment of $7,500 annually.

As for disposition of land, the board had prepared first, back in 1904, for the granting of titles to the occupants of small tracts. The claimants were not required to present a certificate of ownership, which many of them could not do.

Instead, each had to present only a surveyor's description of the boundaries and an affidavit that he or she had occupied the tract for ten years or longer. That applied not only to heirs and assignees of the original tracts but also to lands occupied by others, almost 100 percent Hispanos, who had come later.

The board acted upon each case individually and granted the claim unless somebody else disputed it. In that kind of a case, a member, often the secretary, investigated in order to reach a solution at the next meeting. However, no claim for more than 160 acres would be allowed, but an approved claimant could purchase an additional 160 acres on a payment plan, if able.

When a problem arose in the case of the applicants in the village of San Gerónimo, a plan hit upon for it became the accepted procedure for other villages, too. The board authorized a survey of the village boundaries and its lots and conveyed the entire tract to the village. Then the residents selected a trustee who determined the rightful claimants and made deeds to them. Anyone dissatisfied could appeal his decision to the district court. This expedient happily spared the board from delving into all of the intricacies of claims to lots in the villages.

The board called the small tracts "homesteads." Through the years, much time was devoted to conscientious pursuit of the adopted procedure. The number of cases acted upon passed 800 by 1920, accounting for a total acreage of a little over 17,000, and by the time of the centennial, 1935, the number awarded had exceeded 1,300. In this manner, the board had respected both the initial allocations by the *alcaldes* and the Mexican principle that the remaining lands should be open to colonization.

Up to 1906, the board refused to consider offers to purchase large tracts, and then they began negotiations to that end. In a few instances, it dealt with owners of large ranches already carved out by individuals and companies which somehow had obtained titles to land. In cases wherein their claims to some of the land were shadowed, or overlapped others, the board engaged in negotiations whereby the rancher finally agreed to buy that land or a substitute tract.

As a result, there were a few sales of thousands of acres at a time. Otherwise, the members held to their rule that tracts sold to individuals should not exceed 160 acres.

On April 6, 1906, A. W. Thompson requested the board to sell him 50,000 acres at $1.25 an acre for "colonization." He intended to sell the land for small farms and would pay $10,000 down. The board accepted, and in August, Thompson transferred his contract to Ira G. Hazzard, who would pay $1.75 an acre. Immediately, he reported that he had sold 2,000 acres at $6,00 an acre and that in September he would bring from the Midwest an excursion train full of prospects. By November, he had sold about 19,000 acres, and then he transferred his interests to Fred W. Browne of Chicago, who offered to buy more land. In March 1907, his offer of $2,000 down for the purchase of 100,000 acres at $1.50 an acre was accepted when he agreed to guarantee that within a year he would have seventy-five heads of families settled on the lands. Then he subcontracted with real estate firms to handle the sales. Richard A. Morley, a local Methodist preacher, began "moonlighting" as a salesman and did so well that he quit the ministry in 1907 in order to work full time for sales commissions, whereby he soon became a wealthy property owner in Chicago.

The rapid diminishing of common lands for grazing had so alarmed the Hispanic villagers that in 1907, when spurred on by protests published in *La Voz del Pueblo,* 500 of them met in Las Vegas on August 9 to seek redress. They drafted petitions and raised $800 for an attorney, who in district court sought to get the speculative sales halted or else the Land Grant Board abolished. Attorneys for the board argued for dismissal of the case, which Chief Justice William J. Mills did. From time to time, Browne made payments and took options on more land. Finally, in 1910, the board members rode forth to see if he had settled seventy-five families as specified in his contract of 1907 and found that he had fulfilled that agreement. Actually, that was only a token expression in favor of colonization as against speculative sales.

The boom in the sale of land in those years had been stimulated by a great flurry of interest in dry farming. In

Threshing by treadmill *(Rex Studio)*

April 1906, the board had granted John L. Donahue of Denver, representing the Campbell System, permission to cultivate one section of land for three years to demonstrate that "land could be successfully farmed without irrigation." Simultaneously, G. P. Geiger, representing himself and five others, including W. H. Comstock, was allowed one section for that purpose. For the Campbell System, Donahue engaged in promotional meetings to get the Commercial Club to raise, and advance as a loan, $2,500 to purchase a steam-powered tractor and a special cultivator invented by W. C. Campbell. After the equipment failed to arrive, and after Donahue had run up other bills and had withdrawn the $2,500 from the bank and disappeared, the board in 1907 deeded the Campbell tract to local men, A. C. Erb and Fred Westerman. They had offered to assume the obligation for the lost loan. As they and Comstock cultivated their tracts, both soon displayed a fabulous production. That sparked a boom like those promoted by railroads and speculators elsewhere in the West.

The *Optic* published a special "Mesa Edition" in 1907, promoters had a surveyor plat a town at Onava, a real estate company announced plans to build a hotel out east on the mesa, the county commissioners contracted for the building of a bridge across the Pecos Arroyo, and real estate agents brought carloads of prospects seeking small farms. As happened elsewhere, when the virgin soil of the grasslands first was broken, it produced miraculously for only a few seasons without irrigation. Then the bubble burst. The peak year for land sales, therefore, was 1908, when 81,089 acres yielded receipts of $151,377. Then sales tapered off annually to zero in 1915, followed by small amounts subsequently.

By 1931, the total sum received from sales amounted to $324,133.40. To that date, the board also had received $240,668.55 in interest on outstanding notes, $14,526.65 from leases for grazing, and $9,134.29 from royalties on permits for the cutting of timber where it could stand thinning. At that time, the acreage in sales and homesteads came to 402,962.9, leaving only about 29,000 acres still under board management. The land was almost all gone.

Approximately one-half of the total receipts of about $600,000 went for expenses—salaries of employees, attorneys' fees, surveyors' fees, taxes, firefighting, and the personal expenses of board members along with nominal salaries for them, on the average amounting to approximately $10.00 a month for each member.

After Lorenzo Delgado, county political "boss," became chairman of the board in 1925, other politicians suspected mismanagement and demanded an audit, which was ordered by the governor in 1930. The Albuquerque auditors engaged for that task made a thorough tally of the books in 1931 without finding any irregularities. From their report, the foregoing figures were gleaned.

Quite early, the accumulation of reserve funds began to attract attention. In 1909, the legislature passed an act which specified that the board should invest its surplus in a fund and that the interest earned from the investment should be used to benefit local schools. The board soon developed a project for an irrigation system in which the surplus was invested; nevertheless, it kept account of a sum owed to the schools in what was called "the School Trust Fund." During World War II, another legislative act required the board to spend $30,000 for a veterans' memorial. However, a controversy over whether the memorial should be a school, a hospital, or a monument went to the district court, which ruled that the acts directing how the money should be spent were "special legislation" of the type forbidden by the state constitution. That relieved the board of those obligations.

No longer was there any cash to spare, because the board was investing all of its surplus in the troublesome irrigation project—a story that began even before the board's inception. A depression suitable for a reservoir east of the Hot Springs was located on a tract called the Sanguejuela Grant. Its seventeen claimants, all but one Hispanic, had had their application for that grant rejected in 1898 by the Court of Private Land Claims, because the documents had not been prepared by authorized officials. In 1901, F. A. Manzanares, spokesman for the group, unsuccessfully tried to interest investors in that site, but he did succeed later in getting the attention of acquaintances in Washington. In 1903, federal engineers visited the site four times. Then those claimants became contenders against the Land Grant Board. Isador V. Gallegos, one of the claimants, was also a board member. It was with Manzanares, however, that the board engaged in unsuccessful negotiations. The claimants then brought suit, which led to an agreement, settled out of court, for the board to sell them 16,000 acres elsewhere at $1.50 an acre.

In 1905, government engineers drafted plans for a dam and canals that would irrigate 10,000 acres. That land would be offered for sale at $60.00 an acre, and enough contracts would have to be obtained in advance to cover the cost of the project, estimated at $572,000. There lay the hitch—because all of the local promotional efforts which ensued would not be accepted as a substitute for signatures on the dotted line. Therefore, in 1908, speculation about the federal reservoir ceased.

In 1909, the board initiated negotiations with D. A. Camfield of Greeley, Colorado, who had built reservoirs and established his reputation as "the Western Irrigation King." On September 2, a contract was executed. On the Sanguejuela site he would build a dam that would create a reservoir to irrigate 17,060 acres, which the board would convey to him when the project was finished. For its part, the board promised to secure rights to the floodwaters of the Sanguejuela, Sapelló, and Gallinas rivers, and the Pecos Arroyo, without interfering with prior rights to the normal flow of those streams. Finally, the construction would have to meet specifications required by the State Engineer.

When an attorney for the board filed application number 341 for the floodwater rights, he was informed that it had been superseded by number 320, filed by Andrieus A. Jones. In litigation concluded in 1909, Jones had prevented Thomas B. Catron from obtaining full possession of the entire Pino Grant north of Santa Rosa, later known as the Preston Beck Grant. Instead, Jones, as an inlaw of Beck's partner, had emerged as the owner of 40,000 acres. It was then that he filed for those floodwaters in expectation that he would divert them in a canal far to the south for irrigation on that ranch.

In a petition to the district court, Jones contended that the Land Grant Board had no legal authority to develop an irrigation project, but Judge Mills denied that petition in January 1910. Next, the board members had to make trips to Santa Fe for hearings before both the State Engineer and the Board of Water Commissioners. When his application was denied on the ground that it was "not feasible," Jones appealed that ruling to the district court, which in 1911 rendered a decision that because he had not had the proposed ditch surveyed, he lacked proof that it was feasible. The memory of many citizens of San Miguel County must have been short, because only five years after this attempt by Jones to pull the props out from under local economic development, they joined with others to elect him to the United States Senate.

Meanwhile, in 1910, Camfield had begun work under assurance by the board that if the water rights were not forthcoming, he would be paid anyway for the work done. A "dinky" engine hauled dirt on a track laid over the site of the dam and dumped it as a landfill until May 1911, when Camfield ceased work. Under threat of forfeiture of his bond, he began moving dirt again in August, but then the State Engineer required that much of it be removed and replaced, because it contained too much shale. When he failed to finish the job within the time limit, the board filed a suit against his bondholder. To make matters worse, heavy rains washed out part of the work already done. On September 3, 1912, Camfield reported to the board that, because he had run out of funds, he would have to relinquish his contract. Frustrated and exhausted, he died six months later.

The board repossessed all of the properties by assuming the $60,000 owed by Camfield to his creditors. In the quest for a successor, an offer by R. C. Storrie of San Francisco was finally accepted in June 1916. He agreed to build the dam by March 1918. To that end, the board conveyed to his company 16,957 acres and agreed to make a loan of $200,000 to be paid in installments as the work progressed. A labor shortage created by wartime conditions and bad weather required several extensions of the time limit, until finally, in December 1921, the board accepted the "earthen dam with concrete core" as finished.

In 1922, F. A. Reid of Phoenix, Arizona, incorporated the Las Vegas Land and Water Company to sell land and to store and distribute water. In August, that company bought the project under terms that filled thirty pages of board minutes. Bonds amounting to a quarter of a million dollars were issued to the board as a lien on the 16,957 acres of land. The board transferred titles to the water rights, the lands, the canals, the dams, and the reservoir site, which was described as being bounded by a contour line at 6,600 feet above sea level, or five feet higher than the dam stood at that date. Then the company sent Thomas W. Conway to Las Vegas in June 1922 as manager of the project. By his estimate in an interview years later, the total cost of the project had amounted to about $750,000.

While waiting for the reservoir to fill, Conway operated a demonstration farm in 1923 on which the production was phenomenal. That summer, twenty optimistic families bought farms on the project, and a year later, George W. Gifford, employed by Conway as salesman, had located 145 families on the small irrigated tracts. Already 8,000 acres had been sold under contracts providing for payments in

Storrie Dam under construction *(Rex Studio)*

installments.

In the summer of 1924, the lettuce and peas planted on 1,000 acres were thriving well until on September 16 the earliest frost in twenty-nine years killed nearly all of the plants. A year later, bountiful crops filled 167 freight cars with vegetables, but the net proceeds barely allowed the farmers to subsist, because the high cost of marketing consumed 18 percent of the income. Men fell delinquent in making their payments. In 1927, a severe hailstorm destroyed about one-half of the crops, leaving many of the farmers destitute. Some gave up and moved away.

The outcome was that in 1927 the Land Grant Board filed a foreclosure suit, not only against the company but also against all of the farmers on the project, because they could claim an interest in the irrigation system. The court appointed a receiver. Conway said later that he could still have made a success of it by switching to production of carrots. He thought that the foreclosure had been instituted prematurely because Delgado, then board chairman and Republican "boss," wanted to stamp out the nest of Democrats emerging on the farms on the mesa.

The receiver placed George Gifford in charge for two years. He found that the farms yielded good crops of beets but that the cost of shipping them to a sugar factory in Colorado was prohibitive.

In 1929, in a court sale, the board itself came into possession of controlling interest in the project by purchasing two-thirds of the outstanding mortgages, amounting to $335,314. Through two ensuing years, in the era of the Depression, the board contracted with the local Chamber of Commerce for management, which was pursued by resort to a sharecropping plan that allowed the seventy-two remaining farmers to make payments. Afterward, the board placed Gifford in charge again. Steadily, the few persisting landowners shifted to production of grain, hay, and poultry, along with dairy farming.

Conway, who meanwhile had had to obtain other employment, nevertheless continued to be concerned. In 1944, he finally came up with a plan that met with the approval of the board. He organized a cooperative irrigation district in which farmers on the project would become shareholders at $100 a share. With the funds raised in that manner, he purchased the board's share in the project for $33,875 and the other interests still outstanding for an additional $5,625. The entire project, then, he deeded to the Storrie Project Water Users Association, whose officers continued to employ Gifford, "the Grand Old Man of Storrie Lake."

The few remaining farmers concentrated upon growing forage crops. That was an outcome certainly not foreseen by the early proponents of this project—a scheme that had fallen far short of its promise. Even so, other assets emerged in time. Storrie Lake became popular for fishing and boating, and another lake, McAllister, which was stabilized in a depression near the southern end of the main canal, became the mecca of trout fishermen.

Throughout the entire era, how well had the descendants of the Hispanic pioneers fared? Certainly there could be no complaint that they and Hispanic newcomers in their midst had suffered loss of their *milpas*, because they had been protected in ownership as fairly as possible. Ultimately, the granting of only small tracts to them would be unfortunate. However, at the time when the Land Grant Board, officially designated as the "Trustees of the Town of Las Vegas," was inaugurating the practice of giving title to those "homesteads," that promised to be satisfactory, because simultaneously the board was enforcing resolutions for protection of common grasslands, timberlands, and watering places.

Originally, the Mexican grant had in it an inconsistency in that it authorized the allocating of small farms while also providing for "colonization" of the remaining lands, but "without damage to the common grazing lands and watering places." If the second provision were to be pursued to conclusion, observance of the third one would suffer. That damage might have been alleviated only if the board had attempted an impossibility by trying to halt influx of population in about 1910 in order to grant each village thousands of acres for common watershed and pasture. Even then, probably the board would have had to enforce measures to prevent some of the wealthy *dons* from claiming those lands as private estates upon which the villagers would be their *peones* in the Mexican tradition of that era.

The board and its original sponsors did resort to purposeful deprivation in that the board was created in part to prevent one town and its political "boss" from obtaining control of the common lands in discrimination against other occupants of the land grant. Moreover, it did act vigorously in an effort to deprive overly ambitious *dons* and Anglos from possessing large tracts of land that they were trying to acquire without having defensible titles to them.

Another deprivation occurred circumstantially when the board resorted to a rapid sale of the common lands, much of it speculative, in order to obtain the funds for a promising irrigation project. The filling up and fencing of lands deprived many of the small farmers of access to timberland and pastures once essential for their existence. However, even if that access had been preserved for them, it would have enabled those villagers to sustain only a subsistence economy, like in early times.

In the modern era, the small farmers needed cash income to pay taxes, to acquire a pickup and appliances, to pay medical bills, and to send their children to high school and college. Years later, the board did grant three villages the use of 3,000 acres each, but in an era when small farmers were being squeezed out everywhere, that allocation, although helpful, failed to rejuvenate those villages. If each family could have been given 5,000 acres, the Hispanos would have had a chance to prosper as ranchers under modern conditions.

Another circumstantial deprivation would occur in 1958, when the State Supreme Court ruled in the Cartwright case that water for domestic and public consumption in Las Vegas took precedence over other uses. That put an end to much of the irrigation for agriculture near the town and in villages along the Gallinas River.

Almost everyone has assumed that the decline of the villages and distress of the rural Hispanos had one cause—the loss of access to common lands. This assumption fails to take into account that, without a program for economic redevelopment, the decline no doubt would have occurred anyway due to the simultaneous collapse in the market for wool, the reduced supply of water, the demands of a capitalistic economy, and the inroads of the agricultural revolution.

Any analysis of the turmoil back at the turn of the century must allow for the bias of the newspapers. Although the Republican *Las Vegas Daily Optic* generally supported the candidates for office advanced by the county Republican Romero organization, it opposed the acquisition of all of the common lands by one town and the probable consequent domination of the affairs of the land grant by a Romero. A few attorneys concurred, and one of them obtained signatures on a petition that also persuaded Judge Mills to concur. The motive might be suspect, but a search through the minutes of the Land Grant Board reveals that neither that attorney nor the judge nor the editor nor two land barons, who were shareholders in the Optic Publishing Company formed in 1897, received any land. In fact, one of the latter, Wilson Waddingham, died before the board was appointed. Later, Judge Mills did gain appointment as territorial governor in

1910, and one land baron, Thomas B. Catron (not a local resident), did win election to the United States Senate in 1912, but those advancements were unrelated to the local conflict.

The rival newspaper, *La Voz del Pueblo,* at first Populist and later Democratic, was even more antagonistic toward Republican Romero domination. The editors disregarded the probability that an elected land grant commission or elected town trustees no doubt would have been a Romero board, in order to create, and play up, issues that would incite men to vote for them and others in an effort to overturn the Republican "machine." Certainly they were above any suspicion that they were trying to get any land as their reward, but their agitation in behalf of the White Caps helped win for the publisher, Félix Martínez, election to the Territorial Council in 1890 and 1892. Further, their subsequent playing up of alleged injustices no doubt helped one former editor, Antonio Lucero, to win nomination for the office of secretary of state and another editor, Ezekiel C. de Baca, to become a candidate for lieutenant governor, both in 1912.

Obviously, the partisan articles in those two leading newspapers have to be balanced against each other and tempered by a study of the court opinions and the minutes of the Land Grant Board. Up to about 1908, the considerate policies toward Hispanos maintained by that board belie the interpretation that it had originated as a "tool" of any "boss" or "landgrabber" and that the members had regarded the Spanish Americans as "obstacles in the way of progress," as averred by subsequent critics of the board. Thenceforth, it appears that the wholesale disposition of the vacant lands may have become detrimental to the welfare of many townsmen and villagers; but, as has been shown, other causes made that outcome more circumstantial than intentional and not fully realized until too late for recovery.

Ultimately, nearly everybody who had early claims could protest that he had lost land. That included the disappointed citizens of West Las Vegas, the dependent residents of the villages, and the frustrated *dons* and others who were attempting to create personal estates. All advanced nebulous claims to the common lands, which also were designated in the original grant as reserved for colonization. However, the claims conflicted. If one group were to get those lands, the others would be thwarted, and if colonization by either homesteads or sales were given precedence, then all of the others would lose out. That was the ultimate outcome of this dilemma in which no conceivable solution could have appeased all contenders.

South Pacific Street, about 1875 *(Las Vegas City Museum)*

V | Education Promises Enlightenment

In the Mexican period, education for the masses was informal, even though the distant Mexican government did at times seek to encourage the establishing of schools. In San Miguel del Bado, where the Las Vegas colonists originated, the Mexican census conducted in 1827 reported the presence of one teacher; therefore, the colonists must have had some acquaintance with the concept of formal schooling. However, amid the efforts to subsist at Las Vegas after 1835, there was no report for some time about emulating that example. Instead, most parents instructed children in the speaking of Spanish and in the learning of practical skills.

On the other hand, the *dons* obtained tutoring for their sons and sent them to distant colleges. Several of them emerged later with leadership capabilities by virtue of their literacy and informational background. Local formal schooling, introduced after the crisis of the Civil War had been surmounted, originated as an achievement mainly of church leaders who sought to foster religious education along with inculcation of skills and enlightenment.

Previously, in 1852, Bishop John B. Lamy had persuaded Sisters of Loretto to make the arduous journey to New Mexico and open schools. In 1869, those who had located first in Albuquerque moved to Las Vegas and started a day and boarding school for girls in a three-room adobe house lent to them by Don Rumauldo Baca. There, three of them slept on pallets on the floor at night while instructing their seventy-five initial enrollees in the three Rs and in religion, music, painting, and needlework.

The encouraging response brought in contributions for the construction of a large, two-story frame building near the

The Sisters' Academy in 1885 *(Father James T. Burke)*

Plaza, and in 1876, while it was being constructed, the original quarters burned down. Therefore, the new building was put to use later in that year before it was quite ready. The news reports of the subsequent fund-raising fairs and closing exercises of that academy attest that the Sisters were highly appreciated and well supported. In 1888, they had 180 pupils, both boys and girls, and they graduated their first high school class. Presently, in 1912, they also opened a school in East Las Vegas. In it they started a high school in 1915 and by 1922 had constructed a larger brick building for this Immaculate Conception School.

Simultaneous with the coming of the Sisters in 1869, the Reverend John Annin opened a Presbyterian school in a private home with only four pupils, but a year later he had seventeen. Among later enrollees was Gabino Rendón, who started there only to learn English but became a convert and spent the remainder of his long, active life as a Presbyterian minister.

After Annin and his business manager, José Ýnez Perea, had raised funds to purchase a house from George Chávez on a hill on South Chávez Street, $1,400 came from the East for remodeling, and a boarding school was opened. Competition introduced by Jesuits in 1874 caused this school to go into a slump, which led to its closing in 1880. Three years later, more funds received from the East enabled it to reopen with seven pupils. By 1888, it had close to 150 enrollees receiving instruction by ladies who also had come from the East. The Presbyterians, however, relocated this school in Albuquerque in 1896, where it continued successfully as Menaul School.

The need for a Catholic school for boys was met by Italian Jesuit instructors brought to New Mexico by persuasion of the bishop. Those who first located in Bernalillo moved to Las Vegas in 1874 in response to the offer of Manuel Romero and Francisco López to lend them the use of houses that they owned on South Pacific Street. In the Romero house, call *La Casa Redonda*, they opened their private school for boys in September.

A class in the Jesuit College, 1881 *(Las Vegas City Museum; Mary E. Sowell)*

Immediate success led other Jesuits to join the founders to begin instruction at the collegiate level in 1877 in both the Romero and López houses. In that first year, seven faculty members gave instruction to 132 pupils in elementary and advanced classes in reading, writing, geography, arithmetic, bookkeeping, music, English, Spanish, French, Italian, and Latin.

Relief from the crowded quarters was afforded by the acquisition of a large, new adobe building erected in 1878 down on the flat land between South Gonzales Street and the river. By 1885, the college had an enrollment of 164 students, several of whom had come even from Colorado and from northern Mexico for instruction in what was then described as "the only college in the country in which studies are pursued in the dual languages." By that time, the college had twelve faculty members and a library of 1,500 volumes. It was offering evening classes in Spanish and was sponsoring an orchestra and a debating society.

In 1888, townsmen were startled by the news that the Jesuits were preparing to move their college to Denver, where, as one of them explained, the English-speaking community would better facilitate the learning of English by the boarding students coming from Mexico. Citizens held meetings in an effort to persuade the Jesuits to stay, but to no avail, except that reasons more deep-seated came to light. Because the Jesuits were so popular in Las Vegas, Catholics were supporting their college better than they were their parish church. The priest, the Reverend J. M. Coudert, raised objections. Consequently, the Jesuits concluded that Las Vegas could not well sustain both. General gloom prevailed when the townsmen honored them with a farewell dinner late in the summer of 1888. Then all but the staff of their journal, *Revista Católica,* departed for Colorado to found Regis College in Denver.

Upon the withdrawal of the Jesuits, the Christian Brothers filled that void by opening, in September 1888, their De La Salle Institute, or private school for boys. At first they held classes in St. Joseph's Hall, but within a year they had raised $12,000 for the construction of a two-story stone building on Valencia Street. In it, for a nominal fee of from $1.00 to $3.00 per month (depending upon their grade), 130 pupils, including several boarders, enrolled in grades one through twelve. The popularity of this school also required use of classrooms in the former Jesuit building. For about four decades this school, like that of the Sisters, flourished, as together they served the large Catholic clientele as well as some Protestants.

Other Protestants, who became numerous in the 1880s, founded their own schools. Congregationalists in the East offered to launch one if the townsmen would raise $3,000. That was done, and in 1880, in a brick building on Douglas Avenue that cost $12,000, the Academy began its service. By 1886, it had 121 boys and ten girls enrolled in classes instructed by seven teachers. Five years later, the number was near 500, and the advanced work included collegiate courses for preparation of teachers. Protestant patrons lauded that institution as "the largest and best equipped school in New Mexico," but in the 1890s, the burgeoning public schools caused its decline and demise.

Soon after the opening of the Academy, the Southern Methodists founded their Female Seminary in a building that cost $5,000. This "select" school, opened in 1883, stood a block west of the Methodist Church. Soon the enrollment increased to about ninety girls who were instructed, and strictly supervised, by the seven teachers in both elementary and collegiate studies. However, in the nineties, the school also became a victim of the competition with public schools.

The story of the rise of the public schools begins in the county. Fragmentary evidence indicates that in Old Town, something akin to a county public school was maintained in an adobe building beginning in 1869 and later in St. Joseph's Hall. The feeble territorial school law of that era was replaced by enactment of one not much better in 1884, but at least it did lead to the employment of a school superintendent, M. H. Murphy, by the county commissioners. In the autumn of that year, he organized forty-three districts in which schools were opened, even if, by his own admission, they comprised a "crude system" in which many of the district boards "influenced themselves to employ incompetent teachers." By 1886, thirty-eight schools, mostly rural, were giving instruction entirely in Spanish, five in English, and thirty-three in both languages.

When those school districts were organized, the county allocated district funds to the Sisters and the Jesuits, until Protestants objected in 1887. Then, and later, too, the good patronage of those schools hindered the development of public education in the town. Nevertheless, two buildings were provided in the early 1890s, with three teachers for each. Those schools grew, until in 1900, North Public had 350 pupils and South had 200. Those two county districts were merged into Number One in 1903.

By the decade of the twenties, those schools had close to 800 pupils. Sixteen teachers were employed, and for them two large stone buildings were provided as Public Works projects from 1938 to 1939. Until that time there had been no high school. Finally, District One rented the old Jesuit building in 1947 for use as a secondary school.

In New Town in the spring of 1880, twenty-seven boys and eight girls enrolled in a school maintained by public subscriptions. In 1882, it had expanded into two rented rooms. Then P. D. McElroy, employed as principal, had a former store remodeled into four rooms for three other teachers and himself. Although this was called a "public school," it hardly deserved that title, because it met in rooms provided by private donations and it charged the pupils fifty cents a month.

In 1884, the editor of the *Optic* complained about the large number of children seen on the streets, but, later, when the county superintendent swung into action, the editor remarked, "This begins to look like civilization." In the county district organized then for Precinct 29, a free public school immediately enrolled sixty-five pupils. In 1885, Mr. and Mrs. Andrieus A. Jones of Indiana came as teachers, but three years later Jones passed the bar examination and opened a law office.

By 1889, the rooms were badly overcrowded, and the principal of the dwindling Academy was offering to sell out to the district board. The phenomenal growth of this and other county schools along with that of private schools was set forth in a report in 1890 which revealed that San Miguel County, with 4,119 pupils enrolled, led all counties in the territory.

In the nineties, citizens throughout the territory sought improvements in education, partly to make a demonstration of the "Americanization" of New Mexico as a prospect for statehood. That movement was abetted by the Territorial Education Association, which was founded in Santa Fe in 1885 and held its first convention in Las Vegas during the Christmas holidays two years later. The movement was strengthened, too, by Populist endeavors on behalf of the "common man." They were influential in obtaining the enactment of an improved school law in 1891 and the chartering of two normal schools in 1893.

East Las Vegas was able to respond to the movement promptly be virtue of the great boom and the existence of a municipal government since 1888. As soon as District Number 2 became municipal, the board sought to float bonds for the construction of a building, only to find that school boards of that era did not have legal authority to do that. In 1890, therefore, the town trustees submitted in a referendum a proposal for an issue of municipal bonds amounting to $15,000 and had the original stone Douglas building ready for occupancy by March 1891. For its dedication, a large delegation came from Santa Fe, because this was an auspicious event. Douglas was the first school in the territory to be built by a bond issue approved in a public referendum. Later, the city transferred the building, and the debt for it, to the school district.

In 1897, when the enrollment was above 500, the first four grades were accommodated in Douglas School, the intermediate grades in rooms rented in the Academy building, and the high school in rooms on the second floor of the city hall. It graduated a class of nine in 1898, and then the board contracted with the newly founded Normal University for the offering of secondary work in its demonstration school for four years.

In 1900, the enrollment of 712 so badly crowded the

facilities that the municipality, which had reincorporated as a city in 1895, obtained approval for the floating of bonds amounting to $35,000 for the construction of a stone building for a high school. Since it was designed in the "baronial" style, it was called Castle School.

After 1923, when a new high school was built, elementary grades were taught in Castle School. Next, after a fire gutted Douglas School in 1927, a new one was built a year later. In 1932, the superintendent reported that four buildings accommodated 1,214 pupils, for whom thirty-seven teachers were employed at salaries ranging from $1,044 to $1,620 for the term of nine months.

Mention has been made of a normal university founded earlier. When a bill was introduced in the legislature in 1893 for the opening of one in Silver City, Félix Martínez, Populist member of the council, obtained a revision that provided for one in Las Vegas, too. Consequently Martínez was given the cognomen of "Father of the Normal School." As soon as the governor had appointed a board of regents, the members elected Edward Henry of Albuquerque as their president and Tranquilino Labadie of West Las Vegas as secretary. They also appointed two committees, one for each Las Vegas, as advisers about a site. Several were proposed, and the hassle over the choice became so serious that the legislature intervened and ordered that the institution be located on a small triangular tract on a hill centrally located.

In 1896, as work was progressing on a three-story, stone, "romanesque" building, which would be named after Frank Springer in 1919, funds provided by the state ran out, and local businessmen advanced $19,000 for it to be completed. Meanwhile, three retired regents had been replaced by M. W. Browne as secretary, Charles Ilfeld as treasurer, and Frank Springer as president. A year later, the board employed Dr. Edgar L. Hewett as president, and in the summer of 1898, he selected twelve faculty members, planned the organization of five departments, and announced that classes would be started in makeshift rooms on October 2, because the building was not quite finished.

The initial classes enrolled 103 students. In February

1899, Hewett obtained legislative approval of a change of name from Normal School to Normal University, for which the assembly hall was filled for the dedication on March 4.

As instruction progressed in the teacher training program, the adult preparatory studies, and the demonstration school, prowess in athletics was encouraged, too. The boys had a great field day in June 1900 at which they competed in tennis and in track. One of them was reported to have set a New Mexico record of seven feet, nine inches in the pole vault. Then improvements were made at the field on vacant lots in the north part of the city until it was described as "the finest athletic ground in New Mexico." The Normal Tigers, partly high school boys, defeated the University of New Mexico in a baseball game in May 1900, and in the fall a year later could boast of having an undefeated record in football. That was the year, too, when the first class of thirteen seniors was graduated in June.

Meanwhile, President Hewett had begun investigations in archeology on the Pajarito Plateau. He interested students and gave lectures about ancient Indian pueblos. After 1903,

The first graduates of the Normal University, 1901 *(Highlands University Collection)*

Springer Hall under construction *(Rex Studio)*

he converted this hobby into a profession elsewhere as the promoter of a periodical, as the founder of the Institute of American Research in Santa Fe, and as the author of books on antiquity. One of his faculty members, T.D.A. Cockerell, explored the surrounding area for a study of its plants and insects. In his three years on the faculty, he had eighty research articles published. After his departure, he served as curator of museums for three years, or until he received an appointment, without any academic degree, as Professor of Zoology at the University of Colorado. The production of 3,900 articles, reports, and reviews by him and his wife, also a former faculty member of the Normal University, won them international recognition.

It came as a stunning surprise when Hewett's resignation was announced at the commencement in late May 1903. The news made headlines and provoked discussion about the causes as well as about his achievements. Little was published about the causes, but gradually word got around that a new regent, who opposed Hewett's policies, had won over two other regents, who then began bypassing the president as they meddled internally in the administration. Once the editor of the *Optic* felt called upon to defend scientific research as a proper function of a university. Evidently, Hewett was under fire for promoting research on remote topics instead of orienting the institution directly to the culture and problems of the region.

When Frank Springer, who sympathized with Dr. Hewett, resigned as president of the regents, the governor appointed Charles A. Spiess as his replacement, and then all thirteen faculty members resigned. It took time to recover from that jolt. The enrollment slumped to a figure below 200, the institution had three short-term presidents to 1910, and no collegiate degree was attained until 1912.

Dr. Frank H. H. Roberts, who was president from 1910 to 1921, received praise for his accomplishments. In his first year, a brick dormitory for girls was built, and in 1916, a manual training building was constructed. A Spanish name—*La Casa de Ramona*—was given to the dormitory after a popular novel about Indians in California. For a building occupied mostly by Anglo girls, this represented a beginning, if feeble, of a recognition of the tri-cultural heritage of the locality. Next, the legislature appropriated $75,000 for the building of a stone auditorium, but wartime inflation made that sum inadequate. In 1919, Charles Ilfeld donated $25,000 for its completion as a memorial to his deceased wife.

Two graduates in that early era were destined to attain literary eminence. Aurora Lucero, who placed second in the state collegiate oratorical contest in 1911, won acclaim later as Mrs. White-Lea for her studies of New Mexico culture. This was crowned by the publication, in 1947 and 1953, of her *Los Hispanos* and *Literary Folklore of the Hispanic Southwest.* S. Omar Barker was lauded by a Santa Fe newspaper as the "poet laureate of New Mexico" upon the appearance of his first book of poems in 1928. Later, for his numerous poems and short stories depicting in ranch vernacular the folklore of the cattle country, and especially for two books published in 1966 and 1968, *Little World Apart* and *Rawhide Rhymes,* he attained international recognition. A later graduate, Fabiola Cabeza de Baca, taught homemaking skills in rural areas for thirty years and wrote two popular books in 1949 and 1954, *The Good Life* and *We Fed Them Cactus*.

In 1914, the university regents approved a four-year curriculum leading to a bachelor of arts degree in education. Next, regional orientation was attempted. In 1915, the university advertised an intensive course that would prepare students to teach Spanish in the public schools. The next year, a special rural teachers' training course for bilingual education was initiated, followed in 1920 by a four-year curriculum to prepare welfare workers in Spanish and domestic science. However, those three special programs appeared in the bulletin only once, with no subsequent report about enrollment. They had been introduced fifty years ahead of the demand.

University enrollment slumped, of course, during World War I, but by 1922, it had climbed to 456 in the regular session and to nearly 1,000 in the summer school. Then came another round of troubles. A complete change in the board of regents from Democratic to solid Republican control in 1921 suggested to the members that they should make political capital of their ascendancy. On May 6, 1921, the board declared the office of president vacant and employed Jonathan H. Wagner, who had indulged in clever politicking while employed as state superintendent of public instruction. Immediately Wagner began overspending the stringent budget, and, to make matters worse, a fire gutted Springer Hall on February 2, 1922. In the emergency, classes met in local churches and halls, and then a firebug, who had written anonymous letters to Wagner expressing dislike for him and a desire to burn out the institution, set more fires. The volunteer firemen saved the Oddfellows Hall but not the Baptist Church.

The legislature appropriated $15,000, the regents borrowed $40,000 to rebuild Springer Hall, and Ilfeld Auditorium was brought into use, although it was not quite finished inside. That emergency was bridged, but another one was at hand due to a shortage in operating funds. In 1923, the regents forced the resignation of Wagner on account of his "loose business methods."

To clear the institution of its indebtedness of $107,000,

the regents cut faculty salaries by 10 percent, and the legislature appropriated $25,000 in 1925 and again in 1927. In the latter year, too, an appropriation was forthcoming for the construction of a gymnasium, a heating plant, and a building for the training school, which by then had been reduced to only the elementary grades. The next buildings were WPA projects. One in 1937 combined facilities for a library and administrative offices, and another in 1940 was a girls' dormitory. Then the previous girls' dormitory, La Casa de Ramona, was converted into a boys' dormitory and renamed La Casa de Ramón. Remarkable murals were painted in the halls of the library by a Santa Fe artist, Lloyd Moylan.

Under the presidency of Dr. Frank Carroon, who succeeded Wagner, the enrollment, mostly Anglos, stabilized at about 500 in the regular year, but for the summer sessions it grew to nearly 1,300 due to a law requiring teachers to take refresher courses. A large proportion of them were Hispanos. In that era, no innovations were attempted in efforts to orient to the region, like those that had failed in the presidency of Roberts. The achievements were traditional, like the bringing in of guest professors and the founding of fraternities and honor societies.

Springer Hall after the fire of 1922 *(Highlands University Collection)*

In 1927, another change in the political complexion of the regents instilled a desire to remove Carroon, and an emergency played into their hands. The North Central Association had raised the standards for accreditation of teachers' colleges—standards that this institution had met in 1927 but was no longer able to meet because of its library facilities and faculty qualifications. Abruptly in May, the regents gave Carroon a forced "leave of absence" and replaced him with Dr. H. C. Gossard. By immediate strengthening of the weaknesses, he obtained accreditation in 1932, not by the North Central Association—accreditation that would come later—but by the American Association of Teachers' Colleges. Although Gossard was praised for his achievements, including the launching of graduate work in 1938, he had to buck against the lean years of the Great Depression and the changeable desires of the regents. They relieved him in 1939 and appointed Dr. Edward Eyring, previously head of the department of foreign languages. It was he who obtained a change of name in 1941, by legislative enactment, to New Mexico Highlands University, in order to allow for an expansion to "all kinds of educational pursuits."

In athletics, the record had been spotted in those decades. In the early twenties, the football team, still fielding several high school boys, won a few games, but in basketball the high school girls' team won the state championship in 1921, and the high school boys' team was runner up in the national tournament. Neither fared quite so well until in 1929, after the high school had been closed, when the basketball team defeated the University of New Mexico in two games out of three. In the next year, the football and basketball teams each won all games but one. That was the year when the name was changed from the Tigers to the Cowboys, harmonizing with the local popularity of the Cowboys' Reunion. In 1932, "Stu" Clark began his long and successful career as coach of athletics. His winning record won the enthusiastic support of fans, although they were saddened once in 1937 when Ivan Perkins died of injuries incurred in football practice. His sacrifice was memorialized in the name given to the new stadium built in 1939 as a project of the National Youth Administration.

Meanwhile, another college had come and gone. In 1920, the Commercial Club negotiated a transfer of the former Montezuma Hotel to the Baptist Convention of New Mexico. In it, the Baptists opened a college in 1922 under the presidency of the Reverend Layton Maddox, who selected twelve faculty members for the instruction offered in a grade school and high school and, initially, in the first year of collegiate studies. On the first day, 106 students enrolled, and by 1925, the number had increased to 255, taught by twenty-nine faculty members. Dr. J. M. Cook succeeded Maddox as president in 1924, and two years later, C. W. Stumph became acting president. The college graduated classes of twenty-two in 1926, but only twelve in 1927 and 1928.

As the rural depression grew worse, enrollment declined until in 1930 the Baptists had to close this college. However, it did live on in the nostalgic memories of its alumni, who later contributed their recollections about faculty members, religious life, musical programs, wholesome fun, and competition in sports for publication in a book edited by Tom Wiley.

Although beyond the century covered in this review, a note should be inserted about another utilization of the former Montezuma Hotel. The United States Catholic Conference of Bishops purchased the property in 1937 and made it available to the Society of Jesus for a seminary to educate Mexican youth for the priesthood in their homeland. In 1972, no longer needed for that purpose, the buildings were closed again.

While formal education was being offered by a procession of institutions during the first century of Las Vegas, their achievements became supplemented by agencies combining informal education with other functions. One was the public library, which was established for educational and recreational purposes. As early as 1879, the opening of a reading room was advocated by the *Optic*, and a group of men under the chairmanship of F. O. Kihlberg did arrange in 1885 for the setting aside of a room briefly for that purpose in the Academy building.

In 1887, the Woman's Christian Temperance Union undertook the opening of a reading room so that "young men will come in and out of reach of temptation." Soon they had 250 books in a room in a hotel, which was kept open part-time by volunteer librarians. During the Panic of 1893, when donations dwindled, Mrs. L. N. Higgins of the WCTU reported to the town trustees in East Las Vegas that the ladies would have to close their reading room. She offered to turn the books over to the town if the governing body would provide a room and a part-time librarian. The trustees did make available a room on the first floor of the new town hall, but not a librarian. After it was opened on October 13, 1893, the expense of operation was borne by subscriptions pledged by members of a Reading Room Association. Nevertheless, it was sufficiently "public" that its early founding made of it one of the first such libraries in the territory.

Reports about gifts of Andrew Carnegie to several cities for building library facilities suggested that Las Vegas should apply, which the city council did in 1902. After receipt of Carnegie's donation of $10,000, the council had to fend off efforts of Margarito Romero and others to prevent the building from being located in Hillsite Park. That done, the council had a brick building erected there, and in August 1904, it was turned over to a municipal library board of seven persons headed by E. V. Long, former chief justice. Because the city then appropriated only $250 annually, the bulk of the cost of operation was provided by the membership fees of the Library Association and the benefit events sponsored by it. Nevertheless, the community then had acquired facilities to which citizens could point with pride, and two decades later, those interested could obtain information and recreation by reading some of the 10,000 books available in that Carnegie Public Library.

Among the books in the library were some written by local authors. Eminent among them were the volumes on the history of New Mexico by Ralph Emerson Twitchell and his wife, Estelle Burton Twitchell, written while they still resided in Las Vegas prior to 1913. In addition, available locally were materials produced by local enterprise. They included the religious works and the state reports printed on the presses of *Revista Católica* and *La Voz del Pueblo,* respectively, through many years.

Another educational project was undertaken by the Las Vegas Historical Society, founded in 1932 under the presidency of Louis C. Ilfeld. Some of the members, along with university students, became greatly interested in the artifacts excavated in the Tecolote ruins, and then, largely under the direction of James I. McCullough, a history professor, the society opened a museum on the Plaza in a building remodeled for that purpose by John D. W. Veeder. However, because it had no institutional sponsorship assuring it funds for maintenance, the volunteer attendants were able to continue its operation only to 1940.

Ralph Emerson Twitchell (*Highlands University Collection*)

In the meantime, the radio, although largely recreational and commercial, also had become an agency for informal education. When the first set was installed in the home of A. T. Rogers in December 1922, his family and friends heard a program broadcast from Kansas City "clearly and distinctly." A year later, shoppers were invited to stop in and hear the reception on sets installed in three business houses, and stores were offering parts for sale for the assembling of sets. Beginning in 1924, the *Optic* carried a column announcing the scheduled programs of distant stations offering an opportunity to hear concerts, dance music, comical dialogues, and educational talks. Broadcasting by a local station, KFUN, began in 1941.

The radio was preceded by a series of newspapers, which published materials in part recreational, political, and commercial, but also informational and therefore informally educational. From 1869 to 1935, no less than thirty newspapers emanated from Las Vegas. Many were short-lived, and only a few continued beyond the centennial.

The first newspaper to last more than a decade was the *Las Vegas Daily Gazette*, which Louis Hommel began issuing in 1872. It was bought two years later by J. H. Koogler, a capable and enterprising editor, and it folded up two years after Koogler sold it to another publisher in 1884. Koogler obtained advertisements from the leading local business houses and built up a circulation among subscribers throughout the territory. He made the paper lively with local news, some of it published in Spanish, and he employed catchy alliterations in his headlines.

Another publication, more in the nature of a house journal and one which had long endurance, was *Revista Católica*, which the Italian Jesuits began printing at their boys' school in 1875. While devoted to the propagation of the Catholic faith, it also presented news in pursuit of the editors' objectives to emphasize "the principles of private and public honesty pertaining to controversies about important issues." Because the subscribers were mostly New Mexicans, the articles all were in the Spanish language. In 1918, the Jesuits moved the publication office to El Paso, where they continued issuing the journal until 1951.

A local Spanish-language newspaper also survived from the time of its inception to 1925. Launched in Santa Fe in 1889, *La Voz del Pueblo* was moved to Las Vegas in 1890, where Félix Martínez became its influential publisher. After Martínez died in 1916, the former secretary, Antonio Lucero, became president of the publishing company. Always its output could be counted upon to be intensely political, usually Democratic, but Populist in the early 1890s. Moreover, the editors claimed that the paper had the largest circulation of any weekly in the territory and that it, therefore, was the "most effective medium for reaching the Hispano-American population." It appealed to its clientele by virtue of an incessant campaign in behalf of bilingual education and recognition of Spanish-American contributions and leadership.

Local news was scarce in *La Voz* except as it pertained to politics and personalities. The columns were filled with lengthy reports of county, state, and national conventions, elections, and legislation. Much time must have been devoted to the painstaking translation of all of those news dispatches from English to Spanish. The editors gave indication, too, that they relished the flow and rhythm of their language. Time and again they wrote a column of masterful prose in exposition of a topic that another would have presented tersely in a paragraph of English. In the late nineties, in dull times between political events, they composed poems for publication week after week. Soon readers also contributed poems about anniversaries, abstractions, and politics, and in the late 'teens, the paper reprinted poems extracted from the writings of great poets in Latin America and Spain. Thus, this paper, among other functions, made a significant contribution to informal education.

The newspaper that outlived all others was the *Las Vegas Daily Optic,* which observed its centennial in 1979. When the railroad reached Las Vegas, it brought along Russell A. Kistler, who had first set up a press at Otero, an earlier end of the track, but he soon decided that Las Vegas offered greater opportunity. On July 30, 1879, he began publishing the *Las*

The pressmen of *La Voz del Pueblo*, about 1915 *(Our Lady of Sorrows Collection)*

The *Optic* press and printers in 1914 *(Sandra Trujillo)*

Vegas Weekly Optic, and on November 4, he brought out the first issue of the daily paper, which initially was carried to subscribers in both towns by only one boy. Kistler complained about the poor patronage in advertisements by merchants on the "rich Plaza," but he did soon carry forty advertisements placed in his paper by others, and he supplemented local circulation by employing sales agents in other towns.

Kistler was sarcastically critical of competitors, principally his chief rival, the *Gazette,* but he could also rise to the defense of one if the cause were common. When a Democratic president, Grover Cleveland, appointed Elisha V. Long as chief justice, and Long became a resident of Las Vegas in 1886, local Republicans did not receive him cordially at first. After Louis Hommel, then editor of the *Chronicle,* had written that there would be "no justice" in the district court, Judge Long had him cited for contempt of court. It is a wonder that he did not cite Kistler, too, for writing that "the honest but poor man has to retire from court without receiving justice."

Upon Hommel's appearance in court, Judge Long insisted that the defendant was guilty but said that he was satisfied on that occasion only to refute the allegations fully in public. Kistler was won over. He wrote that the judge's brief comments about fairness in journalism were "the noblest and wisest words ever uttered by a judge from the bench."

Certainly one of the factors contributing to the success of the *Optic* must have been its coverage. It hardly seems possible, but the editor and his assistant must have attended nearly every meeting and event in the community, because they wrote firsthand reports about them. In addition, the *Optic* even surpassed the *Gazette* in its resort to alliteration in the headlines.

In the news items, the editor often injected personal reflections, either complimentary or critical. For example, he objected to the tight lacing of women's clothing, because "men dread the thought of marrying a woman who is subject to fits of irritable temper, to bad headaches, and other ailments" caused by "the compression of the waist." Regularly, too, he wrote witty observations, like the time when he reported that the school board was looking for a "western female teacher, blonde preferred," who could "ratify the multiplication table" and be able to say the "Lord's prayer in Spanish with one hand tied behind her."

Once when three young men from the East, who were wandering about town, happened to blunder into a meeting in a church, they later robbed a man of $85.00 and said in court that they were so moved by the needs of the church people that they wanted the money to put in the collection plate. According to Kistler, "In court the impudent, unwashed, unkempt, unterrified in a masterly manner detailed all the circumstances," and they were "emphatic in their statement that the preacher was guilty of a pulminating enlargement of the elongated variety"; but the judge, "touched by the magnetism, wiped his nose" and gave them "a ticket on the Romero boarding house."

Kistler formed a publishing company in 1897 in which, odd as it may seem, two shareholders were land barons— Wilson Waddingham and Thomas B. Catron. After ownership passed to Colonel M. N. Padgett in 1907, observers of that era felt that the paper suffered a decline: but its quality improved under the ownership of Hub Kane, publisher from 1921 to 1947.

As the community approached its centennial in 1935, the impression conveyed by scanning the columns of the *Optic* was that the place had become rather dull—a circumstance that could be attributed in part to the disheartening effects of the Great Depression. The major reason, however, was the evolution from the old type of journalism to the new.

By 1930, the constant editorial plugging for everything that seemed to matter had given way, with a few exceptions, to "canned" editorials which came in the mail or over the wire. In local news, gone were the witty remarks and personal jibes. Instead, the paper carried a half column of concise personal items picked up by a reporter while making his daily rounds. Moreover, as a substitute for the entertainment once injected by the editor, presumably the subscriber would enjoy reading the syndicated columns on current topics.

In the news coverage, local sports and political events still received considerable attention, since both were spectacular; yet the national political campaigns and the World Series received greater coverage than did the meetings of the city council and the baseball games of the local Maroons. Almost constantly headlined reports about state, national, and international events filled the first two pages, while brief local stories were relegated to the back page. This was the trend of that era in journalism, which reflected a local trend even more profound. No longer was Las Vegas a remote but pulsating center of a great frontier region, in which local events in business, government, and society had great significance. Instead, the railroad, the automobile, the airplane, the mail, the telephone, and the radio had integrated this community into the state and nation, in which it was only one small functional unit. Therefore, what people did in Las Vegas to influence the destiny of their community had to be abetted by favorable conditions in such things as state and national legislation, the stock market, and international relations.

By the end of its first century, Las Vegas had acquired agencies for informal education and related functions comparable to those of other cities—a pattern that would persist through decades to come with one major innovation, the emergence of television. Whatever their purpose in the eyes of the participants—religion, enlightenment, jobs, recreation, or status symbol—the public schools and university also had become stabilized into a pattern that would endure far into the future. As these institutions for formal education expanded, their reputation and their influence in their region regained in part the eminence that Las Vegas had once enjoyed in its commercial heyday.

Aerial view of East Las Vegas in 1923 (*Leslie Bottorf*)

VI | Diverse Peoples Form Many Societies

A distinguishing characteristic of early Hispanic society was the closeness of members of the traditionally large, extended family group, which included all relatives. Those families were the agencies for pleasant fellowship, social controls, and mutual aid.

People gave the entitlement of *don* to the recognized patriarch of the family, since the term expresses their respect for an important person. When used properly, the title was combined with only the Christian name, although some deviated from that practice. For many of them, great wealth was not a criterion for their distinction. The title *doña*, of course, was the female counterpart.

Among the *dons* were several who inherited, or acquired, considerable wealth, and in those instances, the title was not always patriarchal. The sons of a wealthy *don* also were *dons*, because they, too, were important persons who had, if not a large family, others who were responsible to them. Reports handed down, mostly by Hispanos themselves, portrayed some of those *dons* as reasonable, charitable benefactors, but about others the reports were not very complimentary.

Especially in neighboring villages, the wealthy *dons* were said to have enhanced their position by retaining laborers as *peones* by means of debt servitude. One old-timer lamented later that "all but the rich were *peones*," and he gave an example of a muleteer who owed his master sixty *pesos* and was paying off the debt by working for him at two *pesos* a month. Because the *don* charged high prices for essential products, the *peon* continued in debt for life.

There was also the *partido* system by which, according to one observer, *los ricos* obtained sheep from the poor *rancher-*

os at a cost to themselves of about 50¢ a head and sold them at a profit of up to 200 percent. The typical *partido* contract provided that the *pastor* who took sheep on shares would turn in one-half of the annual increase and return the original number of sheep to the *patrón* at the end of a five-year period. Strict compliance with a provision that the *pastor* must make up any losses often ruined many of the poor sheepherders. An elderly pioneer, interviewed in 1937, told about a man in Las Vegas whose name began with "R" and who required him to give a lien on his cattle for the sheep that he took on a share basis. During a severe drought, he lost the sheep and his cattle, too. He was proud to add, "I paid him, though, every cent of debt I paid him."

Along with the recognition that a generalization is inapplicable to the *dons* must be added another—and that is that not all other Hispanic men in Las Vegas were *peones*. Even in early times there was a small emerging class of employees in business establishments and of business proprietors, along with others who rendered skilled services. Although not wealthy, those among them who managed to remain free of burdensome debts were at least fairly independent.

Many wealthy *dons* acquired Indian slaves to do the menial work of the household. Because by Spanish custom Indians taken captive in military campaigns became the property of the captors, a special effort was made to capture women and children. This practice brought several Apaches into Las Vegas for sale to the *dons*. (There are tales, too, about the harrowing experiences of local girls who were captured by Apaches.) Also, since the tractable Navajo girls were much in demand, *dons* bought many of them in the slave market in Taos for $100 to $300 each. A review of the birth and marriage records of Our Lady of Sorrows Parish in the 1860s yielded the names of forty-six women who were designated as "Navajo."

After 1863, when the freeing of Negro slaves in the South became one of the objectives of the Civil War, soldiers at Fort Union received an order to search for Navajo Indian slaves and remove them to Bosque Redondo. The soldiers reported that Indian servitude was almost universal; consequently, they were lax in enforcing the order. Besides, when some did make a search, usually the owners succeeded in hiding their Indian servants. In defense of the practice, spokesmen contended that Indians who had been adopted into their families wanted to stay with them and, if released, would become homeless orphans. Later, in 1868, reports about Indian servitude and peonage in New Mexico led to the adoption of a congressional resolution ordering the military to liberate all persons from peonage; but enforcement again was lax. For example, when 200 persons from several localities were summoned to Santa Fe in 1868 for holding "Navajo captives and others in bondage," a grand jury failed to indict even one of them. Nevertheless, the ban did halt the acquisition of Indian servants, and many of those already acquired married into Spanish-American families.

The eminent *dons* were able to enjoy great influence and luxurious homes. Among them in early times were five

The Baca Mansion in later years *(Museum of New Mexico; Ina S. Cassidy)*

The mansion of Trinidad Romero *(Rex Studio)*

Bacas who were relatives of Luis María C. de Baca. All were wealthy and built fine homes. One, Don José Albino Baca, rapidly increased his *partidos* until he was said to have control of thousands of sheep as well as ownership of hundreds of cattle and oxen and extensive landholdings. He built a three-story mansion in Upper Town between 1850 and 1855. In such palatial homes, the wealthy *dons* entertained their friends with music and dancing, and visitors were impressed by their gracious hospitality and cultural attainments.

As the Santa Fe trade, and then the railroad, increasingly made Las Vegas a commercial center, "new *dons*" emerged. They mastered the English language and copied successfully the Anglo techniques for gaining wealth in mercantile enterprise and in exploiting mineral, land, timber, and human resources. All became anglicized to some extent, and especially this was true of Miguel A. Otero, Jr., who married a lady from Minnesota in an Episcopal ceremony and whose associates were the wealthy sons of merchant and bankers on the east side. Those new *dons,* who adapted quickly to the American system of government, became masters in political organization, too, based in part upon the *patrón* system by which they delivered the votes of many men among whom they were influential.

When an article by Margarito Romero was published in 1912 by *Revista Católica,* it presented a list of thirty-five local *dons* whom he had known and whose property valuation he estimated for each at from $5,000 to $100,000. The list included several whose names weave in and out of these pages, some in the ranching category and others representing the later type of "new *dons.*" Among them were a few men, at least, who engaged in charitable benefactions. Unlike some of the selfishly wealthy *dons,* the Romero brothers were so generous with their money that people were inclined to overlook the means by which they originally had become affluent. Don Eugenio made large contributions for the support of a company of volunteer firemen and a brass band, Don Margarito sponsored Christmas parties for needy children, sometimes attended by 800 of them, and Don Benigno cared for insane persons in his home while standing the expense of his prolonged, successful campaign to attain the building of the Insane Asylum. In addition to those conspicuous contributions, they were said to have engaged quietly in personal aid to distressed families. All of this did more than enable two of them to emerge as political *patrones*; it won for them the everlasting gratitude of many, many families on the west side. Don Margarito also earned the adoration of nearly all fellow townsmen by supporting financially one expensive litigation after another in behalf of causes favoring them in their contention with the growing influence of the city on the east side, as has been described in a previous chapter. When he died in 1917, his funeral was reported to have been attended by the largest crowd ever assembled in Las Vegas for that kind of a tribute to an eminent citizen.

For the great majority of the residents, their social life was oriented to the Church. Within a year after the founding of the town, the pioneers had constructed an adobe church building on the west side of the Plaza. Although one visitor observed that it had a "damp, earthen floor" and was "void of seats," another remarked that it was "decidedly the most civilized object in town." It was originally a mission to which priests rode on horseback from San Miguel del Bado.

Because communicants of the parish, which was delineated in 1852, outgrew that building, they laid a foundation a decade later for the construction of a large one of stone a block west of the old one. Although still unfinished by 1869, it was roofed temporarily with canvas so that it could be brought into use. Due to its imposing appearance, some citizens erroneously called it a "cathedral"; but when a priest in the Jesuit College accompanied the boys there for the first communion in 1880, he had another name for it, "a magnificent refrigerator." The date of the finishing of the interior is indefinite, probably in 1885, when a large, remarkable, water-powered Kilgen pipe organ was installed. For many years this Church of Our Lady of Sorrows was served by priests who came from France upon invitation by the bishop, John B. Lamy. It was one of them, Father J. M. Coudert, who supervised completion of the church edifice.

To that church, the "Hermit"—Giovanni María Augustini—was invited a few times to celebrate mass when he was in town, even though he was not strictly a conformist in all of his interpretations of Catholicism. Augustini had left Italy because of difficulties when he was a young man and, in observance of a vow to serve others while seeking solitude for himself, had traveled across France and Spain and throughout the other Americas. At the age of sixty-two, he joined a caravan of wagons for a journey southwest on the Santa Fe Trail, but he refused the invitation of the wagon master, Miguel Romero, to ride in a wagon and instead walked all the way to Las Vegas.

He arrived in 1863. Because the Hermit's first place of abode in a cave near Romeroville did not allow the solitude

The Hermit before he came to Las Vegas *(Highlands University Collection)*

that he sought, he moved to a cave that he found just below the eastern summit of *El Cerro Tecolote*, or Owl Peak, subsequently known as Hermit's Peak. Soon men from Las Vegas built for him a small cabin over a spring, where he subsisted mainly on mush while carving small religious emblems that he exchanged in town for cornmeal. Each night he built a fire which could be seen by Samuel B. Watrous in distant La Junta. The agreement was that if ever no light appeared, then he was in trouble; but no need ever arose.

On his trips into town, the Hermit walked about with a small bell on his staff so that people could hear him coming, and in the homes of hosts at night, he insisted upon sleeping on the floor. Presently, when restlessness overtook him again, in 1867 he departed for Mesilla, where he sought refuge in the Organ Mountains. There he was found dead, with a dagger in his back, on April 17, 1869. Much later, his devotees in Las Vegas formed the Society of the Hermit, and around the turn of the century, Margarito Romero began promoting annual pilgrimages of the members first to his resort hotel, El Porvenir, and thence worshipfully up the trail to the site of the cabin on Hermit's Peak.

Since Catholics in New Town were partial to the Jesuits, one of the latter began conducting services for them and raised funds in 1885 to build a stone chapel, named the Church of the Immaculate Conception, on Grand Avenue. After most of the Jesuits had moved away, in 1890 the archbishop delineated a large parish east of the Gallinas River and assigned to it Father Manuel Rivera. Others followed, and later, in 1950, the present spacious church building became ready for occupancy by virtue of the endeavors of Monsignor Adrian Rabeyrolle.

Out in the villages, many of the devout Catholic men belonged to *Los Hermanos Penitentes* and worshipped in their *moradas*, or small chapels. Their practices have been so fully described in other works that there is no need here for repetition. Suffice it to say that evidence is abounding about how their prevalence contributed a spirit of togetherness as well as helpfulness in times of need. The members even served as courts for minor offenses in remote localities.

Earliest known view of the first church *(H. T. Wilson)*

One incident in Las Vegas was outstanding. When the archbishop of Santa Fe sought a reconciliation between the *Penitentes* and the Church, Lorenzo López and four others responded affirmatively. They promoted the celebration of the proposed reunion by a great parade and ceremony on November 1, 1891. An estimated 4,000 people participated, of whom 1,500 were said to be *Penitentes*. López then was emerging as an eminent leader in the Peoples' Party. The circumstances suggest that he and others were seeking to weld a union of local *Penitentes* and Populists. The archbishop responded by denouncing certain individuals in San Miguel county who were seeking to win support of the *Penitentes* for their personal political advantage.

The early residents observed the milestones of life with religious ceremonies accompanied by appropriate festivities. A midwife attended the birth of a baby, who was christened in the church forty days later. Children had parties on the anniversary of their patron saint. A proposal and marriage was a protracted procedure involving the families of both parties. A death, of course, was an occasion for solemnity, but it also brought together all relatives and neighbors for the Rosary services and the Requiem Mass. Those who could afford it employed paid mourners so that weeping at the all-night vigil would express appropriately their high regard for the deceased person.

There were *fiestas* on holy days and whenever a significant event occurred. The parishioners celebrated *La Función* from August 14 to 16 by having vespers at the church, a candlelight parade, and a *baile*. They also observed *El Día Santiago* on July 25 by permitting *las señoritas* to ride around the Plaza as a signal that they were eligible for marriage, followed the next day, or *El Día Santana*, by a similar exhibition by *los caballeros*. On both days, the men participated in *la corrida del gallo*, or "rooster pull," in which they divided into teams and took turns at stooping from their galloping horses and grabbing up by the head one partially buried rooster after another. They would then ride to the baseline with the rooster while pursued by, and trying to fight off, the opposing team.

There were many *fandangos*, or common joyous dances, which usually were announced by having the musicians parade in the street and sing lively songs to the accompaniment of their guitars and violins. A visitor in 1856 observed that "they dance with beauty and ease. . . . Some of the musicians play with considerable skill."

The men obtained diversion by engaging in sports— fishing, hunting, promoting cockfights, engaging in horse races, and staging bullfights in an arena located west of their new church building. In addition, as early as 1868, they were spectators at an exhibition baseball game in which the team from Santa Fe defeated the soldiers from Fort Union by a score of seventy-four to thirty-six.

The arrival of visitors was an occasion for excitement. One pioneer related years later how excited she was, as a girl, when Governor Manual Armijo came to call on her father. In order to see that dignitary, she took a tobacco pouch from the workshop of the Indian servants into the parlor to hand it to her mother, who had forgotten to take hers with her. Then, when the first Anglo lady, Susan Shelby Magoffin,, arrived for dinner at a local inn, she wrote that "not only the children but *mujeres y hombres* swarmed around me like bees."

Hospitality and courtesy were virtues of the Spanish culture. Children were taught to remove their hats and to stand when speaking to their elders and not to drink or eat until after all guests had been served. By tradition, all homes were open to guests, and expressions of personal regard preceded the conducting of any business.

Mention has previously been made of the employment of women as midwives. In a community that had no physicians until the 1850s, women also became skilled in treating illnesses with home remedies. Many of the herbs which they used were found later to contain ingredients that really made them effective medicines.

All too concisely, the foregoing presents a glimpse of a society into which the vision of visitors seldom penetrated deep enough for a full view of its many facets. Instead, visitors saw mainly the physical scene, which was not very impressive. In 1846, an approaching army officer thought that he saw ahead a large brickyard, and another a clump of bushes and rocks. With better insight, Dr. George I. Sánchez much later described how the villages in New Mexico had a functional arrangement that blended into their setting, close to nature.

In addition to so-called "Anglos," two other small groups lent variety to the local population. Several Chinese men obtained employment on the railroad and later took jobs in laundries. One was mentioned as the proprietor of a small notions store. They aroused interest because they wore robes and wooden shoes and braided their long hair. Their customs set them apart, too, because they celebrated their New Year's Day in February, a reporter said, with "the sound of the tom-tom, the boom of the boomerang, and the he-yi of the being Celestial. . . ." Presently those people disappeared from the local scene.

In those days, numerous Negroes came, too, for employment mainly on the railroad and in the hotels, although notice was taken of one who was a barber. They had their own dances and maintained their own African Methodist Episcopal Church. A few who were employed at the hot springs organized their Montezuma Social Club and had dances in the old Stone Hotel. In town, although not fully accepted socially, they were not segregated in one residential district nor in the public schools.

Among the black men, one—Montgomery Bell— attained wealth and respect. After being liberated from slavery in Missouri, Bell made his way to Santa Fe, where he saved up enough of his earnings to become a small rancher in the Pecos valley. Next, with money borrowed from Stephen B. Elkins at 18 percent interest, he opened a store in Las Vegas and became such a successful dealer in real estate and livestock that he acquired a reputation as the "wealthiest Negro in the Southwest." News about him in 1903 was that he owned a cafe on Grand Avenue, and with his family he resided in a ten-room mansion located a short distance north of the Plaza.

After Anglos came in numbers, they stirred up a whirlwind of organizational activities for the founding of churches, lodges, and other societies. The first Protestant missionary to arrive was the Reverend John A. Annin, who opened the Presbyterian school in 1869. A year later, he organized a congregation of eight members. Soon more joined, including several from Mora, for whom he found a separate congregation in 1879. He maintained that Catholic converts had to be re-baptized, because "Romish baptism was invalid." The congregation was strict, too, about attendance. Dismissal was the fate of any member who had protracted absences, and one member was dismissed in 1873 for stealing and another in 1876 for intoxication.

With the good assistance of a merchant and rancher, José Ynez Perea, who in his wide travels had become a convert,

The former residence of Montgomery Bell *(Museum of New Mexico; J. W. Buchanan)*

the congregation in 1872 built a long adobe building on South Chávez Street for this first Protestant church to be organized in Las Vegas. By 1880, after fellow townsmen had boycotted Perea's business, he and Annin both departed for services as Presbyterian ministers elsewhere.

When the Reverend John Eastman arrived in 1880, he could find only five members of the Presbyterian mission. Then he enrolled additional members to found a new congregation on the east side, which raised funds for constructing a building on Douglas Avenue in 1881. It is still in use.

The next congregation to be organized was the Episcopalian. A missionary, the Reverend Henry Forrester, came from Santa Fe to Old Town and formed a nucleus of a congregation in May 1879. As membership grew to twenty-three, the congregation became centered in New Town. With mission funds and local contributions, this group had a small adobe building constructed on Blanchard Street, now National Avenue, ready for consecration to St. Paul on November 16, 1879. This was the first Episcopal building in New Mexico and the first of any kind in East Las Vegas.

When an Epsicopalian bishop, the Right Reverend George Kelly Dunlop, made Las Vegas the seat of his diocese in 1880, he undertook the building of a sandstone cathedral in the Gothic style, for which the cornerstone was laid on May 11, 1886. But Dunlop died in 1888. The next bishop revived work on the building, which was finally consecrated on April 27, 1890; but it did not become his cathedral. He assigned to it as rector the Reverend W. J. Roberts. Both of those buildings are still in use.

The founding of a Methodist congregation occurred soon after that of the Episcopalians. Since 1869, a missionary, the Reverend Thomas Harwood, had been working out of La Junta, known also as Tiptonville, where Mrs. Harwood had opened a school. As he traveled by horseback all over northern New Mexico, once he lamented, "What can I do, a lone missionary in this vast field, unacquainted with the language and customs of the people, . . .

After the railroad reached Las Vegas, the arrival of a few Methodists offered Harwood an opportunity. On August 31, 1879, he organized a congregation of fifteen members. Soon afterward, with mission money and local funds, the first minister, the Reverend D. W. Calfee, and a new bishop, the Reverend S. M. Merrill, bought four lots on "Zion Hill," across from the Episcopal building then under construction. As the bishop recalled years later, when he offered to pay his bill at a local hotel, the landlord said that because

> . . . we have some pretty bad men in this town, gamblers, drunkards, thieves, and horse thieves, . . . with the hope that this young preacher will shake all these fellows over the flames of Hell, . . . I am not going to charge you anything.

On February 15, 1880, the Methodists attended the dedication services for their small frame building, which was replaced by a large brick edifice constructed by M. M. Sundt in 1923.

A Southern Methodist congregation of nineteen members also was organized in Las Vegas in December 1881, under the direction of the Reverend W. W. Welsh, presiding elder. It, too, acquired an appropriate brick building in 1923, but in 1939, the Southern Methodists merged with the other congregation.

Homer Newberry, a local teacher and layman, had begun preaching to the Baptists in 1879, until the Reverend M. H. Murphy arrived and organized a congregation—the first in New Mexico—on January 31, 1880. Under the direction of his successor, the Reverend Samuel Gorman, funds were raised for a "handsome frame structure" on Sixth Street, which was ready for dedication in August 1885. After it was burned down during a spell of turmoil at the university, it was replaced in 1923 by a large brick building on Seventh Street.

In 1884, the Jewish community organized their "Montefiore Congregation" of twenty-three members and engaged the services of the Reverend Joseph Glueck as rabbi. When they began work on a stucco building on Douglas Avenue, an observer remarked that he was disappointed that a "denomination so rich" was not putting up a monumental stone edifice. On September 26, 1886, the congregation dedicated that temple, which much later was moved to North Eighth Street in order to make way for a new post office built from 1927 to 1928 on Douglas Avenue. Both that Hebrew congregation and its synagogue were the first in the territory.

Within the first century of Las Vegas, the early churches were joined by others. In 1887, the African Methodists organized and erected a small chapel a year later. A congregation of the Disciples of Christ effected formal organization in 1906 and in 1912 dedicated a stucco church building, which was replaced by the present brick church in 1946. The Lutherans got a firm start in 1911, and eleven years later also built a meeting place, which gave way to a new building in

1967. The addition of a great variety of congregations created a total of twenty-three of them by 1980.

Speaking of the era immediately following the turn of the century, a veteran business proprietor, Milton Taichert, said years later that "we had a wonderful community here in the early days. Everybody helped each other no matter what churches they belonged to."

Much of the spirit of helpfulness can be attributed not only to the churches, but also to the lodges, which multiplied rapidly. The first were the Masons, who founded a lodge at Fort Union in 1862 and moved it to Las Vegas five years later. This Chapman Lodge became Number Two in the Grand Lodge of New Mexico, organized in 1875.

In 1869, the Masons occupied a small temple on West National Street, whence they moved to the new, stone Ward Building on Railroad Avenue in 1882. As organizations of Royal Arch Masons, Knights Templars, and Eastern Star were added, the need arose for a new building; so, a monumental stone structure arose on Douglas Avenue in 1894, when it was dedicated in elaborate ceremonies that attracted numerous visitors from other cities. On that occasion, the ladies sponsored a great three-day fund-raising bazaar. When biographical sketches of the members were published in a brochure in 1903, it became a "Who's Who" of the eminent local business and professional men of that era.

Other lodges that enrolled large memberships in those years were the Independent Order of Oddfellows, founded in 1879, and the Knights of Pythias, organized a year later. Both had auxiliaries for ladies, and both engaged in impressive public activities.

The Catholics, too, had fraternal orders. An early one, the Society of St. Joseph, erected a two-story stone building near the Plaza in 1886. Another, the Catholic Knights of America, founded in 1884, was superseded by the Knights of Columbus, whose charter members were initiated at a banquet on January 17, 1904. Those organizations were supplemented by one not strictly religious. It was *La Sociedad Literaria y de Ayuda Mutua,* which sponsored social functions, made charitable contributions, and acquired a library of books in Spanish for circulation among members.

An influential organization in that era was the Sherman Post of the Grand Army of the Republic, comprised of Union veterans of the Civil War. Founded in 1883, it added a ladies' auxiliary three years later. Together they sponsored the ceremonies on Memorial Day as well as frequent, well-attended social functions.

Several women of the community, desiring to be something more than "auxiliaries," organized a local chapter of the Woman's Christian Temperance Union in 1885. Within a year, the membership grew to 116 ladies, who campaigned against the evils of alcoholism. To that end, among other projects, they had a stone lion, fitted with drinking fountains, erected in Fountain Park on Grand Avenue in 1896, in expectation that an alternate thirst-quencher would reduce saloon patronage. They also sponsored the aforementioned reading room.

In 1887, several women founded a chapter of another society, called Sorosis. The members of this first chapter in the territory convened regularly to present original essays and poems and to distribute their reading assignments.

The first organization having the concept of the subsequently popular service clubs was the Women's Federation, founded in 1903. The members promoted the acquisition of a public library and the making of improvements in the parks. Their "cleanup" campaign that they sponsored in 1903 resulted in the hauling of many loads of rubbish to the dumping place in Pecos Arroyo.

Other lodges offering financial benefits to members found a following. In this category, the Benevolent, Protective Order of Elks, organized locally in 1898 as the first such lodge in the territory, emerged in a position of eminence. They held banquets attended by hundreds, sponsored the building of a new fairgrounds, and engaged in charitable and patriotic activities. In 1912, they acquired a spacious brick clubhouse, built on Douglas Avenue at a cost of $25,000.

Other organizations offering economic benefits were the Ancient Order of United Workmen, three brotherhoods of railway employees, the Fraternal Union, the Red Men, and the Eagles, all founded between 1890 and 1906.

Meanwhile, organizations related to health services also had arisen. Quite early the community acquired a good supply of physicians, several of whom had moved to Las Vegas from the hospital at Fort Union. Eight of them organized the Las Vegas Medical Society in 1881, which became the nucleus around which the New Mexico Medical Society was formed a year later.

Soon afterward, when the plight of several local destitute families came to the attention of the Ladies' Aid Society of the Methodist Church, Mrs. A. D. Higgins sent out a call for help, to which the ladies of four other Protestant churches responded. Together in 1884, they organized the Ladies' Relief Society, which first raised funds for aid to ill persons in indigent families. Later, in 1888, they opened a small hospital in a rented house on Fifth Street, where members took turns as volunteer nurses.

By virtue of fund-raising events, supplemented by a legislative appropriation, the ladies were able to buy and equip a larger house on Mora Avenue in 1890. There eight physicians donated asistance in caring for the needy—and to supplement other funds, chickens and cows were kept in the corral. Ten years later, three rooms were added. At that time, the society was made up of two ladies representing each of seven local churches and five others elected at large. In 1909, that hospital cared for 112 charity patients and 231 paying patrons. Two years later, the Relief Society formally incorporated the Las Vegas Hospital, with ten physicians on the staff. It had then become well established, although it was still hard pressed to keep apace of increasing needs.

Another organization devoted essentially to health improvement came into being in 1900 when a group of men organized a Young Men's Christian Association under the presidency of A. T. Rogers, attorney. In pursuit of its goal to have an athletic center for youth, the international secretary came to Las Vegas in 1903 and launched a financial campaign—the first such high-pressure drive by a professional that the community had experienced. It succeeded. By 1905, work had begun on a building. M. M. Sundt, a local contractor who did most of the building in that era, was to be paid $15,000 for his services. At an open house on March 11, 1906, the visitors viewed the small gymnasium, the swimming pool, the reading room, and the sixteen guest rooms upstairs. It and the program would be sustained by the annual fees of the adult members, whereas the Santa Fe Railroad would contribute the salary of the general secretary.

For two decades, the "Y" was a busy place. The physical director taught swimming and gym classes, organized local athletic leagues, and coached winning football and basketball teams. The executive secretary supervised the plant, conducted membership campaigns, started night classes, laid out tennis courts, established a boys' camp up near El Porvenir, organized the first local Boy Scout troop, and led it on a hike all the way to Santa Fe. In 1908, he reported an average daily attendance of 300.

The Y.M.C.A. began incurring deficits during World War I by providing rooms free to transient soldiers, and afterward, the early depression of the 1920s caused it to go under in 1924. Then the Las Vegas Hospital, by virtue of a bequest from Mrs. Lizzie Carpenter, acquired the vacated building and remodeled it into a hospital, which was opened in April 1926. Meanwhile, the Sisters of Charity had converted St. Anthony's Sanitarium into a general hospital in 1923. Both acquired excellent facilities in new buildings much later, the former in 1952 and the latter in 1957.

In the 1920s, a new type of organization emerged—the "service" clubs, devoted to community improvement and youth activities. A forerunner was the Woman's Club, founded in 1912 as the successor to the Women's Federation. Subsequently, in rapid succession between 1919 and 1926, came the two posts of the American Legion, the Rotary and Kiwanis clubs, the League of Women Voters, the Business and Professional Women's Club, the Chamber of Commerce, the Commercial Club of the Plaza, and the Active Boosters Club. With so many "do-gooders" at work in Las Vegas, it would seem that the community should emerge as a veritable paradise.

Many of the early lodges served a recreational function.

Especially did they become dancing fraternities as they and the volunteer firemen sponsored one ball after another, each of which was reported by the newspaper to have been "the most enjoyable affair of the season." The churches, on the other hand, presented sociables, musical programs, and public lectures so regularly that there was something of that kind going on somewhere nearly every week.

Notable among the purely social organizations was the Montezuma Club, organized in 1884 by the sons of wealthy businessmen—all Anglos except for Miguel A. Otero, Jr. That club outfitted exclusive quarters on the second floor of a business building, until 1895. Then it leased the second floor of the new Masonic Temple and furnished those rooms luxuriously. Each Thursday evening was set aside for entertainment of their lady guests with a dinner, a musical concert, and a dance. In 1903, this club merged into the Commercial Club.

Quite different was the One Lung Club organized at the Plaza Hotel. As tubercular guests became numerous in Las Vegas in the nineties, this club was formed to conduct nonstrenuous social activities which would help members while away their time until their sojourn in the Las Vegas climate would arrest their ailment.

Holidays, of course, especially Thanksgiving, Christmas, and New Year's Day, were the occasion for dinners, parties, and dances. Christmas was the more spectacularly observed because then people, especially on the west side, lighted *farolitos* placed on the roofs of their houses, witnessed folk plays, and handed goodies to children who came around reciting this version of "trick or treat":

> *Oremos, oremos, Angelitos semos*
> *Del Cielo venemos a pedir oremos*
> *Si no los dan oremos*
> *Puertas y ventanas quebraremos.*

Mention has been made previouisly of the inauguration of celebrations on the Fourth of July in 1882, which grew into great annual *fiestas* on the Plaza beginning in 1888. The

The third annual Fiesta (*Museum of New Mexico*)

festive air of a holiday prevailed, too, whenever a circus came to town. The first such performance anywhere in New Mexico was claimed for Las Vegas where the John Robinson Circus erected its big tent in July 1882. Others came regularly at intervals of two or three years.

Because a parade without a band would have been dull, the community had to have a brass band right away. In that era before school bands became prevalent, the musicians were men who participated voluntarily as a form of recreation. As early as November 1879, eight men began practicing. The following summer, they recruited others and appeared as the nattily uniformed Las Vegas Brass Band.

A year later, another unit, the New Mexico Brass Band, was organized on the west side under the sponsorship of a committee headed by Eugenio Romero. By 1887, it had uniforms and was presenting concerts in the Plaza. Since the first band had become defunct, a new one was organized on the east side in 1890 under municipal sponsorship. This one, named the Las Vegas Military Band, was fortunate in having as its director a talented young musician from Chicago, John A. Hand, Jr., until his untimely death in 1898. That band presented concerts in Hillsite and Lincoln parks, led parades, and won prizes in contests in Denver and Albuquerque. As previously noted, it was superseded in the 1920s by the Cowboy Band. There was indeed music in the air in those days, as Hand presented his pupils in recitals, the churches had musical programs, the Montezuma Club held musicales in the clubrooms, and bands presented concerts and led parades. All of this prompted a lady to write an article about the territorial leadership of Las Vegas in the production, and appreciation, of good music.

The demonstration of taste for music was accompanied by popular reception of theatrical performances. In the early 1880s, traveling troupes presented comedies and dramas in the crude local halls then available, until an opera house was equipped in 1882 on the second floor of a building on Railroad Avenue. For four years it was a popular center for plays, lectures, dances, and roller skating. The management, George W. Ward and Charles Tamme, sought to book all companies

A circus came to town *(Rex Studio)*

on tour from New York to San Francisco. Eminent performers in them included David Garrick, George Miln, and Fay Templeton. In addition, amateurs presented well-received, hometown casts in several plays.

The success in that opera house encouraged Charles Tamme to build a new, elaborate one on Douglas Avenue in 1886. It, too, immediately became a popular community center as well as the place to enjoy operas presented by traveling companies. Moreover, home talent really blossomed then in such performances as *The Little Tycoon, Pinafore,* and *Mikado,* directed by John A. Hand, Jr. When technology made possible the substituting of motion pictures, James S. Duncan, the new owner of the opera house, was the first to install a projector, in 1906, for conversion to that form of entertainment.

At least four motion picture houses were opened in Las Vegas between 1908 and 1912, and one of them, the Mutual, or Kiva, or Campus, built on Bridge Street by Obaid Maloof, is still in operation. The larger and more ornate of all of the houses was the Coronado, built in 1919. To it, crowds of patrons came to hear the organ accompaniment of Grace

Roseberry while watching pictures featuring the "stars" of that era, that is, until 1929, when the showing of "talkies" hushed the fine organ. The Coronado also accommodated enthusiastic political rallies and popular bathing beauty contests.

Throughout the years, sports in a great variety had their devotees. Baseball led off after the *Optic* began sponsoring a team that played a few games with teams of other towns in 1886. It evoked great enthusiasm by defeating Albuquerque by a score of thirteen to two. The spark ignited then spread like wildfire in the exciting seasons of 1887 and 1888. Special excursion cars carried crowds of fans to watch their semipro team in action in Santa Fe and Albuquerque in hotly contested games that led to the territorial championship for Las Vegas. One of the participants, Miguel A. Otero, Jr., wrote in his reminiscences that "umpires were hard to get" and often after a game had to ride a horse "to the nearest railroad station to catch a train, no matter what direction it might be going."

Local enthusiasm lagged until in 1904 the Blues won the territorial championship, and again in 1911 to 1912, when the Maroons had winning seasons and surprised even themselves by defeating the visiting Japanese All Stars nine to eight in the tenth inning of a "hair-raiser." Good teams, sponsored by merchants, represented Las Vegas in the twenties and thirties, but by that time fans were giving more support to the high school and university teams and were becoming engrossed, too, in news of the major leagues.

Other early attractions were the carnivals held at the skating rink, the boxing matches promoted in local halls, and the shooting contests of the local gun club. Sportsmen went afield, too, for hunting and fishing, both of which were unbelievably productive in those days.

In the 1890s, a new sport became popular when bicycles were introduced. Cyclists formed a club for riding forth for picnics and pleasure jaunts.

Bicycles were superseded by automobiles as the recreation of a majority of people after World War I. Then they could drive to Wagon Mound for "Bean Day," or to Mora

The bicycle club in 1906 (*Rex Studio*)

for the *fiesta* there, or into the mountains for camping, fishing, and hunting, or to Santa Fe to visit the State Museum, or to Taos to take pictures of the ancient pueblo. In addition, organized programs for youth began to receive emphasis. In 1927, the Kit Carson Boy Scout Council was organized, and service clubs built a campground up in the canyon of the Gallinas River for use alternately by Boy Scouts, Girl Scouts, and Campfire Girls. Next, in 1931, municipally sponsored summer programs of recreational activities for youth were inaugurated.

The growing interest in local history, which usually can be taken as evidence of the maturation of a society, suggested that the founding of the town should be observed appropriately in its centennial, 1935. To that end, Dr. H. C. Gossard, president of the Las Vegas Historical Society, appointed as chairman W. J. Lucas, attorney and amateur historian, and set up committees until the number of appointees came to near 150.

The first centennial program, in June, consisted of meetings honoring descendants of the founders of Las Vegas. The next round of activities, also in June, was a presentation of special historical programs in the university and churches. That was followed in mid-July by Indian Days, when dances were performed by Indians of Tesuque Pueblo and by pupils of Seton Village. In addition, spectators heard the vocal solos of Princess Tsianina, eminent Cherokee soprano.

On August 15, the anniversary of the *entrada* of General Kearny in 1846, a pageant reenacted that event. Men representing soldiers, carrying old borrowed muskets, marched down Bridge Street, where others representing the Hispanic settlers greeted the general at the bridge. Then, heralded by a trumpeter and band music, the "Army of the West" entered the Plaza and unfurled the stars and stripes. Finally, the counterpart of the general climbed a ladder to the roof of the Plaza apartments and read the proclamation of August 15, 1846.

On Friday, August 16, a pageant on horseback and in wagons entered the rodeo arena before a great crowd. It portrayed several events in local history. That evening, Governor Clyde M. Tingley and Ex-governor Miguel A. Otero, Jr.

The first Boy Scout Troop on a hike *(Highlands University Collection)*

addressed those attending a banquet at the Hotel Castañeda. On Saturday, Charles O'Malley, perennial marshal of all local parades, lined up a great procession for a march down Douglas Avenue and to the Plaza. It featured many floats, Indians, the Cowboy Band, stagecoaches, cowboys, the 111th Artillery, and a miniature train sent by the Santa Fe Railroad.

On that Saturday afternoon, the once popular rodeos were revived for this one performance. Besides the typical events, rancher Warren D. Shoemaker exhibited his remarkably trained horse. On Sunday, the program was conducted at King Stadium, where ranch thoroughbreds competed with cavalry horses in exhibitions of polo ponies, five-gaited horses, and jumpers. The summer's program then was concluded by a ranch picnic for which Dee Bibb and J. B. Brown had barbecued a steer.

In retrospect, the pageant on the Plaza can be singled out as the principal historical event of the centennial program. In it, a group of Anglos had marched into the heart of Old Town for a reenactment of the American occupation of New Mexico in 1846. Although few observers seem to have sensed it at the time, that pageant had commemorated the wrong event for the observance of the year 1935 as a centennial. Those who had planned it had presented a performance memorializing what they believed to have been one of the most important events in the history of Las Vegas, which lent itself well to reenactment. Actually, the planners had celebrated the big day in the infiltration of their own predecessors into this community, instead of the event of 1835, which had occurred on April 6 instead of August 15.

A pageant representing the arrival of the procession of Mexican pioneers in 1835, the delineation of the Plaza, and the assignment of tracts of land by the *alcalde* remains yet for enactment at a future anniversary, perhaps at the bicentennial in the year 2035. However, the anachronism in the program of 1935 seems to have passed unnoticed. Some of those who witnessed the event said later that among their *compadres* on the west side they heard no critical comments; rather, all had regarded the performance as a "good show." Neither had there been any expression of resentment at that reminder of having been "conquered"; instead, the prevailing attitude, they said, was one of pride in having had the opportunity to be citizens of the United States. That freedom from serious social discord had enabled the people of the two municipalities to engage in the greatest demonstration of achievement by cooperative endeavor in the history of Las Vegas to that date. The celebration was even more remarkable in that it had been conducted successfully despite the intertown rivalry of politicians and businessmen and despite the economic vicissitudes of the Great Depression.

Previously, evidence has been presented that life in Las Vegas was hazardous for some people part of the time. Now additional evidence establishes that for the majority of the residents, most of the time it was a pleasant, wholesome place in which to share in family, church, and community life. The achievement of such an outcome arose from the choices of diverse groups to attain satisfaction each in its own way.

In the early era for those of Hispanic descent, the formal contacts were largely those of their church and schools; otherwise, they engaged in the informal associations of their primary institutions of family and neighborhood. Those

The distinguished brass band (*Las Vegas City Museum*)

were not the kinds of activities that would engender much publicity or become recorded, other than the registering of births, marriages, and deaths. For them, that type of a pleasant society continued to prevail to a large extent on past the turn of the century.

For the numerous newcomers, on the other hand, this became after 1880 a budding urban environment in which the associations were predominantly secondary. That called for the organizing of groups, the scheduling of activities, the seeking of promotional publicity, and often the keeping of minutes. A count of the organized functions within two decades, from 1880 to 1900, including those described in previous chapters, reveals that there were at least seventy-six, of which fifty-four were long-lived. From all of their records a lengthy volume could be produced, instead of this condensed summary.

After numerous new organizations became well established, one notable change occurred beyond the end of the first century. As the Hispanic population increased on the east side as well as on the west side, the successive generations on both sides adapted well to much of the pattern of institutions then prevailing in Las Vegas and elsewhere in the nation. In fact, after the inception of that pattern locally, they had contributed much to its successful ascendency. While retaining their religion, with a few exceptions, some finally became aware that a deliberate effort would be required to preserve also their language and other cherished features of their cultural heritage.

VII | The Community Becomes Contemporary

In the spring of 1980, City Manager Pat McDermott was joined by the mayor, Steve Franken, and others in an outcry of protest when the census takers released preliminary figures showing that the population of the consolidated City of Las Vegas had declined slightly below the total of 13,835 persons counted in the two formerly adjoining municipalities in 1970.

The Bureau of the Census had estimated the population as having increased to 14,727 by 1978, and other agencies, by use of several projections, had estimated it at 16,000 in 1980. Finally, the director of the local census readjusted the count upward to 14,278, thereby recognizing at least a slight growth in the preceding decade.

Actually, that figure was unbelievable. Subdivisions of new homes had been added, one after another since 1950, until the residential area had occupied formerly large vacant spaces northward by approximately one mile beyond the former fringe. One addition had filled the north half of the large site of the former Camp Luna, and houses had been built along one highway almost to the "third Las Vegas," or "Uppertown," which once had been a populous village. In addition, on the interstate highway, three large motels had arisen recently to supplement others built earlier as a great improvement over the tent camps of the 1920s for tourist accommodations.

In the area of expansion were two school buildings, four large apartment houses, four church buildings, three aggregations of low-income housing units, and two large, busy shopping centers, whose additions had not weakened noticeably the virility of the downtown business district centered on Douglas Avenue. Moreover, hundreds of mobile homes had been anchored down as permanent homes on several tracts, small and large, located all around the urban fringe.

The physical scene was representative of a community that had much the same pattern of economic bases as has been described in the earlier part of this work. After the decline of Las Vegas as a railway and commercial center, the foundations had become largely institutionalized by 1935, which, with some exceptions, has been the terminal date of the previous chronological review of the evolution of the community. This part, therefore, is essentially an epilogue to present the contemporary scene. To that end, flashbacks are included to fill in past contributing events, and the viewpoints of others are injected as indicators of prospects for the future.

Along the way since World War II, more frustrations can be added to those already described. In 1949, a fire destroyed the populous university housing units in the former hospital area of Camp Luna. Next, in 1954, when termination of enrollment under the first GI Bill curtailed financial suport for the university's greatly needed vocational school in facilities in the south part of the site of Camp Luna, the legislature failed to appropriate funds for its overhead, and it had to be shut down. Simultaneously, the introduction of diesel-powered locomotives brought an end to the need for servicing steam engines in the local roundhouse, and a few years later the discontinuance of Las Vegas as a division headquarters reduced greatly the number of railroad employees as local residents.

In 1955, a well-supported campaign made Las Vegas one of the three finalists for the location of the Cowboy Hall of Fame, but Oklahoma City was the winner. In that year, too, local boosters thought that the municipal airport stood a chance for selection as the site of an airforce base; instead, that local airport was destined to continue only as an improved service for private flights.

For many years, charitable and recreational agencies had attempted to conduct independent campaigns, which had raised meagre funds and had required much duplication of efforts. In 1958, a group of interested citizens combined sev-

The renovated Kearny Site of 1846 *(Optic photograph)*

eral of those campaigns into one drive by the United Fund, which they sponsored. It was launched with great enthusiasm and success, but soon too many of the donors tossed in only one dollar each, the volunteer solicitors lagged in their assignments, and the leadership played out. In 1964, this constructive endeavor had to be abandoned, and the cooperating agencies again were left to do the best that they could individually.

Meanwhile, inflating costs of maintenance and increasing competition were working hardships upon the once popular, and superior, institutions staffed originally by Catholic Sisters. In 1963, the Sisters of Loretto had to close their elementary and high schools in their large building on the east side, and in 1972, they also had to cease instruction in the elementary grades in their fairly new building on the west side. A year later, the Sisters of Charity withdrew maintenance of their St. Anthony's Hospital. Loyal patrons of those institutions lamented their demise.

In 1967, the deterioration of the old rodeo pavilion and the exhaustion of leadership led to the termination of the once great annual professional rodeos. In that year, too, the Chamber of Commerce almost obtained the building of a Levi factory in Las Vegas, but it went elsewhere. Meanwhile, a parachute factory located in the former Rosenwald mercantile building on the Plaza through the efforts of a former mayor, Ivan J. Hilton, had been employing sometimes as many as 325 persons, but in the early 1970s, the dwindling of contracts put it out of business. Subsequently, two local industries have been processing timber for building materials, but together in 1981 they had only fifty employees, due largely to a slump in new housing construction.

In 1975, a movement to complete the partially built scenic road of long ago, lately renamed the Elk Mountain Road, had seemingly overcome all obstacles as a culmination of the patient and persistent endeavors of James C. Sampson and others, when a newly elected governor, Jerry Apodaca, persuaded the State Board of Finance to withhold the funds that had been earmarked for it. He contended that the state should not spend so much money on what he misinterpreted to be merely a "recreational project."

In response to promotion endeavoring to make Las Vegas an extension of Hollywood, the producer of *The Shootist* scheduled the making of that film to start in January 1976, in this city and vicinity. Carol Tinker, then executive director of the Las Vegas-San Miguel Chamber of Commerce, engaged places of residence in spacious homes for the stars, John Wayne and Jimmy Stewart, rounded up all of the antique properties that would be needed, and obtained the consent of all merchants around the Plaza for the closing of that block to traffic during the six weeks required for filming there. When everything was ready, John Wayne's physician requested that another location be selected, because he would not permit his patient, who had only one lung, to engage in strenuous work at the high (6,400-foot) altitude of Las Vegas. Although other motion pictures were filmed at this location, as will be related later, that disappointing cancellation eliminated a major production.

After the Jesuits discontinued maintenance of a seminary in the former Montezuma Hotel in 1972, the Chamber of

Commerce and local officials revived the quest for use of those facilities—a task that they had had to pursue intermittently since 1903. This time, a mayor, Fidel "Chief" Gonzales, obtained support for a proposal to have the state buy it for use as a home for rehabilitation of veterans. After the legislature failed to appropriate funds for that purpose, the administrators of the university and the vocational institute developed plans for joint use of the buildings for instruction in hotel management and property restoration, but again, in 1981, the legislature tabled that proposal.

Meanwhile, as a result of technological progress, the Mountain Bell system had closed its district headquarters in Las Vegas; consequently, in this birthplace of telephone service in New Mexico, the employment of sixty-five persons back in the era of manual operation was reduced to only seventeen in 1981.

In a spirit of "never say die," leading citizens did achieve successes in a series of well-planned endeavors. First, in 1942, the district headquarters of the State Highway Department was moved almost overnight to Las Vegas from Springer, where the townsmen said it had been "stolen" by the sly exercising of clout by politicians in San Miguel County. Years later, Ivan J. Hilton, who had been a member of the State Highway Commission of that era, admitted that he had been influential in selecting what he believed to be a better location. In view of the increasing requirements for the building and maintaining of highways, this grew into a major asset for the community on the Meadows. That step was followed in 1947 by another state-sponsored improvement—the beginning of construction of the Meadows Home for the Aged, which has become an adjunct of the State Hospital.

Due to the ever-recurring need for supplying more water for a growing city, the Public Service Company of New Mexico, which had acquired the Agua Pura Company and the Power and Light Company, began work in 1950 on the building of a second large reservoir, to be supplied from the Gallinas River, like the first reservoir. Even so, the storage capacity, increased to near 200 million gallons, would not last long without constant replenishment. During the drought of the late 1950s, therefore, the company drilled four deep wells for pumping during such emergencies. By 1980, this system sometimes was supplying a peak load of about four million gallons daily.

Back in the 1920s, the Masonic Lodges and the Active Boosters Club had begun advocacy of the preservation of the deteriorating buildings of old Fort Union, twenty-eight miles north of Las Vegas, by conversion of the site into a national monument. Intensification of those efforts in the 1950s by James W. Arrott, rancher and industrialist, and by the local Chamber of Commerce, resulted in an agreement with the owners of the large ranch on which the ruins were located. That facilitated congressional acceptance of the site in 1954. Then the National Park Service began stabilizing the ruins and building a combined visitors' center and museum, which was ready for dedication in 1959. Further development of the site as a popular tourist attraction and educational facility has made it an economic asset for Las Vegas, and that advantage was enhanced after the ruins of the Pecos mission and pueblo, forty-five miles to the west, also became a national monument in 1965.

While the Rough Riders were coming to Las Vegas for their annual reunions in the 1950s, twenty of them contributed their mementos for the founding of a museum, and interested citizens sought a sponsor that might assure the institution relative permanence. In 1961, the City of Las Vegas responded. Mayor Leroy S. Wicks appointed a museum board, and the council made an appropriation for a trial period of operation in a rented room with volunteers as supervisors. As the result of good attendance and the contribution of a large collection of other relics of early times in Las Vegas and vicinity, the city made available, and remodeled, a large hall in 1965 in the municipal building on Grand Avenue. There this institution never became a large employer, but it did emerge as an educational and recreational attraction for groups of pupils and interested tourists coming from near and far.

By 1960, the town of Las Vegas west of the Gallinas River had made remarkable physical improvements under the direction of Mayor Junio López by the floating of revenue bonds. As a result, the town was nominated for an award as an All-America City and was one of the eleven that were selected for that honor in that year.

In 1960, another endeavor was crowned with success. This one, chaired for the Chamber of Commerce by banker Al Gerdeman, obtained donations of land around the south side of Storrie Lake and acceptance of it by the legislature for the creation of a state park. Soon afterward, the federal government began acquiring irrigated farms on the mesa for conversion in 1965 into a wildlife preserve around McAllister Lake.

In 1968, the Candido Maestas family, after operating a nursing home since 1957, obtained an issue of municipal revenue bonds for building a well-equipped, 100-bed facility, the Southwest Senior Care, Inc., at a location in a northern subdivision, where it has been well patronized.

In 1968, too, the voters in all precincts in the two adjoining Las Vegases responded in favor of a plan to consolidate the two municipalities, after previous failures of several similar efforts. This time, persuasive contentions by advocates in both communities had led to the appointment of a joint commission in 1967, chaired by District Judge Joe Angel. A year of work on a plan and a city charter had been climaxed by the gratifying response in that referendum. Then the commission devoted two more years of volunteer services in preparation for the combining of functions, which was culminated by the election of officers for the consolidated city in March 1970. Ten years later, a team of specialists from New Mexico State University, who made a study of the impact of consolidation, concluded that it had improved municipal services, had contributed to professionalization in city employment, and had enhanced community solidarity.

In the 1970s, favorable action by the state legislature resulted in additions to the institutional strength of the community. First, an enabling act made possible the opening of a tri-county vocational institute in 1970 in facilities already existing, and in others built in the south part of the former Camp Luna. Because it offered practical training programs

Consolidation achieved: *left to right*, Dr. Lynn I. Perrigo, official adviser; the Reverend Glen McCoy, *vice chairman*; Anna Amelia Silva Ordonez, stenographer; Judge Joe Angel, chairman; Luis Olivas; Floyd Chavez, chairman of the Joint Zoning and Planning Commission; Laurence F. Martinez; and Sam F. Vigil, treasurer. Earlier members, not in the photograph, were Dr. John S. Johnson, Jake Padillo, and John Deeterrick. (*Optic Photograph*)

especially adapted to the needs of the region, it became an immediate success. In 1981, its 988 students in one or more classes amounted to a full-time equivalent enrollment of about 600. Meanwhile, in 1976, in response to local promotional efforts, an appropriation had been forthcoming to acquire the former St. Anthony's Hospital for accommodation of the Northern New Mexico Rehabilitation Center. It also expanded rapidly, because it filled a regional need for specialized medical care.

In recent years the State Motion Picture Promotion Bureau has collaborated with the Las Vegas-San Miguel Chamber of Commerce in efforts to revive movie production in the attractive local setting which was once exploited successfully by Romaine Fielding and Tom Mix. As a result, segments of two major productions were filmed in Las Vegas in 1967 and 1977. One, *Easy Rider*, included action photographed on Bridge Street and around the Plaza, and the other, *Convoy*, along Grand Avenue. In 1977, another motion picture, which enjoyed a popular reception, *The Evil*, was produced in its entirety in the old, vacant Montezuma Hotel. Strictly for televising, three other movies had their setting in this city and vicinity. In 1975, *Sweet Hostage* was produced here for the American Broadcasting Company and *Liza's Pioneer Diary* for the Vision Series. A year later, Yale University produced *Charlie Siringo* to demonstrate that a good "western" could be made by use of authentic subject matter and authentic properties. Although this city lost what could have been a crowning spectacle, *The Shootist,* these other successes were hailed as encouraging harbingers of a productive rediscovery of picturesque, historic Las Vegas.

Mention has already been made of the building of several new church buildings. In addition, new facilities were added in recent years by the university, the public schools, business houses, and professional establishments. Moreover, between 1960 and 1976, joint municipal and federal housing projects were built, one after another, until by the latter date they had available 470 units for low-income families. That development was contemporaneous with a campaign to restore historic buildings, directed for the Chamber of Commerce by

Former Montezuma Hotel, site of a United World College
(Paul Umbarger)

Rheua Pearce as chairwoman. Six districts and almost eighty buildings were designated as state cultural properties, and many were placed on the national register. By 1981, a few of the vacated but sound and magnificent old buildings had been restored for new occupancy in the modern era, and in July the municipality made a generous appropriation for some needed restoration of the historic Plaza, under the direction of the City Design Review Board headed by Elmo Baca.

The previously frustrated quest for appropriate use of the spacious, vacated facilities of the former Montezuma Hotel came to an end in July 1981, when the Armand Hammer Foundation purchased the property for occupancy by a United World College. The governing board under the presidency of Prince Charles of Great Britain was maintaining similar international colleges in Wales, British Columbia, and Singapore, with thirty to forty countries represented in the student body of each of those liberal arts, community-oriented schools. Plans then were made to rehabilitate the

Montezuma buildings for the opening of this unit in the autumn of 1982 to accommodate between 200 and 300 students, with an ultimate objective of world peace through international understanding.

In late October, when a representative of the Armand Hammer Foundation had prepared details of the plans for restoration of the Montezuma properties, he revealed that they included the opening of a bathhouse at the hot springs for revival of salubrious use of the warm mineral water. Simultaneously Wid Slick, Dallas businessman, entered into a partnership with Lonnie and Dana Lucero, owners of the large, historic Plaza Hotel, and announced plans for its complete restoration for inauguration of its occupancy in 1982 once more as a luxury hotel for accommodation of tourists and conventions.

The transition of the economy to an institutional foundation came to full fruition by 1981, as attested by the employment of fifty or more persons by each of the following: the State Hospital, 770; the public schools of the two districts, 650; New Mexico Highlands University, 420; the district office of the State Highway Department, 379; the Las Vegas Hospital, 179; the City of Las Vegas, the Luna Vocational-Technical Institute, and the Santa Fe Railroad, tied at approximately 125; Southwest Senior Care, Inc., 72; Northern New Mexico Rehabilitation Center, 70; San Miguel County, 66; and the New Mexico Department of Human Services (Welfare), 54. Despite these and many smaller providers of jobs, the rate of unemployment in 1980 was 8.6 percent, a full point above the average for the state, and a year later it had risen to 10.2 percent.

As this book was going into production in January 1982, those citizens who had been disappointed by previous failures to acquire small industries could well be happily chagrined by their having expressed publicly their pessimism about the future. Two manufacturing companies announced selection of sites and plans for building factories in the ensuing spring. One, Fairchild Metal Fabricators, would make steel products needed by oil and gas industries, and the other, Montana de Fibre, would produce fiberboard for use in the construction of buildings and the manufacture of furniture. Each expected to employ up to 200 persons when in full operation. This promised quick improvement in employment opportunities by adding manufacturing to the previoiusly almost fully institutionalized economic foundations.

The backbone of the business community was the large number of small enterprises engaging in sales and services for the residents, the university students, the ranch trade, and the tourists either in transit or in pursuit of recreation in the mountain playground. Attractive especially to the latter were the ordinarily equable climatic conditions. Daytime high temperatures averaged 46 degrees in January and only about 82 degrees in summertime, while summer nights were an exhilarating 52 degrees. Hence, Chamber of Commerce slogans had been "The City of Blanket Nights" and "A Breath of Fresh Air." Precipitation averaging fifteen inches annually usually was adequate, but long spells of hot, dry weather occurred occasionally.

Townspeople became gloomy upon the onslought of a drought. A serious one lasting from 1950 to 1955 caused the premature sale of thousands of cattle by ranchers, and their reduced income hurt business in town. In addition, it dried up the fishing waters and required strict rationing of the supply in town, and that in turn impaired temporarily the attractiveness of the city and the mountain resorts. Another bad drought persisted from 1980 to 1981.

Likewise, residents were alarmed by anything that might affect tourism adversely. They suffered when the OPEC embargo caused a shortage of gasoline, and they feared dire consequences as a tripling in the price of fuel was predicted. However, ill effects from that failed to materialize. In 1981, the Chamber of Commerce reported that the returns from a tax on lodging had increased slowly but steadily. People had become so dependent upon automotive transportation that they continued the traffic regardless of the cost. However, in 1981, another cause of alarm was the bypass being built around the city on the interstate highway. Almost everyone was dreading the readjustment which its completion certainly would require. At that time, too, the curtailment of the appropriation for Amtrak made uncertain the future of passenger service for this original center of railway activity in New Mexico.

Otherwise, residents constantly were concerned about any fluctuation that might occur in the institutional basis of the economy. The younger institutions had not yet suffered from serious upheavals, and some of the older ones, as in the case of the Highway Department recently, could endure a shake-up at higher levels without adversely affecting employment. Stabilizing factors were the early effectuation of tenure for teachers in the schools and university and the later adoption of merit systems for most other institutional employees. The eroding away of sources of patronage for politicians, along with the introduction of voting machines, had deprived local elections of their fighting spirit. It has been a long time since they were accompanied by fisticuffs, the impounding of ballots, and the calling out of the National Guard.

Early in the 1970s, when chicano activists resorted to mob demonstrations against the school board on the east side, the turmoil resulted in the employing of a Hispano as superintendent and the revising of some educational policies. Subsequently, the district on the west side experienced a prolonged round of infighting by board members in a power struggle. It involved, too, a few administrators, and it even led to contests in court. Both uproars were causes of embarrassment in the community and sources of distress for teachers and pupils, yet they did not result in any great economic losses. Unlike the voluntarily enrolled university students, the 5,300 pupils in the public schools were captives of the systems, and their presence required that budgets be maintained and work be continued, regardless. That there really was no overwhelming desire to escape is revealed by the enrollment of only 107 in the two private schools in 1980. A different type of alarm arose a year later when the slashing of federal expenditures imperiled the continuation of funding upon which both public systems had become more and more dependent for specialized programs.

At the State Hospital, periodic administrative strife and

political meddling once had such far-reaching effects that there used to be a saying that the institution had two shifts of trained employees, one when state government was under Democratic control and another when Republicans were dominant. Resistance to extreme fluctuations was effected by the development of a merit system since 1965. Once, a large number of employees was needed simply to attend to the physical needs of long retained patients and mounting admissions, until the number rose to 1,200. Then an improved percentage of recoveries, along with transfers to other institutions, began reducing the number, for example, from 977 to 671 in 1965, and since then to approximately 500. The change that this wrought in employment was not so much in numbers as in types. More and more of the staff became specialists trained for several kinds of therapeutic treatment, for medical services, and for psychiatric guidance. Conflicts with a recently removed administrator caused a big turnover in the professional staff in the 1970s, but stabilization and reorientation by 1981 led to expectations that soon the name might be changed to something like the New Mexico Psychiatric Institute.

One institution, a major employer, which almost precipitated a chill in the local climate in the early 1970s, was the Las Vegas Hospital. Upon the retirement of a few physicians and the departure of others, the medical staff became seriously depleted, while simultaneously poor collections and rising expenses created mounting deficits. Not until afterward did the trustees reveal that in 1973 the crisis had become so acute that the community almost lost that hospital. However, a campaign to attract more nurses and physicians resulted in an increase in the latter to eighteen by 1980, in addition to five dentists. Meanwhile, strenuous efforts under new management had resulted in balanced budgets. In 1981, therefore, the administration was able to prepare plans to enlist additional specialized surgeons and to launch immediately a four million dollar expansion program that would serve seven counties under a new name, the Northeastern Regional Hospital.

Another large employer, the university, was watched like a barometer, because it was especially responsive to periodic crises. Beginning in 1951, the appointment of a Republican majority on the Board of Regents provided an opportunity for a few ambitious, disgruntled faculty members to team up with one of the new regents for a campaign of harassment of Dr. Edward Eyring, the president, whose politics and pertinacity made him vulnerable. After a bitter, protracted battle, a year later the regents dismissed him but then decided that they should have conducted a hearing first and called one after the deed had been done. The president then contended that his firing had been illegal and refused to leave his office until the regents obtained a court order and had a police officer evict him. For that and other irregularities, the North Central Association placed the institution on probation for two years, and immediately the enrollment slumped from nearly 1,000 to about 500.

As president the regents employed Dr. Thomas C. Donnelly, previously dean of arts and sciences at the University of New Mexico. He concentrated first upon a thorough reorganization and an adoption of sound policies in order to clear the institution of the stigma of probation . Then he encouraged great emphasis upon research in the physical sciences, by aid of federal financial grants, and upon the development of athletic teams which for several years made Highlands a contender, among small colleges, for national titles in major sports. The publicity, along with the strengthening of the faculty and facilities, attracted a steadily increasing enrollment until it became a cosmopolitan assemblage of 2,500 students by 1970.

Actually, the policies were a throwback to those of the first president, Dr. Edgar L. Hewett, only on a grander scale, and, as in 1903, they also provoked a reaction, especially among Hispanos who wanted this institution to be oriented more to the special needs of its service area. Instead, it had become a combination of a "little MIT" and a "little Notre Dame." For the first time, a president was permitted to serve until his age qualified him for retirement. When that time arrived in 1970, and the regents at first selected a Midwesterner as his successor, young chicano activists, encouraged by local politicians, went on the warpath. They staged a prolonged sitdown strike in the administration building and resorted to threatening demonstrations without actually damaging any property.

The outcome was that a year later the appointment of a majority of Spanish Americans to the board led to their employment of one, Dr. Frank Angel, as president, the first in the nation, and four years later he was succeeded by Dr. John Aragón. Again the turmoil had caused a decline in enrollment, this time to 1,800.

Under Hispanic leadership in nearly all administrative offices and in many faculty positions, the institution became reoriented and attained recognition for its devotion to multicultural studies, continuing education, and "affirmative action" employment of minorities. Actually, the Hispanic "minority" in its immediate service area was a majority. On the 1980 census forms, 81 percent of the respondents in the San Miguel County designated themselves as "Spanish-American."

The new administration deemphasized the recruiting of prospective professional athletic stars from a distance. Thenceforth, for a few years the teams in major sports competed mostly for entertainment of the spectators. Only once in a while did they win a game. (By the end of the decade they were faring better). Slowly but steadily during the troublous era of readjustment, the enrollment picked up again until it passed the 2,000 mark in 1981, at a time when a slight decline was being experienced by most other universities.

In the frontier epoch, Las Vegas had had a distinct entity, but changing conditions had caused the decline and ultimate extinction of the once great local mercantile houses. Local businesses, which arose in their place, by 1930 had come into competition with a few chain stores. That trend has continued. In 1981, there were only four independent department stores as against eight branches of big businesses common to many cities. Among the restaurants, ten were local and eleven were members of chains, mostly of the new fast-food variety. Other community services were becoming likewise standardized.

For recreation, there was nothing comparable to the

manifold program of the defunct YMCA in its heyday. Nevertheless, in 1980, the *Community Profile* listed numerous activities and facilities much like those in other cities of comparable size, that is, two libraries, a concert series, three motion picture theatres, two radio stations, a T.V. translator, a T.V. cable system, city parks, bowling alleys, tennis courts, a swimming pool, a golf course, a skating rink, school sports, summer baseball leagues, etc. Distinctly local were the Old Town fiestas conducted annually since 1888 and the rodeos of the Jaycees inaugurated in 1974 in a new arena.

Noteworthy among contemporary agencies were several that in one way or another were striving for improvements. In this category, besides the several schools and churches, were the Las Vegas-San Miguel Chamber of Commerce, the Rotary, Kiwanis, Lions, Jaycee, Pilot, Women's, and other clubs, the Hispanic Chamber of Commerce, the Elks Lodge and other fraternal orders, the veterans' organizations, the Boy Scout and Girl Scout councils, the 4-H clubs, the Future Farmers of America, the County Fair, the Environmental Improvement Division, the League of Women Voters, the Citizens for Historic Preservation, the Municipal Design Review Board, the City Planning and Zoning Commission, the Municipal Industrial Park, the City Energy Conservation Committee, the San Miguel Solar Energy Society, and the Las Vegas Arts Council.

For persons having troubles of various degrees and all kinds, the community had numerous aids. They included, of course, the police officers and firemen, the courts, the hospitals, and a typical battery of state agencies for assistance with employment, economic relief, and health services. Noteworthy, too, were the Crimestoppers, Alarm Systems, Crisis Center, American Red Cross, Salvation Army, Volunteer Shelter Bed Program, Foster Grandparents, Alcoholism Center, Methadone Drug Treatment Program, Weight Watchers, and Health and Fitness Center. Obviously, local distresses were extensions into this community of conditions prevalent elsewhere in the nation.

For an analysis of opinions about the problems and progress of contemporary Las Vegas, questionnaires were distributed among observant persons representing the east and west sides, the two major cultural components, both sexes, and age levels from young adults to senior citizens. Several expressed themselves quite candidly on those unsigned responses, especially about conditions which they condemned as detrimental.

At a time when one of those occasional droughts was a source of annoyance, naturally almost everyone listed shortage of water as a serious handicap, and one even regretted that the municipality never had acquired ownership of the water and power utilities. Also ranking high among opinions about detriments to progress were county and school board politics as well as several replies that were similar in their deploring of disorder. They mentioned drugs, drinking, vandalism, petty crime, broken homes, litter, lack of pride in neatness, and poor respect for law and property. Three respondents added old districts having "broken windows and boarded-up stores," and another called attention to areas of "rundown houses."

A few were even despondent about the future. One wrote, "The community seems to be at a standstill, and until our youth are educated to respect other people's property and stop their destructive ways, nothing the merchants and progressive citizens do will help our community," and another, "I believe if a sense of pride and worth were emphasized, the population could make the town a showplace rather than the dumping ground it seems to be."

Several also lamented the lack of industry, the unemployment, the departure of young people in quest of jobs, the loss of railway employment, the draining of talent out of the area, the pervasive poverty, and the great dependence upon public assistance; but herein were a few discordant notes. One advised that those who sought salvation by industrialization were misdirecting their efforts, because transportation of materials in and products out at such a great distance never would permit it, and another agreed but for a different reason—the relatively high cost of utilities for commercial uses. Moreover, whereas several felt that a good supply of labor was available, a few others were of the opinion that efforts to utilize it would be futile, because the unemployed lacked "incentive to take advantage of the opportunities they have."

Ranking less noticeably as causes of complaint were inadequate recreation and supervision for youth, excessively divisive chicano agitation, the "haphazard urban sprawl" northward, and the budget slashing by President Ronald Reagan. Beyond that, almost everybody had individualized ideas about liabilities of a minor nature, not recognized by others. Apparently the participants had been well selected to obtain views of the city from many angles.

The foregoing could not be accepted as a severe condemnation of Las Vegas specifically, because several of the ailments were recognizable as reflections of the pervasiveness of distresses in the macrocosm—a social malaise which once had been the subject of a nationwide appeal in a speech by President Jimmy Carter. Critics have grumbled about similar, if not exactly the same, faults in other cities, and besides, nearly all of the persons who wrote the criticisms of Las Vegas expressed effusively their praise for other attributes of the community.

As present assets contributing great promise for the future, the State Hospital and the university were singled out by most respondents. The university was valued not only as an employer but also "for its many programs and activities affecting the community." One reply elaborated at length upon "its tremendous potential for influencing the entire region."

Ranking next in incidence were the Luna Vocational-Technical Institute, the national forests with their natural beauty, recreational facilities, and timber resources, the lakes for recreation, the "ideal climate" and "clean air," the highway connections and services, and "the excellent city government, police force, and fire department." Close to the above were "ranching assets," small business enterprise and competition," a large variety of organizations with their "growing spirit of volunteerism," the several state agencies, the health services making this a "second-to-none medical community," the outstanding "historic appeal," and the remarkable "blending of cultures." About the latter, however, one dissenter saw in it only an unfortunate source of "antagonism."

Incidentally, in supplementary casual conversations, several persons of both major cultural affiliations expressed the hope that the absence of any serious disturbances in recent years indicated that the "antagonism" and "divisive chicano agitation" may have subsided permanently, due to improvement in the employment of qualified Hispanos and the advancement of several to positions of leadership in business, government, and education. One young scholar of Spanish descent pointed out that locally even their use of the term chicano was waning in popularity.

Among other quotable optimistic observations about the community were these, gleaned from the questionnaires: "Its climate, pure water and air, the fact that it is not beset by overpopulation and its accompanying pollution and other problems, makes Las Vegas a real land of opportunity, a good place in which to live." Also, "Over the past five years Las Vegas has experienced a healthy growth. Not big, but healthy. One very positive factor has been the influx of new business, which has caused some of the old establishments to be more competitive. With prices down and more goods and services available, more people will shop in Las Vegas and create more jobs."

Again, the great diversity of individual viewpoints was reflected in a long list of assets. Practically every institution and activity previously mentioned in these pages received favorable notice by at least one or two of the observers. One summed it up with praise for the "harmonious, compatible, economic living conditions."

In remarks about how Las Vegas had found a new identity to supplant its outstanding distinction in the frontier epoch, only a few individualized viewpoints appeared. One said, "its peculiar brand of politics," three liked its "relaxed, frontier atmosphere," three mentioned its "ideal size," and one commended its "blend of urban and ranch life." Even one damaging tendency was suggested as contributing a special identity, and that was "an unfair, deceitful, negative portrayal of its character and reputation."

Almost all of the citizens were impressed in one way or another by the qualities of the population. The people were portrayed as "friendly," "helpful," "permissive," "accepting all classes," and "enriched by cultures from abroad at the university." Some put it simply as "a special people," and one elaborated upon that further: "Every town has people, but ours are special in that when the chips are down they never fail to band together for specific causes."

Many remarked about the enrichment by a "cultural blend," or "human mosaic," and the generally smooth intercultural accommodations. About this one wrote, "There is a rich Spanish culture here (not to be confused with the radical chicano group) which makes social life that much more delightful." Also highly regarded as identifying characteristics were the good educational facilities from the public schools through the university and the rich historical background reflected in the "architectural charm" of old buildings.

Finally, complete unanimity placed at the head of the list the physical environment, "where high plains meet snow-capped mountains." Nearly all emphasized the salubrious climate along with the inspiring scenery and the recreational facilities of the alpine location.

The several traits of special identity were those most appreciated, and commented upon, by visitors, some of whom expressed the conviction that by and by "many people surely will discover Las Vegas." One such visitor, Oka Stanton Flick, who was a guest faculty member in the summer session of 1949, expressed his appreciation for having had that opportunity by handing to his department head a penciled copy of this previously unpublished verse which he had composed as his tribute to New Mexico:

In the shadow of Old Mexico, New Mexico,
A youth among the sisterhood of states
But ancient with the lore of ages past—
Conquistadores, pueblo, padre, and wagon train—
The three-fold trysting place of man:

From the eastern sea, the sturdy Anglo-Saxon,
From the land of Old Castile
That race who taught the world
To love and suffer and be gay,
And from the plain and from the mountain-side
Those who would see in mountain and in plain,
In lightning flash, in water-fall, in sun and star
The all pervading Spirit which conceived the world
And keeps it now
In the everlasting circle of the heavens.
Rich therefore thy heritage
Born of the grandeur of thy peaks
And the sweep of thy desert vistas
The silence of thy canyons,
The awe of thy eternal rocks,
The snows, defiant of summer sun,
The muted ruins of long ago
Speak to the souls of men
Of the souls of men and things,
The meaning and destiny of the Earth.

Bibliography

Public Records

City of Las Vegas, Board of Health, Record of Births 1901–1917, Deaths 1901–1917, Nuisances 1914–1918; City Council Minutes and Record of Ordinances 1895–; and Official Plat Book of 1919 (City Hall).

Fourth Judicial District (County Library, Courthouse).

A. A. Jones v. Las Vegas Land Grant Board, Cause 6865–6.

Board of Education of the Town of Las Vegas . . . , v. Board of Trustees of the Town of Las Vegas . . . Cause 14338.

Board of Trustees of the Town of Las Vegas v. Margarito Romero, Cause 6366.

Board of Trustees of the Town of Las Vegas v. Teodoro Pena, Cause 6974.

Board of Trustees of the Town of Las Vegas v. LeRoy Bish, et al., Cause 10936.

Board of Trustees, Las Vegas Land Grant, v. Las Vegas Land and Water Co., et al., Cause 10166.

Court Order of 1874 (E. V. Long Papers, State Records Center).

Criminal and Civil Docket, 1868–1875 (Special Collections, University of New Mexico).

La Fraternidad de Nuestro Padra Jesus de Nazareno . . . v. Concilio Original de Nuestro Padre Jesus Nazareno . . . et al., Cause 13761.

Milheiser v. Padilla, Cause 2680

The Sanguejuela Co. v. Board of Trustees, Cause 6152.

Higher Courts

Board of Trustees of the Town of Las Vegas and Donaciano Marruja v. Elauterio Montano et al., 481 P. 2d 702.

Cartwright et al. v. Public Service Company of New Mexico, 343 P. 2d 654.

Jaremillo v. Romero, *Supreme Court Reports, Territory of New Mexico, 1852–1879* (San Francisco, 1881), pp. 190–208.

Pablo Maese et al. v. Binger Herman, 183 U.S. 572, 46L. Ed. 335.
Re Las Vegas Grant, Rehearing by Secretary of the Interior (Andrieus A. Jones Papers, State Records Center).
Waddingham v. Robledo, 6 N.M. 347.
United States, Department of the Interior, General Land Office, *Cases Relating to the Public Lands*, vol. 27, 29, 30 (Washington, D. C., 1899, 1900, 1901).

Las Vegas Carnegie Public Library
Constitution, and Circulation Records, 1902–.

Las Vegas Land Grant Board (County Library, Courthouse).
Audit Reports, 1902–1931, by Horton and Gould;
Cash Journal, 1903–1921; Court Orders, 1909–;
Journals, 1903–1931; Minutes, 1903–1906 (E. V. Long Papers State Records Center); Minute Books, 1906–.

Las Vegas Municipal Schools, District #2, Superintendents' Annual Reports, and Board Minutes, 1891–1922 (School Office).

New Mexico Department of Public Welfare, San Miguel County, File of Inactive Cases (Welfare Office).

New Mexico National Guard, File on Improvements at Camp Luna (State Records Center).

San Miguel County
Books of Testamentos, 1862–1867, and 1874–1879 (Special Collections, University of New Mexico).
Deed Record Books, 1852–, and Direct and Indirect Indices (Office of County Clerk).
Commissioners' Minutes, 1882– (Office of County Clerk).
Justice of the Peace Dockets, 1881–2, 1896– (City Hall).
Plat Books (Office of County Clerk).
Ulibarri y Duran, Jose de Jesus, The Las Vegas Grant, Deed Record Book No. 1 (Office of County Clerk), pp. 119–129.
Town of East Las Vegas, Trustees' Minutes, 1888–1895 and Record of Ordinances 1888–1895 (City Hall).

Federal
United States Army, Las Vegas Post Returns, 1848–1851, (Arrott Collection, New Mexico Highlands University).
United States General Land Office, Las Vegas Grant Patent (District Court Office, Court House).

Private Records
Benevolent Protective Order of Elks, #408, Charter (Lodge Room).

C. de Baca, Ezekiel, Papers (State Records Center).
East Las Vegas Fire Department, Minutes, 1909–1916, and Manuscripts (Fire Station).
E. Romero Hose and Fire Company Constitution, 1882, and Minutes, 1887– (Fire Station).
First Baptist Church, List of Pastors; Minutes of Covenant Meetings 1880–1912; Minutes of Monthly Conferences, 1922– (c/o Mrs. Frank J. Wesner).
Grand Army of the Republic, Sherman Post, Dues and Treasurer's Record, 1889; Minutes 1914–1920 (New Mexico Highlands University).
Gross, Kelly Co., Business Papers (Special Collections, University of New Mexico).
Harris, D. U., Abstract of Title 5826, in Storrie Project (County Library, Court House).
Historical Society of Las Vegas, The Centennial Celebration, (Bound Mss., 1935, New Mexico Highlands University).
Ilfeld, Charles, Business Papers (Special Collections, University of New Mexico).
Ilfeld, Charles, Personal Papers (State Records Center).
Las Vegas Land and Water Co., Auditor's Report, 1927 (County Library, Court House).
Las Vegas Lumber Co., Abstracts of Title 1436 and 12812 (Company Office).
Las Vegas Water Users Association, Inventory of 1926 (County Library, Court House).
Long, E. V., Papers (State Records Center).
McKissick, George O. and Aileen Marie, Abstract of Title 3027 (Bank Safe Deposit).
Montefiore Congregation
Constitution of 1886 and 1898; Building Contracts, 1886; Indenture of 1888; Subscription Lists of 1884–1886; Statement, 1886; Ladies' Benevolent Society Minutes, 1904–1920 (c/o Milton Taichert).
Historical Film Collection, Romaine Fielding and Tom Mix Reports, Letters, and Papers (State Records Center).
Our Lady of Sorrows Church, Baptismal, Marriage, and Burial Records, 1852– (Office in Rectory).
Perrigo, Lynn I., Abstracts of Title #1649–10,053 to Personal Property (Bank Safe Deposit).
Plaza Hotel, Visitors' Register, 1892–3, 1912 (New Mexico Highlands University).

Prince, L. Bradford, Papers (State Records Center).
Public Service Company, Scrapbooks, 1918-49, 1922-7 (Las Vegas Office).
Raynolds, Jefferson, Appointment Books (Special Collections, University of New Mexico).
Relacion escrita por Demetrio Perez (Read Collection, State Records Center).
Romero, Secundino, Papers (Special Collections, University of New Mexico).
Rosenwald, Emanuel, Papers (Special Collections, University of New Mexico).
San Miguel County Title and Abstract Company, Deed Record Books 1-3 (Company Office).
Serna, Mrs. Rose, Abstract of Title #9285, to former Jesuit property (Safe Deposit).
Spanish Presbyterian Church, Session Minutes, 1891-1931 (Office, United Presbyterian Church).
St. Paul's Church, Legal Documents (State Records Center).
Storrie Project, Lease Book, 1930 (County Library, Courthouse).
United Presbyterian Church, Session Minutes, 1869- (Church Office).
United Methodist Church, Brown, Higgins, Hoffman, Long, Morley Manuscripts; Historical Sketch; Board Minutes; *Christian Mirror* of 1882; Dedication program, 1923; and *The Calendar*, 1930 (Church Office).

Newspapers

Arrott Collection (New Mexico Highlands University). *Revista Catolica* (Las Vegas), 1875-1909.

Mills Collection (New Mexico Highlands University).
The Chronicle (Las Vegas), daily 1884-6, weekly, 1886.
El Independiente (Las Vegas), weekly, 1907-1908.
Las Vegas Daily Gazette, 1879-1886, lacking some issues.
Las Vegas Daily Optic, 1879-1901, 1903-1912, 1920-1931, 1932-1934, 1935-, lacking a few months. Also, Booster Edition, 1915, and Centennial Souvenir Edition, 1935.
Las Vegas News, weekly, 1887-1888.
Las Vegas Sunday Courier, weekly, three months of 1888.
Weekly Optic and Stock Grower (Las Vegas), 1910-1917.
La Voz del Pueblo (Las Vegas), weekly, 1889-1919, lacking some months.

San Miguel County Star (Las Vegas), weekly, 1928, 1931, 1933–1935.

Museum of New Mexico Collection
The Acorn (Las Vegas), weekly, 1875, a few issues.
Santa Fe Republican, some issues, 1847.
Santa Fe *New Mexican*, 1863–.
Santa Fe *Weekly Gazette,* 1852–1864.

Books
Barker, S. Omar. *Little World Apart* (Garden City, N.Y.: 1966).
Callon, Milton W., *Las Vegas, New Mexico: The Town That Wouldn't Gamble* (Las Vegas: 1962).
Carruth, A. J. *First Annual Directory . . . (Las Vegas: 1895).*
City and Business Directory of Las Vegas, New Mexico (Las Vegas: 1900).
City, Town, and Business Directory of Las Vegas, New Mexico (Las Vegas: 1908).
Farley, C. A. *A Mile and a Half Toward Heaven* (Lubbock, Texas: 1972).
History of the Las Vegas Grant (Las Vegas: 1890).
A Journey Through New Mexico's First Judicial District in 1864. William S. Wallace, ed. (Los Angeles: 1956).
Kelly, Daniel T., and Beatrice Chauvenet. *The Buffalo Head* (Santa Fe: 1972).
Landmann, Robert S., *New Mexico State Hospital* (Albuquerque: 1965).
Medina Ascensio, Luis, S. J. *Historia del Seminario de Montezuma* (Mexico, D. F.: 1962).
Montoya, Vicente, and F. C. de Baca. *Directory of Las Vegas, New Mexico* (Las Vegas: 1939).
Nahm, Milton C. *Las Vegas and Uncle Joe* (Norman, Okla.: 1964).
Otero, Miguel A. *My Life on the Frontier,* 2 vols. (New York: 1935, 1939).
Parish, William J. *The Charles Ilfeld Company* (Cambridge, Mass.; 1961).
Porter, Gay E. *City Directory of Las Vegas, New Mexico* (Las Vegas: 1882).
Rendon, Gabino, with Edith Agnew. *Hand on My Shoulder* (New York: 1953).
Stanley, F. (Crocchiola). *The Las Vegas (New Mexico) Story* (Denver: 1951).
Stanley, F. *The Montezuma, New Mexico, Story* (Pep, Texas: 1963).

Threinen, Ellen. *Architecture and Preservation in Las Vegas* (Las Vegas: 1977).
Wiley, Tom, and others. *Montezuma Memories* (n.p., 1972).
Wilson, H. T., *Historical Sketch of Las Vegas, New Mexico* (Chicago: 1880).

Pamphlets

Annual Cowboys Reunion: Souvenir Program (Las Vegas, 1915–1932).
Atcheson, Topeka, and Santa Fe Railroad, *Las Vegas Hot Springs, New Mexico* (Chicago, 1887).
Baca, Carlos C. de, *Vicente Silva, New Mexico's Vice King of the Nineties (Las Vegas, 1938).*
Baca, Carlos C. de, *Vicente Silva, the Terror of Las Vegas* (Truchas, N.M., 1968).
Baca, Manuel C. de, *Historia de Vicente Silva, Sus Cuarentos Bandidos, Sus Crimenes y Retribuciones* (Chicago, n.d.).
Baca, Manuel C. de, *Vicente Silva and his 40 Bandits* (Washington, D. C., 1947).
Bodrall, Constance C., *The Centennial of the Italian Hermit* (n. p., 1969).
Chamber of Commerce, *Las Vegas, Scenic, Historic, Romantic* (Las Vegas, 1927).
The Climate of New Mexico and Las Vegas Hot Springs (Chicago, 1885).
Consolidation of Municipal Governments: Las Vegas (Las Cruces, 1980).
Gould, George T., *Illustrated Las Vegas* (Las Vegas, 1903).
Higgins, C. A., *Las Vegas Hot Springs and Vicinity* (Chicago, 1897, 1898, 1899).
Historical Society of Las Vegas, *Las Vegas Centennial, 1835–1935* (Las Vegas, 1935).
Las Vegas Hot Springs (Springfield, Ohio, 1883 and 1887).
Las Vegas Woman's Club, 1920–1921 (Las Vegas, 1921).
Lucas, W. J., *Historic Las Vegas* (Las Vegas, 1927).
McGrath, Tom, *Vicente Silva and his Forty Thieves* (Las Vegas, 1960).
Mills, T. B., *San Miguel County, Illustrated* (Las Vegas, 1885).
Montezuma College, *Bulletins* (Las Vegas, 1922–1930).
New Mexico Bureau of Immigration, *San Miguel County* (Santa Fe, 1907).

New Mexico Department of Public Welfare, *San Geronimo*, and *Villanueva* (n. p., 1937).
New Mexico Highlands University, *Bulletins* (Las Vegas, 1898-).
Perrigo, Lynn I., *Historic Sites in and near the "Meadow City"* (Las Vegas, 1963).
Perrigo, Lynn I., *Las Vegas and the Rough Riders* (Las Vegas, 1961).
Romero, Margarito, *El Secreto de la Riqueza* (Las Vegas, 1912).
Stanley, F., *Dave Rudabaugh, Border Ruffian* (Denver, 1961).
Ward, Charles L. G., Robert Taupert, and R. E. Twitchell, *Las Vegas Gallinas Park and the Scenic Highway* (Las Vegas, 1904).

Articles

Antoneides, Anthony, "The Other Las Vegas," *New Mexico Architecture*, vol. 16 (July-August, 1974), pp. 11–20.
Arellano, Anselmo, "Hispanics in Las Vegas," *Las Vegas Daily Optic*, July 27, 1979.
Arellano, Anselmo, "People Versus Trustees . . . ," *NMHU Journal*, II, 1 (July, 1980), pp. 33–42.
August, Jack, "Desperados Arrive," *Las Vegas Daily Optic*, July 27, 1979.
Baca, Elmo, "Old Town Plaza," *Las Vegas Daily Optic*, July 27, 1979.
Ballenger, Mrs. H. L., "Churches of Las Vegas," in *Las Vegas Centennial* (Las Vegas, 1935), pp. 10–11, 14–15.
Barker, S. Omar, "Another Gun-Slinging Billy," Empire Section, *The Denver Post*, August 5, 1956, pp. 9–10.
Barker, S. Omar, "Billy with a Gun," *True West*, vol. 16, no. 2 (Dec. 1968), pp. 16–17, 51–53.
Barker, S. Omar, "New Mexico Normal University," in *Las Vegas Centennial* (Las Vegas, 1935), pp. 16–17, 20.
Beatson, James, "New Mexico and Fort Union in Civil War," *Las Vegas Daily Optic*, July 27, 1979.
Booth, Mary W., "Music in Las Vegas," *El Palacio*, vol. LIII, no. 6 (June 1946), pp. 163–5.
Brooks, Mary J., "Along the Avenue," in *Annual Cowboys' Reunion: Souvenir Program* (Las Vegas, 1948), pp. 19–20.
Callon, Milton W., "Boxing's Greatest Fiasco," in *The Denver Westerners Roundup*, vol. XXVII, no. 7 (Sept. 1972), pp. 3–19.

Callon, Milton W., "Chanukah Comes to Las Vegas," *The Denver Westerners Monthly Roundup*, vol. XXVI, no. 9–10 (Sept.-Oct. 1970), pp. 22–33.

Callon, Milton W., "Las Vegas and the Dodge City Gang," *Frontier Times*, vol. 42, no. 3 (April-May 1968), pp. 12–17, 62–4.

Callon, Milton W., "The Merchant Colonists of New Mexico," in *Brand Book of the Denver Westerners*, ed. by Arthur L. Campa, vol. XXI (1965), pp. 1–26.

Callon, Milton W., "The Montezuma Hot Springs Hotel," in *Brand Book of the Denver Westerners*, ed. by Raymond G. Colwell, vol. XV (1959), pp. 187–206.

Callon, Milton W., "The Sheriffs of San Miguel," *True West*, vol. 20, no. 6 (August 1973), pp. 6–13, 46–7.

Callon, Milton W., "The Tunnel of Death," *Frontier Times*, vol. 44, no. 4 (June-July 1970), pp. 24–5, 66–7.

Campa, Arthur L., "Hispanic Customs of the Southwest," in *Brand Book of the Denver Westerners*, vol XXI, ed. by Arthur L. Campa (Boulder, Colo., 1960), pp. 161–179.

Clark, Ann Nolan, "The House of the Dons," in *This Is New Mexico*, ed. by George Fitzpatrick (Santa Fe, 1948), pp. 16–26.

Cole, T. C., "Victory! For Las Vegas Baptists," *Baptist New Mexican* (July 1946), pp. 6–7.

Dlugach, Susan, "Church Takes Lead," *Las Vegas Daily Optic*, July 27, 1979.

Donnel, F. S., "When Las Vegas Was the Capital of New Mexico," *New Mexico Historical Review*, vol. 8, no. 4 (Oct. 1933), pp. 265–272.

"The First One," *Southwest Churchman* (Jan. 1950), pp. 5, 8.

Gillespie, Pat, "The Fire Queens," *New Mexico Magazine*, vol. 44, no. 1 (Jan. 1966), pp. 3–5, 36.

Hollenberger, F. X., "The Indian Days at Las Vegas," *Las Vegas Centennial* (Las Vegas, 1935), pp. 18–20.

"The Hot Springs of Las Vegas," *The Daily Graphic*, vol. XXVII (April 1882).

Ivers, Louise Harris, "The Hotel Castaneda, Las Vegas, New Mexico," *New Mexico Architecture*, vol. 16, no. 5–6 (May-June 1974), pp. 19–24.

Ivers, Louise Harris, "The Pride of Las Vegas," *New Mexico Architecture*, vol. 12, no. 3–4 (March-April 1970), pp. 15–17.

Knowlton, Clark, "The Town of Las Vegas Community Land Grant...,"*Journal of the West,* vol. XIX, no. 3 (July 1980), pp. 12–21.

Lancaster, Harry, "Las Vegas Builds on the Past," *New Mexico Magazine,* vol. 53, no. 9 (Sept. 1975), pp. 10–17.

"Las Vegas," *Miner and Manufacturer,* vol. V, no. 6 (June 1904), pp. 9–37.

"Las Vegas Railway and Power Company," *Street Railway Journal,* vol. 29, no. 4 (1907), pp. 130–134.

Laumbach, Verna, "Las Vegas before 1850," *New Mexico Historical Review,* vol. 8, no. 4 (Oct. 1933), pp. 241–264.

Leach, Leah, "Penitentes and Politics," *Las Vegas Daily Optic,* July 27, 1979.

"Leonard Hoskins Post 24, American Legion," *Annual Cowboys Reunion, Souvenir Program* (Las Vegas, 1942), p. 9.

Lux, William, "Land Grant Problems," *Las Vegas Daily Optic,* July 27, 1979.

McGuire, Sandra, and others, "Las Vegas Newspapers," *Las Vegas Daily Optic,* March 7, 1973.

Olsen, Michael, "Agriculture in 1900," *Las Vegas Daily Optic,* July 27, 1979.

"Palace of Frontier Grandeur," *New Mexico Magazine,* vol XXVII, no. 11 (Nov. 1959).

Paul, Richard, "First Cowboy Reunion," *Las Vegas Daily Optic,* July 27, 1979.

Perrigo, Lynn I., "The Eminence of Las Vegas in the Territorial Period," *Las Vegas Daily Optic,* July 27, 1979.

Perrigo, Lynn I., "Historical Review," *Las Vegas Daily Optic,* August 13, 1976.

Pullen, Clarence, in *Harper's Weekly,* "A Ranch among the Clouds," vol. XXXIV, no. 1750 (July 5, 1890); "The Las Vegas Hot Springs," vol XXXIV, no. 1749 (June 28, 1890); "Scenes about Las Vegas," vol XXXIV, no. 1751 (July 12, 1890).

Rasch, Philip J., "Dave Rudabaugh, Gunman," *Real West,* vol. 166, no. 22 (Nov. 1979), pp. 17–20, 47–8, 62.

Redden, Gail, "First Masonic Meeting," *Las Vegas Daily Optic,* July 27, 1979.

Rendon, Gabino, "La Corrida de Toros in Las Vegas," *New Mexico. Folklore Record,* vol. IV (1949–50), p. 23.

Riggs, Arthur S., "Hewett, the Realist," *So Live the Works of Men,* ed. by Donald D. Brand and Fred E. Harvey (Albuquerque,

1959), pp. 35-42.
Rodrigues, Raymond, "The Blackest Day for Texas," Santa Fe *New Mexican*, Jan. 14, 1973.
Rosenbaum, Robert J., "Las Gorras Blancas of San Miguel County," Renato Ronaldo and others, *Chicano: The Evolution of a People* (Minneapolis, 1973), pp. 128-136.
Roybal, Paul, "Republican Politics," *Las Vegas Daily Optic*, July 27, 1979.
Schlesinger, Andrew B., "Las Gorras Blancas, 1889-1891," *Journal of Mexican American History*, vol. 1, no. 2 (Spring 1971), pp. 87-143.
Schoonmaker, Rodney, "The Strange Story of Giovanni," Santa Fe *New Mexican*, Dec., 14, 1931.
Simmons, Marc, "On the Trail of the Comancheros," *New Mexico Magazine*, vol. 39, no. 16 (May 1961), p. 30.
Shirley, Lyna, "Young Movie Industry," *Las Vegas Daily Optic*, July 27, 1979.
Silva, Richard, "Legislature Creates University," *Las Vegas Daily Optic*, July 27, 1979.
Simpson, Audrey, "Gateway to Conquest," *New Mexico Magazine*, vol. 46, no. 10 (Oct. 1968), pp. 18-19.
Vigil, Sister Carmelita, "Early Mission Service," *Las Vegas Daily Optic*, July 27, 1979.
Vigil, Maurilio E., "Vegans Have Distinctive Political Role," *Las Vegas Daily Optic*, July 27, 1979.
Vigil, Veronica, "Local Publishing Company Renewed," *Las Vegas Daily Optic*, August 6, 1979.
Walter, Paul A. F., "A Half Century of Achievement," *So Live the Works of Men*, ed. by Donald D. Brand and Paul E. Harvey (Albuquerque, 1959), pp. 43-48.
Walter, Paul A. F., "Octaviano Ambrosio Larrazolo," *New Mexico Historical Review*, vol. VII, no. 2 (April 1932), pp. 97-104.
White, Aurora Lucero, "Folkways and Fiestas," *This Is New Mexico*, ed. by George Fitzpatrick (Santa Fe, 1948), pp. 260-265.
Winston, Steve, "Moonshine Once Lively Industry," *Albuquerque Journal*, Nov. 18, 1979.
Works Progress Administration, "Spanish Baptismal Customs," *El Palacio*, vol. XLIX, no. 3. (March 1942), pp. 59-62.

Theses and Research Papers

Anonymous, "The Penitente Brotherhood" (Ms., Carnegie Libra-

ry, n. d.).
Arellano, Anselmo, "Don Ezekiel C. de Baca and the Politics of San Miguel County" (Thesis, New Mexico Highlands University, 1975).
Bachicha, Tony, "The Penitentes of New Mexico" (Ms., Carnegie Library, 1976).
Barker, S. Omar, "Hermit of the Mountain" (Bound ms., Carnegie Public Library, 1949).
Beimer, Dorothy S., "Pioneer Physicians in Las Vegas, New Mexico" (Bound ms., both local libraries, n. d.).
Bohme, Frederick D., "A History of Italians in New Mexico" (Dissertation, University of New Mexico, 1958).
Brown, Linda, "Electric Street Car" (Ms., Public Service Co., Las Vegas, n. d.).
Emrick, Lois, "Valmora: The Story of an Institution" (Thesis, New Mexico Highlands University, 1962).
Fitzgerald, James M., "The Development of Las Vegas, 1920–1930" (Thesis, New Mexico Highlands University, 1952).
Fulgenzi, Mary A., "Bits of History of Nuestra Senora de Los Dolores de Las Vegas" (Ms., Carnegie Public Library, 1935).
Gard, David M., "History of Public Service Company of New Mexico" (Ms., Public Service Co., Las Vegas, 1966).
Giese, Dale F., "Social Life at Fort Union, New Mexico, in the 1880s" (Thesis, New Mexico Highlands University, 1964).
Goldstein, Richard Lee, "New Mexico Outlaws Reported in the Weekly *New Mexican* from 1865 to 1885" (Thesis, New Mexico Highlands University, 1968).
Grant, Clinton, "Law and Order in Las Vegas during the Territorial Days" (Ms., New Mexico Highlands University, n.d.).
Gray, Seth B., Jr., "A Historical Sketch of Montezuma" (Bound ms., Carnegie Public Library, n.d.).
Hernandez, Andres, "Origin of the Names of the Streets in the Town of Las Vegas, New Mexico" (Bound ms., both local libraries, 1954).
Howell, Peter S., "The Summer of 1890: The People's Party" (Carnegie Library, ms., 1974).
Hummel, Sister Patricia, S. L., "The Effects the Frontier Had on the Missionary and the Missionary Had on the Frontier" (Thesis, New Mexico Highlands University, 1969).
Johnson, Claude E., "The Municipal Government of the City of Las Vegas for the Year 1909" (Thesis, New Mexico Nor-

mal University, 1935).
Knowlton, Clark S., "The Town of Las Vegas Community Land Grant" (Ms., 1978).
LeGault, Dorothy Lee, "Footlights in the Foothills" (Thesis, New Mexico Highlands University, 1971).
Lucas, W. J., "Why Fort Union" (Ms., New Mexico Highlands University, n.d.).
Malone, Patrick F., "Periodicos Hispanos en Nuevo Mexico desde 1834 y Observaciones Historicas" (Thesis, New Mexico Highlands University, 1971).
Martinez, Edward Eloy, "Los Hermanos Penitentes" (Bound ms., both local libraries, 1955).
McMillan, Myrtle, "History of the Growth of Education in Las Vegas, New Mexico" (Thesis, New Mexico Normal University, 1935).
Montano, Patricio M., "Observations of the Penitentes" (Carnegie Library, 1968).
Moore, Ruth, "St. Paul's Episcopal Church" (Ms., c/o Mrs. J. D. W. Veeder, n.d.).
Mosley, Marion, "Las Vegas before the University" (Bound ms., both local libraries, 1948).
Murphy, Michael M., "A History of the Pecos Missions, 1540–1834" (Thesis, New Mexico Highlands University, 1968).
Nichols, Landon, "The History of the Las Vegas Municipal Airport" (Thesis, New Mexico Highlands University, 1965).
Olivas, Arthur, "Montezuma's Revenge . . . "(Bound Ms., New Mexico Highlands University, 1973).
Otero, Miguel A., "Events of 1879–1882" (Ms., Carnegie Library, n.d.).
Parker, Newman R., "Survey of the Municipal Government of the City of Las Vegas, New Mexico, for the Year 1908" (Thesis, New Mexico Normal University, 1931).
Perrigo, Lynn I., compiler, American History Seminar: Chapters in the History of Las Vegas; containing Clinton Grant, Las Vegas to 1846; Fred G. Martinez, The Jesuits in New Mexico and the Revista Catolica; Patrick F. Baca, Prominent Facts in the History of the Immaculate Conception Parish, Las Vegas, New Mexico; William A. Cordova, History of the Presbyterian Church; Frutoso Lopez, History of Emmanuel Lutheran Church; Wm. A. Gerdeman, The Hermit; Phillip Schroeder, The Millenium Has Come; Brantley C. Nelson, The Montezuma; Robert M. Olson, El Por-

venir (Bound mss., both local libraries, 1948–9).

Perrigo, Lynn I., compiler, American History Seminar: Papers on Local History; containing, Joe Aldaz, A Study of New Mexico Rough Riders with Emphasis on the Cowboys Reunion; Jane Morgan, A History of Highlands University Buildings; Kenneth L. Strate, History of the E. Romero Hose and Fire Company (Bound mss., both local libraries, 1961).

Perrigo, Lynn I., compiler, Historical Methods Seminar: Las Vegas in the 1880s; containing Joe E. Boettcher, Las Vegas from November, 1879, to November, 1880; D. I. Galindo, The Related Events of the Year 1880; William A. Cordova, *Las Vegas Daily Gazette*, 1881; Elmer Henry, What Happened in Las Vegas in 1881, from the *Las Vegas Gazette*; Clinton Grant, The Optic's Las Vegas of 1882; Joe L. Lujan, A Collection of Facts from the *Las Vegas Daily Optic* of 1883; James E. Bell, A History of Las Vegas, New Mexico, in 1883; Amy Lyster, Las Vegas in 1884; Roscoe T. Lauderdale, News Items Taken from the *Daily Optic* for the Year 1885; Frutoso Lopez, A History of Las Vegas during 1886; Atilano Valencia, Improvements and Institutions of Las Vegas in 1886; Robert C. Nuse, The Growth of Las Vegas in 1887; Patrick F. Baca, A History of Las Vegas from April 15, 1887, to April 7, 1888; Roy W. Tolliver, Historical Events of Las Vegas from the *Las Vegas Daily Optic* for the Year 1888; Frederick G. Martinez, A Chapter in the Early History of Las Vegas, New Mexico, from La Voz del Pueblo, 1890–1891 (Bound mss., both local libraries, 1948–1949).

Perrigo, Lynn I., compiler, History Seminar, Papers on Local History; containing Jon B. Montgomery, The Birth of a Monument; Leonila P. Duran, Los Penitentes (Bound mss., both local libraries, 1962).

Perrigo, Lynn I., compiler, History Seminar Papers on New Mexico; containing Diana Chavez, Spanish Wedding Customs (Bound mss., both local libraries, 1954).

Perrigo, Lynn I., compiler, History Seminar: Papers on the Southwest; containing Sister Mary Caroline Caffrey, S.C., A Brief History of Catholic Sisterhoods in Las Vegas; Reynoldo Crespin, San Miguel del Bado; Deborah Shillinglaw, Senator A. A. Jones and the Frontier (Bound mss., both local libraries, 1963).

Perrigo, Lynn I., compiler, History Seminar: Papers on the Southwest; containing Carlos J. Craig, The Penitentes: David King, White Caps; Byron C. Lewis, Vislumbres de Nuevo Mexico; Kathryn Ramsey, Adventure and Fulfillment in the Southwest (Bound mss., both local libraries, 1965).

Perrigo, Lynn I., compiler, History Seminar: Papers on Las Vegas and Highlands University; containing Anselmo Arellano, Vicente Silva and the White Caps: James A. Pollock, New Mexico Normal University, 1893–1902; Benito Martinez and Marian Mosley, Growth of the Normal University, 1910–1938; George F. Adelo, Normal University Athletics, 1910–1920; Nada Henry, The Physical Plant, NMHU, 1898–1948 (Bound mss., both local libraries, 1968).

Perrigo, Lynn I., "Concerning the Plaza" (Bound mss., both local libraries, 1972).

Perrigo, Lynn I., "The Methodist Church: A Historical Pageant" (Bound ms., both local libraries, 1954).

Perrigo, Lynn I., "The Original Las Vegas, 1835–1935" (Bound ms., both local libraries, 1975).

Price, Hugh, "A History of New Mexico Normal University" (Thesis, New Mexico Normal University, 1931).

Quintana, Patricio G., "The Pettit Documents" (Thesis, New Mexico Highlands University, 1958).

Rieniets, Thomas H., "A History of Montezuma Hot Springs, Hotels, and Bathhouses, 1847–1937" (Thesis, New Mexico Highlands University, 1966).

Roberts, Lucien E., "The Penitentes in Court" (Bound ms., New Mexico Highlands University, 1957).

Rutledge, Ada Blanche, "Critical Analysis and Calendar of Las Vegas *Optic*, Las Vegas, New Mexico, November, 1885, December 1885, and January, 1887" (Thesis, New Mexico Normal University, 1934).

Salazar, David R., "Las Gorras Blancas" (Ms., Carnegie Library, n. d.).

Sarabia, Luis, "Mexican Administration of New Mexico, 1822–1824" (Thesis, New Mexico Highlands University, 1970).

Schufle, J. A., "Fragments from the Stream of Time" (Bound ms., both local libraries, 1968).

Schufle, J. A., "Preparing the Way" (Bound ms., both local libraries, 1970).

Skinner, Norman, "The Churches of Las Vegas" (Ms., Carnegie

Library, 1907).
Steere, Edward, "Fort Union" (Bound ms., New Mexico Highlands University, 1951).
Thatcher, Gladys, "The Origin and Development of the Las Vegas Hospital, 1883–1926" (Bound ms., New Mexico Highlands University, 1961).
Thompson, Lulu, and Audrey Simpson, "George Gifford, Grand Old Man of Storrie Lake" (Bound ms., Carnegie Public Library, 1958).
Vollmar, Edward R., S. J., "History of the Jesuit Colleges of New Mexico and Colorado, 1867–1919" (Thesis, St. Louis University, 1939).
Welch, Vernon E., "Las Vegas and the Adjacent Area during the Mexican Period" (Thesis, New Mexico Highlands University, 1950).
Wilson, James B., "The Agua Pura Co." (Bound ms., Public Service Co., Las Vegas, 1922).
Woodward, Dorothy, "The Penitentes of New Mexico" (Dissertation, University of New Mexico, 1935).
Yara, Robert, "Wool Business in New Mexico" (Ms., Carnegie Library, 1976).

Photographs, Maps, and Relics

Benevolent Protective Order of Elks, #408; photographs of Past Exalted Rulers, in lobby.
Beisman, H. E., Camp Luna Map, 1965 (District Court Office).
Bible, Lloyd, album of snapshots of local aviation.
Brown, W. E., and Clyde Arquero, Santa Fe Trail Map (City Museum).
Burke, Father James T., negatives of photographs of early Las Vegas.
Camp Luna, Post Engineer, Camp Luna Map, 1943 (c/o J. B. Clark).
City Museum, photographs and relics of early Las Vegas.
City Museum, Rough Riders' photographs and mementos.
Cochran, Harold, Photographs of Storrie Project.
East Las Vegas Fire Department, photographs (Fire Station).
Kihlberg, Frank O., Plat of Las Vegas in 1868 (c/o H. E. Beisman).
Los Artesanos, Collection of Photographs.
Masonic Temple, photographs of Past Masters, in hall.
McGrath, Tom, collection of photographs and relics of Las Vegas,

City Museum.
Morley's Map of New Mexico, 1873 (Arrott Collection, N. M. Highlands University).
Morrison, G. E., Map of the Plaza, 1915 (c/o H. E. Beisman).
Museum of New Mexico, Photographic Archives, Las Vegas file.
Naylor, Alvin, collection of rodeo photographs.
New Mexico Highlands University, Donnelly Library Collection.
New Mexico State Records Center, photographs of Camp Luna.
Our Lady of Sorrows, photographs of Las Vegas printed in church *Bulletins*, 1965-1973.
Our Lady of Sorrows Parish, collection of photographs.
Photo Survey of Las Vegas, collection.
Public Service Company, Las Vegas, file of pictures.
Rex Studio, collection of glass negatives, Las Vegas, 1890-1925, donated to the State Museum.
Rosenwald, Emanuel, Papers, including album of snapshots, 1900-1920 (Special Collections, University of New Mexico).
Sanford Insurance Maps, Special Collections, University of New Mexico.
Stoner, J. J., Birds' Eye View of Las Vegas, N. M. (Lithograph, Milwaukee, 1882).
United States Department of the Interior, General Land Office, Berthrong Map of New Mexico, 1912 (City Museum).
United States Department of the Interior, General Land Office, Map of the Johnson Survey of the Las Vegas Land Grant, 1899-1900 (District Court Office).

Interviews

Cooke, Phillip St. George, with Lehn G. Englehart, about movie making, Feb. 11, 1970 (Historical Film Collection, State Records Center).
Hernandez, Andres S., This They Said (Bound ms., both local libraries, 1955).
McCain, Alonzo Earl, The Recollections and Memories of Ludwig Ilfeld (Bound ms., both local libraries, 1959).
Perrigo, Lynn I., compiler, Historical Methods Seminar: Interviews with Pioneers; containing William E. Cheatham with Jacobo Lujan, Frederick G. Martinez with Josefita Gonzales de Montoya, James E. Bell with Byron Truman Mills, Noe B. Lucero, with Senior Citizens, Patrick Baca with Msgr. Rabeyrolle, Larry Deutsch with The Rev. Gabino Rendon, Bevington Reed with Rodney B. Schoonmaker, Roscoe T.

Lauderdale with William Hopkins Stapp, Roy W. Tolliver with William Hopkins Stapp, and Elmer Henry with Jim Whitmore (Bound mss., both local libraries, 1948–1949).

Perrigo, Lynn I., compiler, History Seminar: Papers on the Southwest, containing Maria Elba C. de Baca, Reminiscences of Senior Citizens (Bound mss., both local libraries, 1963).

Perrigo, Lynn I., compiler, History Seminar: Papers on the Southwest, containing Bob McQuarie, interview with Manuel Otero Henriquez; Dolores Trujillo, Speaking of Las Vegas; Loretta Lesperance Estrada, Memories of Two Pioneers (Bound mss., both local libraries, 1965).

Perrigo, Lynn I., compiler, History Seminar: Papers on Las Vegas and Highlands University, containing Steve Carter, The Leroy Wicks Story (Bound mss., both local libraries, 1968).

Perrigo, Lynn I., interviews with:

Angel, Joe, District Judge and counsellor to the Land Grant Board.

Baca, Eduardo F., life-long resident and merchant, now deceased.

Bacharach, Herman, son of eminent merchant, now deceased.

Barker, S. Omar, author and early student at the Normal University.

Beisman, Henry, civil engineer since the 1920s.

Beltz, Wilbur, printer and trainee at Camp Luna during World War I.

Bibb, Mrs. Mabel, widow of early rodeo champion.

Bible, Lloyd, proprietor of private aviation service since the 1930s.

Brown, J. B., rancher, business proprietor since 1916, and rodeo participant.

Burke, Father James T., former O.L.S. pastor and a specialist in local history.

Charlton, Claude, business proprietor who as a youth participated in local activities of the 1930s.

Clark, J. B., developer of Luna Linda Estates.

Comstock, Mrs. Edward S., erstwhile "Harvey Girl."

Conway, Thomas W., in Santa Fe, early supervisor of Storrie Project, now deceased.

De Aragon, Ray John, teacher, publisher, and historian.

Di Domenico, Nick, former teacher and coach in the I. C. School.

Egan, Evelyn, co-proprietor of the Johnson Memorial Mortuary.

Encinias, Luis, teacher in Old Town in the 1930s and subsequently county superintendent.

Erb, William L., retired real estate and insurance agent, active in civic affairs since the 1920s.

Escudero, Epifanio, jeweler, in-law of the Romeros and great grandson of Albino Perez, Mexican governor.

Fish, William, retired Army officer, who drafted plans for Camp Luna buildings, 1942, now deceased.

Fulgenzi, Mary A., retired teacher of long experience in Old Town.

Goddard, G. A., manager of the Las Vegas Lumber Company in the former Exchange Hotel building, 1916–23 and 1929–59.

Gonzales, Fidel "Chief," former mortician, eminent civic leader and former mayor of Town and consolidated City.

Greer, Tom, former operator of a ranch as a tourist attraction in historic Glorieta Pass, now deceased.

Gross, Edward L., merchant, grandson of Jacob Gross, pioneer.

Guerin, Gene, early printer and long-time co-proprietor of food market in Old Town.

Kaemper, Elmer, retired utilities manager, now deceased.

Karelitz, Leon, attorney and specialist on the Land Grant.

Korte, John, merchant and secretary-treasurer of the Land Grant Board.

Lingnau, Ben W., Sr., mechanic in the Roundhouse in the 1920s and subsequently prominent rancher, merchant, and mayor.

Lopez, "Gillie," employee of Town Schools since 1947.

Marquez, George, retired postal employee and participant in local activities, now deceased.

McGrath, Tom, resident since 1900, erstwhile rancher, politician, and public employee, now deceased.

Moore, Sketchley, early druggist and later secretary of the company.

Naylor, Alvin, rancher and rodeo participant since 1916.

Noble, James V., of Santa Fe, erstwhile attorney in Las Vegas.

Pettit, David C., son of A. E. Pettit, deceased, both former proprietors of local abstracting service.

Reeve, Dr. Frank D., former professor at U.N.M. and author of volumes on New Mexico history, now deceased.

Shoemaker, Warren D., rancher, and rodeo promoter in the 1930s.

Sundt, Martin, former proprietor of local brick factory, and participant in campaign to apprehend Pancho Villa, now

deceased.
Taichert, Milton, prominent merchant since 1909, and trustee of the former Montefiore Congregation.
Tinker, Carol, civic leader and former legislator, who was a youthful participant in activities of the 1930s.
Van Sickle, N. G., retired railroad fireman and engineer, now deceased.
Veeder, Mrs. J.D.W., widow of early prominent attorney.
Wesner, Mrs. Frank J., resident since 1908 and clerk of First Baptist Church since 1955.
Wicks, Leroy S., former truck and bus proprietor and mayor of East Las Vegas.

Partially Pertinent Public Records

Cabeza de Baca, Luis Maria, Last Will and Testament (File, 103, U. S. Bureau of Land Management, Santa Fe).
Diputacion, Journals, 1828–1837 (U.S. Bureau of Land Management, Santa Fe).
Mexican Archives of New Mexico (State Records Center; Microfilm N.M. Highlands University), Rolls 1–42.
New Mexico, *Acts of the Legislative Assembly* (Santa Fe, 1880, 1893, 1903).
New Mexico, *Compiled Laws* (Santa Fe, 1897).
New Mexico, Corporation Classification, 1870–1911 (State Records Center).
New Mexico, Department of Public Welfare, *Biennial Report* (Santa Fe, 1940), and *Annual Report* (Santa Fe, 1947).
New Mexico National Guard, Adjutant General, Orders and Correspondence, 1904–1916, 1923–1935; Field Training Program, 1930–1935 (State Records Center).
New Mexico, *Statutes Annotated* (Denver, 1915, and Indianapolis, 1953).
New Mexico, *Report of the Governor* (Washington, D.C., 1902).
Pablo Montoya Land Grant, San Miguel County Deed Record Book A (Office of the County Clerk).
United States, Bureau of the Census,
  Seventh Census, 1850 (Washington, 1853);
  Ninth Census, 1870 (Washington, 1872);
  Tenth Census, Part I, 1880 (Washington, 1883);
  Eleventh Census, Part I, 1890 (Washington, 1895);
  Twelfth Census, Part I, 1900 (Washington, 1901);
  Twelfth Census, Vol. V, Part I, Agriculture (Washington,

1902);
Thirteenth Census, Vol. III (Washington, 1913);
Fourteenth Census, Vol. I (Washington, 1920);
Fourteenth Census, Vol. VI, Part 3, Agriculture (Washington, 1922);
Sixteenth Census, Vol. I (Washington, 1942);
Sixteenth Census, Vol. VI, Part III, Agriculture (Washington, 1942);
United States, Bureau of Mines, *Mineral Resources of the United States,* annually, 1882–1931 (Washington, 1883–1934), and *Minerals Yearbook, 1938* (Washington, 1938).
United States, *Statutes, 36 Cong., Sess. 1,* ch. 167 (Washington, 1960), Confirmation of Land Grants, pp. 71–2.
United States, War Department, *Confederate Victories in the Southwest,* compiled by Calvin Horn and Wm. S. Wallace (Albuquerque, 1961).
United States, War Department, *Union Army Operations in the Southwest; Final Victory,* compiled by Calvin Horn and Wm. S. Wallace (Albuquerque, 1961).

Partially Pertinent Books

Abert, James W. *Western America in 1846–1847,* John Galvin, ed. (San Francisco: 1966).
Abert's *New Mexico Report* (Albuquerque: 1962).
Adams, Samuel H. *The Harvey Girls* (New York: 1942).
Anderson, George B. *Illustrated History of New Mexico,* 3 vols. (Los Angeles: 1907).
Bailey, Lynn R. *Indian Slave Trade in the Southwest* (Los Angeles: 1966).
Balbas, Antonio, ed. *Recopilacion de Leyes de Las Indias* (Madrid: 1756).
Bancroft, Hubert Howe. *History of Arizona and New Mexico* (San Francisco: 1889; Albuquerque: 1962).
Bancroft, Hubert Howe. *History of the North Mexican States and Texas,* 2 vol. (San Francisco: 1884).
Barbour, Sister Richard Marie. *Light in Yucca Land* (Santa Fe: 1952).
Benavides' Memorial of 1630, translated by Peter P. Forrestal and edited by Cyprian Lynch (Washington: 1954).
Bennett, James A., *Forts and Forays,* ed. by Clinton E. Brooks and Frank D. Reeve (Albuquerque: 1948).
Bloom, Lansing B. *New Mexico in the Great War* (Santa Fe: 1927).

Bolton, Herbert E. *Coronado on the Turquoise Trail* (Albuquerque: 1949).
Boyd, E. *Popular Arts of Spanish New Mexico* (Santa Fe: 1974).
Bryant, K. L. *History of the Atchison, Topeka and Santa Fe Railway* (New York: 1974).
Burke, Rev. James T. *This Miserable Kingdom* (Las Vegas: 1973).
Campa, Arthur L. *Treasure of the Sangre de Cristos* (Norman, Okla.: 1963).
Chase, C. M. *New Mexico and Colorado in 1881* (Fort Davis, Texas: 1968).
Chavez, Fray Angelico, O.F.M. *Archives of the Archdiocese of Santa Fe 1628–1900* (Washington, D.C.: 1957).
Chavez, Fray Angelico. *Origins of New Mexico Families in the Spanish Colonial Period* (Santa Fe: 1954).
Clarke, Dwight L. *Stephen Watts Kearny, Soldier of the West* (Norman, Okla.: 1961).
Coan, Charles F. *The County Boundaries of New Mexico* (Santa Fe, 1965).
Coan, Charles F. *A History of New Mexico*, 3 vols. (Chicago: 1925).
Cockerell, T.D.A. *Recollections of a Naturalist* (Boulder, Colo.: n.d.).
Colton, Ray C. *The Civil War in the Western Territories* (Norman, Okla.: 1959).
Cooke, Philip St. George. *The Conquest of New Mexico and California* (Oakland, Calif.: 1952; Albuquerque: 1964).
Cooke, Philip St. George, and others. *Exploring Southwestern Trails, 1846–1854*, ed. by Ralph P. Bieber (Glendale, Calif.: 1938).
Curtis, Edward S. *The North American Indian*, vols. 1 and 19 (New York: 1907, 1970).
Davis, William W. H. *El Gringo, or New Mexico and Her People* (Santa Fe: 1938).
Denslow, Ray V. *Transactions of the Missouri Lodge of Research* (St. Louis: 1948).
Ellis, George F. *Bell Ranch As I Knew It* (Kansas City, Mo.: 1973).
Emmett, Chris. *Fort Union and the Winning of the Southwest* (Norman, Okla.: 1965).
Emory, Wm. H. *Lieutenant Emory Reports*, Ross Calvin, ed. (Albuquerque: 1951).
Falconer, Thomas. *Letters and Notes on the Texan Santa Fe Expedition, 1841–1842*, F. W. Hodge, ed. (New York. 1930).
Field, Matthew C. *Matt Field on the Santa Fe Trail*, John E. Sunder,

ed. (Norman, Okla.: 1960).
Fitzpatrick, George, ed. *This Is New Mexico* (Albuquerque: 1962).
Gibson, George R. *Journal of a Soldier under Kearny and Doniphan, 1846–1847*, Ralph P. Bieber, ed. (Glendale, Calif.: 1935).
Gregg, Josiah. *Commerce of the Prairies*, R. G. Thwaites, ed. (Cleveland, Ohio: 1905); ed. by Max L. Moorhead (Norman, Okla.: 1954).
Grivas, Theodore. *Military Governments in California, with a Chapter on Their Prior Use in Louisiana, Florida, and New Mexico* (Glendale, Calif.: 1963).
Hafen, LeRoy R. *The Overland Mail, 1849–1869* (Berkeley and Los Angeles: 1952).
Hafen, LeRoy R., and Carl Coke Rister. *Western America* (Englewood Cliffs, N.J.: 1950, 1957).
Haley, James Evetts. *Charles Goodnight, Cowman and Plainsman* (Boston: 1936).
Hall, Martin H. *Sibley's New Mexico Campaign* (Austin, Texas, 1960).
Hammond, George P., ed. *Onate, Colonizer of New Mexico*, 2 vols. (Albuquerque, 1953).
Hammond, George P., and Agapito Rey. *The Rediscovery of New Mexico, 1580–1594* (Albuquerque, 1966).
Harwood, Thomas. *History of New Mexico Spanish and English Missions of the Methodist Episcopal Church from 1850–1910*, 2 vols. (Albuquerque, 1910).
Henderson, Alice C. *Brothers of Light* (New York, 1937).
Hertzog, Peter. *A Directory of New Mexico Outlaws* (Santa Fe, n.d.).
The Historic Preservation Program for New Mexico. 2 vols. (Santa Fe, 1973).
Hollister, Ovando J. *Boldly They Rode* (Lakewood, Colo., 1949).
Holmes, Jack E. *Politics in New Mexico* (Albuquerque, 1967).
Horka-Follick, Larayne Ann. *Los Hermanos Penitentes* (Los Angeles, 1969).
Horn, Calvin. *Climbing a Rainbow* (Albuquerque, 1966).
Hoyt, Henry F. *A Frontier Doctor*, ed. by D. B. Nunis, Jr. (Chicago, 1979).
Inman, Henry. *The Old Santa Fe Trail* (New York, 1897).
Johnston, Abraham R., and others. *Marching with the Army of the West, 1846–1848*, Ralph P. Bieber, ed. (Glendale, Calif., 1936).
Keleher, William A. *The Fabulous Frontier* (Albuquerque, 1945,

1962).
Keleher, William A. *Troublous Times in New Mexico* (Santa Fe, 1952).
Kendall, George Wilkins. *Narrative of the Texan Santa Fe Expedition* (New York, 1844; Austin, Texas, 1935).
Kenner, Charles L. *A History of New Mexican-Plains Indian Relations* (Norman, Okla., 1969).
Kidder, Alfred V. *Southwestern Archeology* (New Haven, Conn., 1924, 1962).
Klasner, Lily, with Eve Ball. *My Girlhood Among Outlaws* (Tucson, Ariz., 1972).
Kupper, Winifred. *The Golden Hoof: The Story of the Sheep Industry of the Southwest* (New York, 1945).
Lamar, Howard R. *The Far Southwest, 1846–1919; A Territorial History* (New Haven, Conn., 1966: New York, 1970).
Larson, Robert W. *New Mexico Populism* (Boulder, Colo., 1974).
Larson, Robert W. *New Mexico's Quest for Statehood* (Albuquerque, 1968).
Leonard, Olen E. *The Role of the Land Grant . . . of a Spanish American Village in New Mexico* (Baton Rouge, La., 1943).
Long, Margaret. *The Santa Fe Trail* (Denver, 1954).
Loomis, Noel. *The Texan-Santa Fe Pioneers* (Norman, Okla., 1958).
Loomis, Noel M., and Abraham Nasater. *Pedro Vial and the Roads to Santa Fe* (Norman, Okla., 1967).
Magoffin, Susan Shelby. *Down the Santa Fe Trail into New Mexico*, ed. by Stella M. Drumm (New Haven, Conn., 1926).
Marshall, James L. *Santa Fe: The Railroad That Built an Empire* (New York, 1945).
McCall, G. A. *New Mexico in the 1850s: A Military View*, ed. by Robert W. Frazer (Norman, Okla., 1968).
McGregor, John C. *Southwestern Archeology* (New York, 1941).
McHugh, Tom. *The Time of the Buffalo* (New York, 1972).
Meinig, C. W. *Southwest: Three Peoples in Geographic Change, 1600-1700* (New York, 1971).
Meline, James F. *Two Thousand Miles on Horseback: Santa Fe and Back* (New York, 1867; Albuquerque, 1966).
Mix, Olive (Stokes), with Eric Heath. *The Fabulous Tom Mix* (Englewood Cliffs, N. J., 1957).
Moncus, H. H. *Prairie Schooner Pirates* (New York, 1963).
Monroe, Harriet. *John Wellborn Root, Planner of Cities* (Boston, 1921).
Moody, Ralph. *Stagecoach West* (New York, 1967).

Myers, John M. *Doc Holliday* (New York, 1955).
New Mexico, Adjutant General. *History, National Guard of New Mexico, 1606–1963* (Santa Fe, 1964).
New Mexico Blue Book (Santa Fe, 1915).
Otera, Miguel A. *My Nine Years as Governor of the Territory of New Mexico, 1897–1906,* ed. by Marion Dargan (Albuquerque, 1940).
Otero, Nina. *Old Spain in Our Southwest* (New York, 1936).
Pearce, T. M., ed. *New Mexico Place-Name Dictionary* (Albuquerque, 1949–1950).
Perrigo, Lynn I. *The American Southwest* (New York, 1971, Albuquerque, 1975).
Perrigo, Lynn I. *The Rio Grande Adventure: A History of New Mexico* (Chicago, 1964).
Pino, Pedro B., and others. *Noticias Historicas y Estadisticas . . . de Nuevo Mexico* (Mexico, D. F., 1849; Las Vegas, N. M., 1972).
Prince, L. Bradford. *Historical Sketches of New Mexico* (New York, 1883).
Prince, L. Bradford. *New Mexico's Struggle for Statehood* (Santa Fe, 1910).
Read, Benjamin. *Illustrated History of New Mexico,* translated by Eleuterio Baca (Santa Fe, 1912).
Reeve, Frank D. *History of New Mexico,* 3 vols. (New York, 1961).
Richmond, R. W., and R. W. Murdock. *A Nation Moving West* (Lincoln, Neb., 1966).
Robertson, M. S. *Rodeo* (Berkeley and Los Angeles, Calif., 1961).
Roosevelt, Theodore. *The Rough Riders* (New York, 1904).
Ryden, Hope. *Mustangs* (New York, 1972).
Sanchez, George I. *Forgotten People* (Albuquerque, 1940, 1967).
Smith, Alfred, ed. *Whispering Pines* (Las Vegas, 1926).
Sprague, Marshall. *The Great Gates* (Boston, 1964).
Stanley, F. (Crocchiola). *The Civil War in New Mexico* (Denver, 1960).
Stanley, F. *Dave Rudabough, Border Ruffian* (Denver, 1961).
Stanley, F. *Fort Union, New Mexico* (Denver, 1953).
Stoney, Rt. Rev. James M. *Lighting the Candle: The Episcopal Church on the Upper Rio Grande* (Santa Fe, 1961).
Taylor, Morris F. *First Stagecoach West* (Albuquerque, 1971).
Thomas, Alfred B. *After Coronado: Spanish Exploration Northeast of New Mexico, 1696–1727* (Norman, Okla., 1935, 1966).
Thomas, Alfred B. *The Plains Indians and New Mexico* (Albu-

querque, 1940).
Turner, Henry S. *The Original Journals of Henry Smith Turner ...,
1846–1847*, ed. by D. L. Clarke (Norman, Okla., 1966).
Twitchell, Ralph E. *The History of the Military Occupation of New
Mexico from 1846 to 1851* (Denver, 1909).
Twitchell, Ralph E. *The Leading Facts of New Mexico History, five
volumes* (Cedar Rapids, Iowa, 1911–1917; Albuquerque,
1963).
Twitchell, Ralph E. *The Spanish Archives of New Mexico, two
volumes* (Cedar Rapids, Iowa, 1914).
Underhill, Ruth M. *Red Man's America* (Chicago, 1953).
United States Army, Corps of Topographical Engineers. *Notes of a
Military Reconnaissance*, by William H. Emory (Washington, D. C., 1848).
United States, Office of Indian Affairs. *The Official Correspondence
of James S. Calhoun* (Washington, D. C., 1915).
Vigil, Maurilio E. *Los Patrones: Profiles of Hispanic Political Leaders
in New Mexico* (Washington, D. C., 1980).
Walker, Henry P. *The Wagonmasters: High Plains Freighting* (Norman, Okla., 1966).
Waters, Lawrence L. *Steel Trails to Santa Fe* (Lawrence, Kansas,
1950).
Webb, James Josiah. *Adventures in the Santa Fe Trade, 1844–1847*,
ed. by Ralph P. Beiber (Glendale, Calif., 1931).
Weber, William A. *Theodore Dru Alison Cockerell, 1866–1948*
(Boulder, Colo., 1965).
Weigle, Marta. *Brothers of Light, ...* (Albuquerque, 1976).
Wentworth, Edward N. *America's Sheep Trails* (Ames, Iowa,
1948).
Westermeier, Clifford P. *Man, Beast, Dust: The Story of the Rodeo*
(Denver, 1947).
Westermeier, Clifford P. *Who Rush to Glory* (Caldwell, Ida., 1958).
Westphall, Victor. *The Public Domain in New Mexico, 1854–1891*
(Albuquerque, 1965).
Westphall, Victor. *Thomas Benton Catron and His Era* (Tucson,
Ariz., 1973).
White, William Allen. *The Autobiography of ...* (New York,
1946).
Whitford, William C. *The Colorado Volunteers in the Civil War*
(Denver, 1906; Glorieta, N.M., 1971).
Wislezenus, Adolphus. *Memoir of a Tour to Northern Mexico* (Albuquerque, 1969).

Works Progress Administration. *New Mexico: A Guide to the Colorful State* (New York, 1940).
Wright, Arthur A. *The Civil War in the Southwest* (Denver, 1964).

Partially Pertinent Pamphlets

Chavez, Fray Angelico, *The Old Faith and Old Glory, 1846-1946* (Santa Fe, 1946).
Drum, Ross, *Scenic 85 thru the Land of Enchantment* (Torrington, Wyo., 1955).
Grand Army of the Republic, *Roster, Department of New Mexico, 1916-1917* (Las Vegas, 1917).
McCarty, Frankie, *Land Grant Problems in New Mexico* (Albuquerque, 1969).
Mills, T. B., *New Mexico* (Las Vegas, 1889).
Stanley, F. (Crocchiola), *Giant in Lilliput: The Story of Donaciano Vigil* (Pampa, Texas, 1963).
State Planning Office, *New Mexico Historic Sites* (Santa Fe, 1967).
Tate, Bill, *The Penitentes of the Sangre de Cristos* (Truchas, N.M., 1968).
Utley, Robert M., *Fort Union National Monument, New Mexico* (Washington, D. C., 1962).
Weigle, Marta, *The Penitentes of the Southwest* (Santa Fe, 1970).

Partially Pertinent Articles

Barker, S. Omar, "The Penitentes," *Overland Monthly*, vol. 82, 1924, pp. 178-180.
Beck, Warren A., "The Penitentes of New Mexico," *Chicano: Evolution of a People* (Minneapolis, 1973), pp. 137-145.
Bloom, Lansing B., "Early Vaccination in New Mexico," in *Publications* of the New Mexico Historical Society, (Santa Fe), May, 1949.
Bloom, Lansing B., "Edgar Lee Hewett," in *So Live the Works of Men* ed. by Donald D. Brand and Fred E. Harvey (Albuquerque, 1959), pp. 13-34.
Bloom, Lansing B., "New Mexico under Mexican Administration," *Old Santa Fe*, vol. V, no. 1 (July 1913), pp. 3-49.
Bolton, Herbert E., "French Intrusions into New Mexico, 1749-1752," in *Pacific Ocean in History* (New York, 1917).
Burton, Bennett, "The Taos Rebellion," *Old Santa Fe*, vol. I, no. 2 (Oct. 1913), pp. 176-209.
Callon, Milton W., "Scouting the Utes," *True West*, vol. 16, no. 5 (May-June 1965), pp. 12-17, 52-55.

Chavez, Fray Angelico, "Early Settlements in the Mora Valley," *El Palacio*, vol. LXII, no. 11 (Nov. 1955), pp. 319–323.

Chavez, Fray Angelico, "The Penitentes of New Mexico," *New Mexico Historical Review*, vol. XXV, no. 4 (Oct. 1960), pp. 265–283.

Clark, Robert E., "The Pueblo Rights Doctrine in New Mexico," *New Mexico Historical Review*, vol. XXXV, no. 4 (Oct. 1960), pp. 265–283.

Edwards, George, "The Lost Highway Out of Santa Fe," Santa Fe *New Mexican*, July 21, 1974.

Frazer, Robert W., "Purveyors of Flour to the Army," *New Mexico Historical Review*, vol. XLVII, no. 3 (July 1972), pp. 213–238.

Greenleaf, Richard E., "Land and Water in Mexico and New Mexico, 1700–1821," *New Mexico Historical Review*, vol. XLVII, no. 2 (April 1972), pp. 85–107.

Herstrom, Guy M., "A Pygmy among Giants," in *Brand Book of the Denver Westerners*, vol. XV, ed. by Raymond G. Colwell (Boulder, Colo., 1960), pp. 235–278.

Jenkins, Myra Ellen, "The Diocese of New Mexico and Southwest Texas," *The Southwest Churchman*, vol. XIII, no. 3 (Dec. 1971), p. 5.

Kenner, Charles, "The Eastern New Mexico Frontier during the 1850s," in Renato Rosaldo and others, *Chicano: The Evolution of a People* (Minneapolis, 1973), pp. 114–122.

Kidder, Alfred V., "The Story of the Pueblo of Pecos," in *Papers of the School of American Research*, no. 44 (Santa Fe, 1951).

Libke, Aileen Stroud, "Magee's Money Eater," *Kiwanis Magazine* (Dec.-Jan. 1965-6), pp. 39–40, 86.

Rist, Martin, "Methodist Beginnings in New Mexico," Denver Posse of Westerners, *The 1967 Brand Book*, ed. by William D. Powell (Boulder, Colo., 1967), pp. 75–91.

Schufle, J. A., "The Young Cockerell," New Mexico Academy of Science, *Bulletin*, vol. XIV, no. 1 (June 1973), pp. 12–15.

Vollmar, E. R., S. J., "The First Jesuit School in New Mexico," *New Mexico Historical Review*, vol. 27, no. 3 (July 1952), pp. 27–30.

Index

Active Boosters Club, 175, 193
Agriculture, 1, 5, 34, 39, 40, 126, 128, 203
Agua Pura Co., 28, 45, 96, 191
Airports, 59, *60*, 61, 188
Alcaldes, 1, 12, 13, 22, 67, 101-103, 105, 121, 185
Alcoholism Center, 203
Allen, James, 73
Allison, Clay, 77
American Legion, 56, 93, 175, 203; Red Cross, 203
Ancient Order of United Workmen, 173
Angel, Frank, 202; Joe, vi, 193, *194;* Paula, 68
Anglos, 35, 69, 81, 89, 93, 106, 112, 117, 129, 143, 145, 167, 169, 183
Annin, John A., 135, 168, 169
Anton Chico, 3
Apache Indians, 2, 31, 158
Apodoca, Jerry, 191
Aragon, John, 202; Ray John de, vi
Arango, Doroteo, 53
Archebeque, Antonio, 93
Archeology, 1, 2, 141, 149
Architecture, 65, 140, 171, 207
Armijo, Luis, 93, 95; Manuel, 167
Arrott, James W., 192
Arts, 27, 52, 133, 151, 203
Atchison, Topeka & Santa Fe Railroad, 17-20, 27, 36-39, 62, 87, 175, 183, 189, 197, 199
Atkins, F. A., 43, 77
Augustini, Giovanni Maria, 162, 164
Austin, "Tex," 55
Automobiles, 34, 39, 56-58, 181, 199

Aviation, 48, 59-61

Baca, Eduardo F., 46; Chata, 69; Elmo, v, 196; Federico, 93; Jose Albino, 160; Rumauldo, 19, 133; y Sandoval, Francisco, 46
Baca's Folly, *18,* 19
Bands, brass, 27, 55, 178
Bank of Las Vegas, 27
Banks, 26-27, 36, 62
Baptist churches, 145, 171; College, 147
Barker, Elsa, vi; S. Omar, vi, 143
Barr, John W., 93
Baseball, 45, 141, 155, 166, 180, 203
Beck, Preston, 125
Becknell, William, 3
Bell, Montgomery, 168, *169*
Bell Ranch, 4, 35
Bent, Charles, 13
Bibb, Dee, 56, 183
Bible, Lloyd, 62
Bicycles, 181
Billy the Kid, 22, 73, 75
Blanchard, Charles, 8, 31
Borne, "Dutchy," 73
Boyle, "Sport," 73
Boy Scouts, 175, 182, *183,* 203
Brewery, 27
Brick kiln, 27
Bridges, 21, 81, 83, 87, 89, 123
Brown, "Hoodoo," 71-72; J. B., 183; Wm. T., 43, 63
Browne and Manzanares Co., 25
Browne, Fred W., 121; M. W., 140
Buddecke, William, 33
Buffalo: Hall, 8, *69;* hunting, 7
Bursom, Holm A., 90

237

Business and Professional
    Women's Club, 175

Calfee, D. W., 170
Callon, Milton W., 48
Camfield, D. A., 124-126
Campbell, W. C., 123
Campfire Girls, 183
Camp Luna, 53-54, 187, 189, 193
Carnegie Public Library, 147-148
Carpenter, Lizzie, 175
Carriage factory, 27
Carrillo, Leo, 51
Carroon, Frank, 145-146
Carson, Joe, 71; Kit, 17
Carter, Jimmy, 205
Cartwright Case, 130
Castaneda Hotel, 27, 43, 57, 86
Castello, Joseph, 71
Caston, Theodore, 71
Catholic churches, 1, 137, 147,
    163, 165; Knights of
    America, 172
Catron, Thomas B., 35, 125, 131,
    154
Cattle, 35, 118, 198
C. de Baca, Alvar Nunez, 5;
    Ezekiel, 90, *91*, 92, 115, 117,
    131; Fabiola, 143; Luis
    Maria, 5, 101, 105, 160;
    Manuel, 85
Centennial, The, 182-184
Chacon, Eusebio, 117
Chain stores, 63, 202
Chamber of Commerce, 39, 51-
    52, 63, 99, 128, 175, 190,
    191, 192, 193, 195, 198
Chaperito, 74
Charities, 37, 63-64, 161,
    188-189
Charles Ilfeld Co., 9, 11, 25, 35
Charles, Prince, 196
Chautauqua, 51
Chavez, George, 134; Manuel, 93
Chicanos, 199, 201, 205, 206,
    207
Chinamen, 167-168
Christian Brothers, 136-137
Churches, 1, 69, 163, 164, 168-
    172, 175, 177

Circuses, 178, *179*
City Hall, 82, 139
Clark, "Stu," 146
Climate, 43, 198, 205, 207
Cockerell, T.D.A., 142
Colorado Telephone Co., 31
Comancheros, 7
Comanches, 2, 7
Commercial Club, 39, 45, 55, 56,
    88, 97, 110, 122, 147, 175,
    176
Comstock, W. H., 123
Congregational Academy, 137,
    138, 139, 148
Connelly, Henry, 9, 16, 105
Consolidation, municipal, 81,
    89, 97, 117, 193
Contemporary observations, 204-
    207
Continental Airlines, 61
Conway, Thomas W., 51, *60*,
    126-128
Cook, J. M., 147
Cortez, Manuel, 14
Coudert, J. M., 127, 162
Court of Private Land Claim, 124
Courthouses, 67, 81, 108, 110
Cowboy Band, 55, 178; Hall of
    Fame, 188
Crime, 67, 71-74, 82-85, 96, 203,
    205
Crimestoppers, 203
Crisis Center, 203
Curley, Jack, 46

Dances, 8, 23, 55, 69, 166, 169,
    176, 178, 183
Daughters of the American
    Revolution, 56
Davidson, George, 73
Davis, George, 74; S. B., 23
De La Salle Institute, 137-138
Delgado, Lorenzo, *60*, 88, 93, 94,
    95, 123
Depressions, 25, 37, 62-63, 129,
    146, 155
Design Review Board, 196, 203
Disciples of Christ, 171
District Court, 71, 81, 94-95,
    107, 108, 109, 110, 115,
    121, 124-125

Dold, Andres, 8
Donahue, John L., 122
Donaldson, Antonio and Julian, 22
Donnelly, Thomas C., 201
Dons, the, 35, 64, 79-80, 105, 108, 109, 111, 113, 129, 133, 157-161
Doran, Thomas, 97
Dorsey, John, 71
Droughts, 2, 62, 63, 192, 199, 204
Duncan, James S., 179
Dunlop, George K., 170

Eagles Lodge, 174
Eastman, John C., 169
Economy, capitalistic, 15, 113, 130; subsistence, 5-6, 113, 129
Edison, W. R., 43
Edmonson, D. B., 14
Education, 113, 123, 133-155, 188, 189, 193, 197, 199, 200-202
Electric lights, 24, 30, 33-34
El Fidel Hotel, 27
El Indepiendente, 93
El Porvenir, 33, 36, 89, 164, 175
Elk Mountain Road, 190
Elks Lodge, 44, 173, 203
Employees', railway, 42, 62, 173; contemporary, 199
Energy conservation, 203
English language, 64, 104, 135, 136, 160
Episcopal Church, 161, 169-170
Epperson, E. L., 33
Erb, A. C., 122; William L., vi
E. Romero Hose and Fire Co., 29-30
Esquibel, Felix, 116
Exchange Hotel, 8, 19, 68, 71, 117
Eyring, Eward, 146, 201

Fairchild Metal Fabricators, 197
Fairgrounds, 44-45, 55, 173
Fall, Albert B., 94
Fielding, Romaine, 48-49, 195

Fiestas, 89, 166, 177, 203
Finances, educational, 138-139; municipal, 97; land grant, 119, 123, 124, 126; university, 144-145
Firemen, volunteer, 28-30, 77-78, 88, 145, 205
Fires, 22, 24, 77-78, 141, 144, *145*
First National Bank, 26
Flick, Oka S., 207
Floods, 25, 45, 87-88
Flour mill, 27, 35
Flynn, Jim, 46-48
Folsom Man, 1
Football, 141, 146, 175
Ford, "Bob," 77
Fornoff, Fred, 48
Forrester, Henry, 169
Fort Sumner, 17, 75
Fort Union, 15, 34, 35, 37, 172, 174; National Monument, 192
Foster Grandparents, 203
Fransiscan friars, 3
Franken, Steve, 187
Fraternal Union, 173
Future Farmers, 203

Gallegos, Isador V., 116, 125; Rafael, 85
Gallinas: Canyon, 35, 45, 117; River, 1, 3, 4, 29, 81, 86, 89, 97, 103-104, 191
Gambling, 68-69, 97
Garcia, Felix, 93; Miguel, 107
Garner, Charles A., 93
Garrett, "Pat," 74-75
Garrick, David, 179
Gas lights, 23, 31
Geiger, G. P., 122
Geoffreon, O., 107
Gerdeman, A. H., 193
Gibbons, Mrs. James D., 97
Gifford, George W., 127, 129
Girl Scouts, 183, 203
Glorieta Pass, 3, *4*, 13, 17, 57, 62, 99
Gleuck, Joseph, 171
Gonzales, Fidel, 191; Hilario, 67, 103, 104

Index   239

Gorman, Samuel, 171
Gortner, Mrs. W. E., 92
Gossard, H. C., 147, 182
Government, 70, 71, 80-82, 88-92, 96-98, 192, 205
Grand Army of the Republic, 173
Grant, Ulysses, S., 24
Green, Billy, 84-85
Gross, Blackwell (Kelly) Co., 25
Gross, Jacob, 77
Guadalupe Hidalgo, Treaty, 103

Hammer, Armand, 196-197
Hanna, Richard, 95
Harvey, Fred, System, 23, 27, 43, 57; H. A., 35
Harwood, Thomas, and Mrs., 170
Hatch, Alexander, 105
Hays, May, 107
Hazzard, Ira G., 121
Hebrew congregation, 171
Hendley, J. R., 13
Henry, Edward, 140; Tom, 71
Hermit, the, 162-164
Herrera, Juan Jose, 110-111; Nicanor, 110; Pablo, 110-112
Hewett, Edgar L., 140-142, 201
Higgins, Mrs. A. D., 174; Mrs. L. N., 148
Highways, 56-57, 89, 191, 198, 205
Hilton, Ivan J., 190, 191
Hinkle, J. F., 195
Hispanic Chamber of Commerce, 203
Hispanos, 16, 19, 55, 64, 69, 89-90, 108, 110, 112, 118, 120, 128-129, 144, 158, 182, 184, 199, 201, 202, 206
Historic Preservation, 66, 195-196, 202
Holidays, 30, 82, 88, 167, 173, 176
Holliday, "Doc," 74
Hollister, Ovando J., 7
Homesteads, 107, 119-120, 129
Hose and Fire Co., No. 1, 29-30, *31*

Hoskins, Leonard, 93
Hospitals, 21-22, 79, 174, 193, 195, 199-200
Hotels, 8, 23-25, 27, 37, 42, 45, *69*, 86, 97
Housing, low income, 187, 195; mobile, 188; original, 6
Hunker, George, 95
Hunter, R. H., 76
Hunting, 7, 180

Ice Industry, 21, 33, 42
Ilfeld Auditorium, 143
Ilfeld, Charles, 8, *10*, 11, 25, 34, 63, 116, 117, 140, 143; Louis C., 149; Ludwig, 49, 53, 86
Immaculate Conception: Church, 164, *165;* School, 134
Indians, 1-5, 13, 15, 17, 30, 45, 47, 55, 182; as servants, 25, 158-159, 167
Industrial park, 203
Irrigation, 103, 123-128, 131

James, Jesse, 22, 77
Jaramillo, Benigno, 107
Jaycees, 203
Jesuits, 135-136, 138, 147, 151, 162, 190
Johnson, F. M., 102, 117; Jack, 46-48
Jones, Andreius A., 92, 125, 138

Kane, Hub, 154
Kearny, Stephen W., 12-13, 182
Kelliher, Michael, 73
KFUN, 150
Kihlberg, F. O., 8, *9*, 11, 147
King, N. L., 54; Stadium, 54, 183
Kistler, R. A., 68, 70, 73, 80, 151-153
Kiwanis Club, 175, 203
Knights: of Columbus, 92, 173; of Labor, 110-111; of Mutual Protection, 83; of Pythias, 44, 172
Knowlton, Clark S., 2
Koogler, J. H., 68, 80, 150

Labadie, Tranquilino, 140
Ladies' Relief Society, 174
Lamy, John B., 133, 135
Land grants, 3-5, 35, 101-132
Larrazolo, O. A., 60, 90, 92, 117
Las Gorras Blancas, 82, 110, 112, 118
Las Vegas: *Advertiser*, 39; Arts Council, 203; Brass Band, 178, *185*, city of, 59, 61, 79, 81, 83, 96-97, 141, 193, 203; College, 136; *Daily Gazette*, 68, 75, 80, 151; *Daily Optic*, 27, 51, 73, 76, 80, 89, 111, 112, 130, 138, 143, 147, 150, 151-155, 180; Historical Society, 149, 182; Hospital, 174, 175, 197, 200; Land Grant, 4, 101-115; Land Grant Board, 116-128; Land and Water Co., 126-128; Medical Society, 174; Military Band, 178; Old Town, 5-13, 77, 78, 137, 157, 169; Savings Bank, 27; Street Railway Co., 33; Telephone Co., 30-31; town of, 82, 88, 89, 97, 105, 109, 113, 117, 139, 149, 192, 193; Upper Town, 1, 34-35, 103, 160, 189
La Voz del Pueblo, 80, 89, 90, 92, 111, 113, 121, 131, 149, 151
League of Women Voters, 175, 203
Leahy, David J., 94-96
Letcher, Adolph, 8
Library, public, 147-149, 203
Lindberg, Charles, *58*, 59
Lions Club, 203
Lodges, 172-174, 175, 203
Long, Elisha V., 109, 116, 117, 148, 153
Lopez, Arturo, 93; Francisco, 8, 104, 135; Junio, 193; Lorenzo, 80, 81, 83-84, 89, 107, 109, 110, 113, 165
Los Alamos, village of, 11, 31, 83
Los Hermanos Penitentes, 164-166

Lucas, W. J., 68, 182
Lucero, Antonio, 90, 92, 131; Aurora, 143; Dana and Lonnie, 197
Luna, Maximiliano, 54
Luna Vocational—Technical Institute, 191, 193-194, 197, 205
Lutheran Church, 171
Lynch, J. W., 35

Maddox, Layton, 147
Maes, Herman, 115; Patricio, 83
Maese, Juan de Dios, 13, 14, 67
Maestas, Candido, 193; Herman, 84
Magee, Carl C., 94-96
Magoffin, Susan Shelby, 167
Maier, Frank, 77
Mail carriers, 15, 61
Mallet, Peter and Paul, 3
Maloof, Obaid, 179
Manufactures, 27, 190, 197, 204
Manzanares, F. A., 90, 107, 124
Martin, Joe, 71
Martinez, Alejandro, 93; Felix, 106, 111, 131, 140, 151; Gregorio, 93
Masonic Lodges, 172, 193
Mather, Dave, 71, 73
McAllister Lake, 128, 193
McCoy, Frank, 71
McCullough, James I., 149
McDermott, Pat, 187
McDonald, W. C., 47, 92
McElroy, P. D., 138
McMillen, R. C., 48
Meadows: Home, 191; Hotel, 27, 96
Medical services, 21-22, 24, 167, 174-175, 195, 197, 199-200, 205
Meline, James, 64
Menaul School, 135
Mercantile houses, 9, 11, 25, *26*, 37
Merrill, S. M., 170
Methadone Treatment Center, 203
The Mesa, 59, 121-122, 127, 193

Index   241

Methodist: churches, 121, 168, 170-171, 174; Female Seminary, 137
Milheiser, Philip, 109, 110, 111
Militia, 30, 85, 86
Mills, Wm. J., 90, 116, 119, 121, 125, 130
Miln, George, 179
Mineral Hill, 34
Mining, 34
Mishler, Robert E., 2
Mitchell, E. F., 8
Mix, Tom, 49, 51, 195
Montana de Fibre, 197
Montefiore Congregation, 171
Montezuma: Baptist College, 147; Club, 177; Hotels, 23, 22-25, 31, 33, 39, 45, 47, 147, 190, 196; Hot Springs, 22, 24, 197
Montoya, Pablo, 4; Phillip B., 93; Salvador, 101
Moore, W. S., 22
Mora, 3, 13, 34, 168, 181
Morehead, James, 73
Morley, R. A., 121
Morrison, Arthur, 16, 107; Charles, v
Motels, 187
Motion pictures, 44, 49-51, 179-180, 190, 195, 203
Mountain Bell Co., 191
Moylan, Lloyd, 145
Mullen, William, 71
Murphy, M. H., 137, 171
Museums, 149, 182, 192
Music, 136, 137, 151, 176, 178, 179, 203

Nahm, Milton C., 57, 96
National monuments, 192
Navajo Frank, 76
Navajo Indians, 17, 55, 158
Naylor, Alvin, 56
Negroes, 158, 169
Neill, H. G., 71
Newberry, Homer, 171
New Deal agencies, 63, 145, 147
New Mexico: Department of Public Welfare, 65, 197; Education Association, 139; Highlands University, 2, 61, 146, 188, 191, 197, 200-202, 205; Highway Department, 59, 191, 197, 198; Insane Asylum, 33, 39-42, 86; State Hospital, 43, 191, 197, 199-200, 205; Medical Society, 174; Militia, 30, 85; National Guard, 50-55, 96; Normal University, 55, 94, 139-147; Volunteers, 16-17
Newspapers, 68, 81, 82, 89, 93, 150-155
Northeastern Regional Hospital, 179, 201
Northern New Mexico Rehabilitation Center, 195, 197

Oddfellows Lodge, 25, 144, 173
Oil boom, 51
O'Malley, Charles, 46-47, 53, 60, 183
Onate, Juna de, 3
Onava, 59, 122
Opera houses, 55, 98, 178-179
Ortiz, Antonio, 4, 5, 35, 101
Otero Guard, 30, 85, 86
Otero, Miguel, A., Jr., 23, 68, 70, 76, 85, 91, 176, 180, 182; Miguel A., Sr., 26, 31
Otero, Sellar Co., 25
Our Lady of Sorrows Church, 1, 163

Padgett, M. N., 154
Parachute factory, 190
Parker, Frank W., 94-95
Parks, 27, 83, 87, 148, 173, 177
Partido system, 34, 113, 157-158, 160
Patron system, 79-80, 111, 157-158, 161
Patterson, B. J., 55
Pearce, Rheua, 196
Pecos Arroyo, 123, 125, 173; Pueblo, 2, 3, 22, 193; village, 45, 67
Penitentes, 164-165
Peones, 80, 111, 129, 157

Peoples Party, see Populists
Perea, Jose Ynez, 134, 169
Perkins, Ivan, 146
Peterson Reservoir, 29
Pena Blanca, 3, 5
Physicians, 22, 174, 200
Pickett, Tom, 75
Pierce, F. H., 45
Pilot Club, 203
Pino, Juan Esteban, 4, 125
Pioneer Airlines, 61
Plaza, the, 1, 8, 11, 12, 19, 26, 27, 29, 33, 68, 69, 77, 78, 82, 102, 103, 107, 134, 176, 182, 183, 190, 195; Hotel, 27, 43, 48, 176, 197
Policemen, 71, 80, 88, 205
Politics, 80, 88-97, 130-131, 144, 151, 199-201, 204
Population, 3, 20, 35, 36, 64, 65, 82, 103, 187, 202
Populists, 80, 83, 89, 111, 139, 165
Post offices, 88, 171
Poverty, 63-64, 204
Presbyterian Church, 168-169; school, 134-135
Price, Stanley, 93; Sterling, 13
Prince, L. Bradford, 71, 111, 113
Prostitution, 70
Public Service Co., 191
Pueblo Indians, 1-2, 13, 47
Pugilism, 46-48, 180

Rabeyrolle, Adrian, 164
Radios, 150, 203
Railroad: brotherhoods, 173; Hospital, 21-22
Ranches, 4, 14, 15, 34-36, 108, 198
Randall, William, 71
Rankin, R. C., 52
Raynolds, Jefferson, 26, 33, 92, 111, 113, 116, 117; Joshua, 26, 95
Reagan, Ronald, 205
Recreation, 45, 51-52, 55-56, 68-70, 166, 174-175, 180, 202, 203, 207
Red Men, lodge, 173

Regis College, 136
Reid, F. A., 126
Rendon, Gabino, 68, 135
Resorts, 22-25, 35-36, 51, 198
Revista Catolica, 113, 136, 149, 151
Rice, R. B., 108
Rivera, Manuel, 164
Roberts, Frank H. H., 143; W. J., 70
Rociada, 31, 34
Rodeos, 45, 49, 55-56, 87, 183, 189-190, 203
Rogers, A. T., 60, 99, 150, 174
Romero, Benigno, 26, 27, 39, 161; Cleofes, 84, 89, 93, 112; Eugenio, 80, 81, 90, 106, 112, 116, 117, 161, 178; Hilario, 77, 80; Juan, 106; Manuel, 135; Margarito, 33, 35, 36, 86, 91, 116, 117, 161; Miguel, 5, 9, 25, 80, 106, 162; Secundino, 89, 90, 92, 94, 95; Trinidad, 25, 43, 90, 107, *160*
Romero Mercantile Co., 25, *28*
Romeroville, 34, 89, 162
Roosevelt, Theodore, 85, 86, *87*
Root, John Wellborn, 22
Roseberry, Grace, 180
Rosenwald store, 77, 190
Rotary Club, 175, 203
Rough Riders, 54, 55, 85-86, 192
Roundhouse, the, 37, *41*, 42, 75, 188
Rudabaugh, Dave, 71-75

Saloons, 68-69, 96, 173
Salvation Army, 63, 203
Sampson, James C., 190
San Antonio, 1
Sanchez, George I., 167
Sandoval, Doroteo, 112; Gabriel, 83; Pablita, 68
San Geronimo, 80, 120
Sanguejuela tract, 124
Sanitaria, 43-44
San Jose, 3
San Miguel del Bado, 1-5, 67, 101, 133, 162

Index 243

San Miguel: Bank, 26; County, 30, 33, 34, 67, 91, 107, 125, 197
Santa Fe Trail, 5, 6, 7-8, 13, 15, 17, 56, 57, 162
Sapello, 5, 71, 76, 101, 125
Scenic Road, 45, *46,* 190
Schools, see Education
Service clubs, 57, 173, 175, 203
Seward, F. W., 43
Sheep, 4, 5, 34, 113, 118, 157
Sheriffs, 67, 74, 77, 84-85, 89, 93, 95
Shoemaker, Warren, 56, 183
Shupp, W. H., 27
Silva, Emma, 83-84; Telesfora, 83-84; Vicente, 82-84
Sisters: of Charity, 43, 63, 175, 189; of Loretto, 63, 133-134, 138, 189
Slick, Wid, 197
Slough, John P., 16
Smallpox, 78-79, 81
Smith, Orlando, 11
Snyder, Floyd W., 2
Sociedad Literaria y de Ayuda Mutua, 172; de San Jose, 172
Sorosis Club, 173
Southwest Senior Care, Inc., 193, 197
Spanish Americans, see Hispanos
Spanish: culture, 68, 143-144, 164-167, 176, 186, 207; explorers, 2-3; language, 69, 117, 133, 137, 139, 145, 150, 151, 154, 173, 196
Spiess, Charles, 90, 115, 117, 143
Sports, 44-45, 54-56, 141, 166-167, 175, 180, 201, 202
Springer, Frank, 143; Hall, 140, *142, 145*
Stagecoaches, 8, 15-16
St. Anthony's: Sanitarium, 43, 47; Hospital, 175, 189, 195
Starbird, Nelson, 73
Statehood, 89-90
Stern and Nahm Co., 25
Stewart, Jimmy, 190
Storrie: Dam, 51, 125-126, *127;* Project, 126-128; Resort, 51; State Park, 193

Streetcars, electric, *32,* 33-34; horse, *32,* 33
Street improvements, 83, 97, 193
Stumph, C. M., 147
Suazo, Thomas, 71
Sulier, D. A., 97
Sulzbacher, Louis, 107
Sumner, Edwin Vose, 15
Sundt, M. M., 55, 171, 174

Taichert, Joseph, 62; Milton, 62, 172
Tamme, Charles, 178
Taos, 8, 13, 84, 158, 182
Tecolote: Land Grant, 3, 101-102, 119; Pueblo, 2, 149; village, 11, 57
Telegraph, 8, 21
Telephones, 30-33, 191
Television, 155, 195, 203
Templeton, Fay, 179
Theatres, 178-180, 203
Thompson, A. W., 121
Thornton, Wm. T., 83
Timber, *100,* 108, 116, 117, 123, 190
Tingley, Clyde M., 182
Tinker, Carol, vi, 190
Tipton, W. R., 39-40
Tiptonville, 170
Train wrecks, 20
Transcontinental Air Transport, 59
Trolley cars, *32,* 33-34, 44
Truder, Thomas, *60,* 97
Tsianina, Princess, 182
Tuberculosis, 43-44, 176
Tuttle, J. J., 74
Twitchell, Estelle B., 148; R. E., 40, 53, 148, *149*

Ulibarri y Duran, Jose de Jesus, 102
United Fund, 188-189
United World College, 196-197
United States Army, 13-17, 22, 85; Air Corps Ferrying Command, 54; cavalry detachment, 15; First Regiment of Volunteer Cavalry, 85;

200th Regiment of Coastal artillery, 54
Upper Town, 1, 34-35, 103, 160, 187
Utility companies, 28, 30-31, 33, 97, 191

Valdez, Antonio, 73
Valerio, Procopio, 93
Valmora Sanitarium, 43, 63
Vasquez de Coronado, Francisco, 2
Veeder, John D. W., 117, 119, 149
Victory Missionary Sisters, 63
Vigilantes, 11, 71, 74-76
Villa, Pancho, 53, 57
Vocational schools, 188, 193, 197, 205

Waddingham, Wilson, 35, 108, 130, 154
Wagner, Jonathan A., 94, 144
Wagon Mound, 15, 180
Ward, George W., 40, 178
War, Civil, 16-17, 173; Indian, 13-15, 17; Mexican, 12-13; Spanish-American, 31, 85; World, 54, 61, 92-93, 175
Water, domestic, 28, 96-97, 191, 198, 204
Watrous, Samuel B., 164; village, 11
Wayne, John, 190
Webb, J. J., 71-75
Welsh, W. W., 171
West, James, 71
Westernman, Fred, 122
Westphall, Victor, 108
White Caps, 82, 110-112, 118
White, Charlie, 74
Whiteman, R. H., 52
Whitney, James G., 107
Wicks, Leroy S., 57, 192
Wildlife Preserve, 193
Wiley, Tom, 147
Wilson, Billy, 75
Woman's: Christian Temperance Union, 148, 173; Federation, 173

Women, 6, 12, 51-52, 56, 68, 69-70, 83-84, 92, 97, 133-134, 137, 138, 143, 146, 148, 153, 157, 172-174, 175, 190, 196, 197, 203
Women's Club, 51, 175, 203
Wood, Leonard, 85
Woodworth, O. H., 22
Wool, 20, 34, 130

Young Men's Christian Association, 92, 174-175

Zimmerman, John L., 119

www.ingramcontent.com/pod-product-compliance
Lightning Source LLC
Chambersburg PA
CBHW022109150426
43195CB00008B/332